The Work of Psycl

MW00775189

The majority of psychoanalysts today agree that the analytic setting faces them daily with certain aspects of their work for which the answers provided by an analytic theory centred exclusively on the notion of representation prove insufficient.

On the basis of their experience of analytic practice and illustrated by fascinating clinical material, César and Sára Botella set out to address what they call the work of figurability as a way of outlining the passage from the unrepresentable to the representational. They develop a conception of psychic functioning that is essentially grounded in the inseparability of the negative, trauma and the emergence of intelligibility, and describe the analyst's work of figurability arising from the formal regression of his thinking during the session, which proves to be the best and perhaps the only means of access to this state beyond the mnemic trace which is memory without recollection.

The Work of Psychic Figurability argues that taking this work into consideration at the heart of the theory of practice is indispensable. Without this, the analytic process is too often in danger of slipping into interminable analyses, into negative therapeutic reactions or, indeed, into disappointing successive analyses.

César Botella and **Sára Botella** are child and adult psychoanalysts in private practice. They are training analysts at the Société Psychanalytique de Paris and, in 1983, received the International Prize Maurice Bouvet for their article 'On the auto-erotic deficiency of the paranoiac'.

THE NEW LIBRARY OF PSYCHOANALYSIS
General Editor Dana Birksted-Breen

The New Library of Psychoanalysis was launched in 1987 in association with the Institute of Psychoanalysis, London. It took over from the International Psychoanalytical Library, which published many of the early translations of the works of Freud and the writings of most of the leading British and continental psychoanalysts.

The purpose of the New Library of Psychoanalysis is to facilitate a greater and more widespread appreciation of psychoanalysis and to provide a forum for increasing mutual understanding between psychoanalysts and those working in other disciplines such as the social sciences, medicine, philosophy, history, linguistics, literature and the arts. It aims to represent different trends both in British psychoanalysis and in psychoanalysis generally. The New Library of Psychoanalysis is well placed to make available to the English-speaking world psychoanalytic writings from other European countries and to increase the interchange of ideas between British and American psychoanalysts.

The Institute, together with the British Psycho-Analytical Society, runs a low-fee psychoanalytic clinic, organizes lectures and scientific events concerned with psychoanalysis and publishes the *International Journal of Psycho-Analysis*. It also runs the only UK training course in psychoanalysis that leads to membership of the International Psychoanalytical Association – the body that preserves internationally agreed standards of training, of professional entry and of professional ethics and practice for psychoanalysis as initiated and developed by Sigmund Freud. Distinguished members of the Institute have included Michael Balint, Wilfred Bion, Ronald Fairbairn, Anna Freud, Ernest Jones, Melanie Klein, John Rickman and Donald Winnicott.

Previous General Editors include David Tuckett, Elizabeth Spillius and Susan Budd. Previous and current Members of the Advisory Board include Christopher Bollas, Ronald Britton, Donald Campbell, Stephen Grosz, John Keene, Eglé Laufer, Juliet Mitchell, Michael Parsons, Rosine Jozef Perelberg, David Taylor, Mary Target Catalina Bronstein, Sara Flanders and Richard Rusbridger.

ALSO IN THIS SERIES

THE NEW LIBRARY OF PSYCHOANALYSIS

General Editor: Dana Birksted-Breen

The Work of Psychic Figurability

Mental States without Representation

César Botella and Sára Botella

With an Introduction by Michael Parsons

Translated by Andrew Weller
with the collaboration of Monique Zerbib

Brunner-Routledge
Taylor & Francis Group

HOVE AND NEW YORK

First published 2005
by Brunner-Routledge
27 Church Road, Hove, East Sussex BN3 2FA

Simultaneously published in the USA and Canada
by Brunner-Routledge
270 Madison Avenue, New York NY 10016

Brunner-Routledge is an imprint of the Taylor & Francis Group

Copyright © 2005 Delachaux et Niestlé-Loway

Translation © Andrew Weller

Typeset in Bembo by
Keystroke, Jacaranda Lodge, Wolverhampton
Printed and bound in Great Britain by
TJ International Ltd, Padstow, Cornwall
Paperback cover design by Sandra Heath

This publication has been produced with paper manufactured to strict
environmental standards and with pulp derived from sustainable forests.

British Library Cataloguing in Publication Data
A catalogue record for this book is available from the British Library

Library of Congress Cataloging-in-Publication Data
Botella, César.
[Figurabilite psychique. English]
The work of psychic figurability: mental states without representation / by
César Botella and Sára Botella; translated by Andrew Weller, with the
collaboration of Monique Zerbib.
p. cm. – (The new library of psychoanalysis)
Includes bibliographical references and index.
ISBN 1-58391-814-0 (alk. paper) – ISBN 1-58391-815-9 (pbk.: alk. paper)
1. Psychoanalysis. 2. Freud, Sigmund, 1856–1939. I. Botella, Sara. II.
Title. III. Series: New library of psychoanalysis (Unnumbered)

BF173.B68513 2004
150.19′5–dc22
2004010784

ISBN 1-58391-814-0 (hbk)
ISBN 1-58391-815-9 (pbk)

CONTENTS

Contents

Prospero. You do look, my son, in a mov'd sort,
As if you were dismay'd: be cheerful, sir.
Our revels now are ended. These our actors,
As I foretold you, were all spirits and
Are melted into air, into thin air:
And, like the baseless fabric of this vision,
The cloud-capp'd towers, the gorgeous palaces,
The solemn temples, the great globe itself,
Yea, all which it inherit, shall dissolve,
And, like this insubstantial pageant faded,
Leave not a rack behind. We are such stuff
As dreams are made on, and our little life
Is rounded with a sleep. Sir, I am vex'd;
Bear with my weakness; my old brain is troubled:
Be not disturb'd with my infirmity.
If you be pleased, retire into my cell,
And there repose: a turn or two I'll walk,
To still my beating mind.
Ferdinand. Mira. We wish your peace.
                              [Exeunt.
Prospero. Come with a thought [*To them*] I thank thee,
Ariel: come.

        Enter ARIEL.
Ariel. Thy thoughts I cleave to. What's thy pleasure?
Prospero. Spirit,
We must prepare to meet with Caliban.

William Shakespeare. *The Tempest*, Act IV, scene I

FOREWORD

Science is constructed according to the data furnished by a corner of space. Perhaps it does not agree with all the rest that we are ignorant of, which is much vaster, and which we cannot discover.
Gustave Flaubert, *Bouvard et Pécuchet*, 1880

The majority of psychoanalysts today agree that the analytic setting faces them daily with certain aspects of their work for which the answers provided by an analytic theory centred exclusively on the notion of representation prove insufficient.

Freud handed down to us a system of thought of remarkable coherence and explicatory power based on a series of concepts. What do these concepts, which cemented the foundations of psychoanalytic practice, represent for the psychoanalyst today?

It is now over a century since *The Interpretation of Dreams* (1900) was published and the best part of a century since Freud's death. Klein, Bion, Winnicott and others have opened up new horizons for Freudian concepts, revealing possibilities for enlarging the scope of analytic practice. And yet there is a contemporary trend that is forever relativising them, on the assumption that they have reached the term of their development. Some, victims of their desire for modernisation, no longer attribute them with anything but a historical value; while, at the other extreme, others immobilise them by repeating, out of a need for reassurance, their application to clinical facts, thereby defending the immutability of concepts. Such extreme positions lose sight of the real value of Freudian concepts – namely, that they are the product of long years of conceptualisation based on ideas, experiences, intuitions and discoveries; and, while they are inevitably marked by the culture and scientific spirit of the epoch, they convey a revolutionary mode of thought that is independent of the knowledge of the moment. On the contrary, this thought is the vehicle of the rupture it introduces. In fact, it is only the manifest contents of the concepts, and not the thought that creates them, that are in concordance with the scientific requirements of the epoch in which they emerge. Let us recall here the first lines of *Instincts and their Vicissitudes* (1915b), which are particularly eloquent in this respect: 'We have often heard it maintained that sciences should be built up on clear and sharply defined basic concepts.' They are followed by a series of considerations for and against this way of seeing things, which conclude as follows:

> The advance of knowledge, however, does not tolerate any rigidity even in definitions. Physics furnishes an excellent illustration of the way in which even 'basic concepts' that have been established in the form of definitions are constantly being altered in their content.
>
> *S.E.* XIV, 117

In order to continue to explore the psychic domain, envisaged from a psychoanalytic point of view, should the psychoanalyst today create new conceptual means? Or rather, should he 'modify' the manifest content of those advanced by Freud, making them gain ground in 'extension'?

Nowadays, the psychoanalyst is in the presence of a scientific ideal modified by the widely accepted notion of rigorous experimentation, scientists having discovered just how far the latter depends on the conditions of observation. One only has to think of quantum physics and the disconcerting property that matter and energy possess of being able to *present* themselves under the double nature of wave and corpuscle, even though they can only *be represented* in the form of a duality. Two contradictory statements, then, concerning the same object – a duality that only exists as a means of thinking about this strange property. What are the implications of this, then, for the psychoanalyst and for the analytic process?

An analytic concept must remain like a living organism, ready, if needs be, to shatter its secondary representational order in favour of another mode of intelligibility. For instance, what could be better for 'modifying' the manifest content of the concept of 'primal phantasies' than the metaphor of substitution in chemistry, the notion of 'precipitate' used by Freud himself? It shatters the temporo-spatial idea of the primal in favour of something actual that does not belong to the present, however, and whose continuity with the past cannot be represented.

On the basis of our experience of analytic practice, we shall be developing in the pages that follow a conception of psychic functioning that is essentially grounded in the inseparability of the negative, trauma and the emergence of intelligibility – a primordial process of psychic life unfolding in the indivisible state between negative implosion and hallucinatory flash. From *non-representation* to *figurability*, from the amnesic trace of *memory without recollection* to *dream memory*, there occurs a vital transformation for the continuity of our psychic life. The analyst's *work of figurability* arising from the formal regression of his thinking during the session, proves to be the best and perhaps the only means of access to this state beyond the mnemic trace, which is *memory without recollection*. Consequently, taking this work into consideration at the heart of the theory of practice is as indispensable as the *prise en considération de la figurabilité* [1] is for the theory of dreams. Without this, the analytic process is too often in danger of slipping into interminable analyses, into negative therapeutic reactions or, again, into disappointing successive analyses. Our aim, then, is to succeed in demonstrating this. In its broad outline, this book respects the chronological order of the publication of our works, spreading over almost 20 years, chosen for their thematic unity. All of them have been revised and brought up to date and certain unpublished texts have been added.

January 2001

Note

1   Translator's note: the standard French translation of the German term 'Rücksicht auf Darstellbarkeit' (*S.E.* 'Considerations of Representability' in Chapter VI of *The Interpretation of Dreams* (1900)). I have left the French formulation untranslated here, for the sake of coherence, because it is the author's wish to retain the French neologism '*figurabilité*' throughout the book. His concept refers essentially to the complex work of the analyst during the session, when his thinking is in a state of formal regression, which is akin to certain processes in the dream-work. By virtue of his *work of figurability*, which should be understood, I think, as a sort of intuitive, visionary work of the imagination resulting in a 'flash', a visual representation such as 'wolf' or 'gas chamber' (examples from the text) that will make it possible for the analysand to form a representation of that which had formerly remained irrepresentable, because of its traumatic origins.

INTRODUCTION

Michael Parsons

One of the hardest things to think clearly about in psychoanalysis, but one with which analysts are constantly confronted, particularly by their more disturbed patients, is the question of experience that will not go into words. Freud wrote about it in terms of 'thing-presentations' and 'word-presentations', emphasising the importance of the latter for adequate mental functioning. The concept of representation is central to analytic thinking. The capacity to symbolise depends on forming internal representations and it is when representations arouse intrapsychic conflict that repression or other defence mechanisms come into action. The analyst's free-floating attention and avoidance, so far as possible, of preconscious assumptions are in order to detect traces of representations that the patient has needed to remove from consciousness. The analyst tries, by interpretation, to put these back into words. This habitual mode of analytic understanding, centred on the concept of representation, leaves out what is not representable: that aspect of experience which will not 'go into words' because it will not, so to speak, 'go into thought' in the first place. César and Sára Botella stress how important it is to take full account of the unthinkable and they set out to offer, in this book, a view of psychoanalysis that can do so.

The authors' clinical examples show the analyst finding his or her own capacity for representation subverted. With Thomas (pp. 31–33), for example, and notably in the session with Florian, which is described at length (pp. 71ff.), the analyst found himself in a kind of nightmare state. These patients' com-munications were not merely meaningless to the analyst's normal mode of understanding, but they provoked a sense of unreality in the analyst himself. In the case of Aline (pp. 123ff.), the analyst found he could not remember the patient's name and again experienced a sense of derealisation. The final paragraph of Chapter 5 (p. 49) is a helpful summary of how the authors understand such moments. The analyst picks up, at an unconscious level of awareness, the patient's experience of non-representation. The analyst's own word-presentations are disinvested and there is a rupture with the world of representations. The analyst is subjected to something that by its nature is not capable of representation. The sense of a void, which this can produce, may have a quality of horror. The authors' experience of such states in the analyses of psychotic children leads them to say that what is at stake is psychic survival itself.

The German word *Darstellbarkeit* is usually translated into English as 'representability'. *Figurabilité* is a neologism in French, first used in 1967 as a translation of *Darstellbarkeit* in *The Interpretation of Dreams*. César and Sára Botella, in the present translation of their book *La Figurabilité Psychique*, carry the neologism over into English with the word 'figurability', in order to emphasise that what is irrepresentable cannot be psychically apprehended by the same processes that allow representations to be understood. The modes of intelligibility, as the authors put it (p. 21), are different. The clinical episodes just mentioned are examples of a retrogressive movement – 'formally' regressive in the sense of Chapter 7 of *The Interpretation of Dreams* (Freud, 1900: 548) – into a realm of non-representability. Figurability is a specific mode of internal perception arising from such a movement. The analyst's 'work of figurability' is the achievement of allowing his or her own mind to undergo this retrogressive movement, when that is needed in order to accompany the patient's mind. 'Achievement' because the experience can be disturbing and disorganising for the analyst as well as the patient. But the analyst's mind, being more mobile along this axis of representability/non-representability, may be able psychically to register a perception of the void and bring it into the realm of the representable. The analyst may then be able to find a way of articulating it to the patient as a representation that can be made use of. It is important that this work of figurability 'originates in community with the patient's psychic functioning' (p. 71). This means that when the understanding in terms of representation can finally be reached, it has a sense of meaning and conviction for the patient.

For many years this kind of clinical sequence and the shifts within it between retrogressive and progressive movement in the patient's and analyst's minds have been a central object of study for César and Sára Botella. They are both training analysts of the Paris Psychoanalytical Society and have long been respected in France for their contributions to psychoanalytic thinking. They came to psychoanalysis through their work as child and adolescent psychotherapists and they have also studied the psychosomatic approach of Pierre Marty, Michel Fain and Michel de M'Uzan. If it still feels courageous, for some British readers of psychoanalysis, to embark on a French analytic text, the title of the book's first chapter offers reassurance. It indicates the Botellas' longstanding interest in British analytic thought. They were the first to invite Frances Tustin to France and the earliest analytic publication by either of them, a case study of Sára Botella's, appeared, at Frances Tustin's instigation, in English! Winnicott and Klein have been important to their thinking about children and Bion is another significant point of reference. Among French analysts their work is closest, perhaps, to that of André Green, whose writing is already well known in English (Green, 1986a, 1999a, 1999c). The Botellas' book is Gallic in the conceptual demands it makes on an English reader, but the same reader will be at home with the constant grounding in experience with patients that gives an unambiguous sense of clinical relevance and accessibility.

Throughout the book readers will discover their own resonances, particularly with those British analysts who have also been interested in what cannot be expressed in words. The links to Bion seem especially noteworthy. At the beginning of Chapter 2 (p. 21), the authors imply the need for a theory of transformations. But in Chapter 5 (p. 48) Bion's notion of reverie is said to differ from figurability. It would be interesting to consider further how far the irrepresentable corresponds to Bion's beta-elements, and the relation between the work of figurability and alpha-function. Another important statement is that the analyst's work of figurability gives access to a state that César and Sára Botella call 'memory without recollection' (*mémoire sans souvenir*). This refers to an inchoate awareness of something having occurred, or some state having obtained, at some time other than the present moment; but an awareness that cannot be psychically represented. Instead of a mnemic trace there is what may be called an *amnesic trace*. As the authors put it, 'the absence of representable content does not mean an absence of an event' (p. 164). This seems to echo Winnicott's idea, in his paper 'Fear of breakdown' (1974) that 'clinical fear of breakdown is the fear of breakdown that has already been experienced'. Winnicott, however, is somewhat ambiguous about what he means by 'experienced'. He also says that the patient needs to go on 'looking for the detail which is not yet experienced', because 'the original experience of primitive agony cannot get into the past tense unless the ego can first gather it into its own present time experience' (Winnicott, 1974: 104–105). Bion, again, was addressing the same question when he wrote of people who 'feel pain but will not suffer it and so cannot be said to discover it' (Bion, 1970: 9).

A reference by César and Sára Botella (p. 116) to Winnicott's paper suggests that the ambiguity about what it means for something to be 'experienced' may be clarified by the concept of the negative. The idea of the negative, which goes back beyond Freud's (1925b) paper 'Negation' (see p. 19), has played an important role in French psychoanalysis, notably summarised and developed in André Green's (1999c) *The Work of the Negative*. A central theme of the present book is 'a conception of psychic functioning which is essentially grounded in the inseparability of the negative, trauma, and the emergence of intelligibility' (p. xii). How are these three linked? Analytic thinking is traditionally orientated along the progression from drive, through fantasy, conflict and subsequent repression. The aim of psychoanalytic work is a regressive movement back down this line so as to undo the repression, uncover the fantasy and find a more satis-factory resolution of the conflict. The Botellas propose an additional sequence that runs from drive, through object-representation, to thought. If progression along this line is disturbed, the result is not repression but the negating of representation, leading to disavowal. Instead of the reality of objects, what is experienced is a negative. Because this negative is by its nature irrepresentable, however, to speak of 'experiencing' it is a kind of contradiction in terms. Instead of being able to 'have an object', the person is left with a void. It is important to realise that an object-representation is not simply a memory, the internal record of a perception. It is a representation not just of the object, but also of the significance it carries for the subject. Object-representations are complex structures, involving a network of meanings at different levels and, in this way, they 'guarantee the constancy, the permanence of our psychic functioning' (p. 27). Loss of an object can be dealt with provided the capacity to represent the lost object remains. If the object-representation is lost, all that the object ever meant to the person disappears into a void. This is, I think, how the Botellas understand the nature of trauma and it explains the link between trauma and the negative. The further step back, to the loss of the capacity in general for object-representation, leads to a psychotic state. The function of figurability, for the analyst, is to overcome the negative by contacting the irrepresentable within the void. The analyst's work of figurability may be able to awaken the same capacity in the patient also, so that what is not representable can become representable and thus possible to think about. This depends on the analyst's being open to a process of formal regression in his or her own thinking, which leads back from secondary process thinking towards non-verbal perception and non-representation. This is the same regressive movement that has taken over the patient's psyche, but the analyst, by virtue of training, experience and personal analysis, is able to undergo it while at the same time fully 'experiencing' it and making perceptive use of it.

At the end of Chapter 2 (pp. 27–28) there is a commentary on the *fort-da* game. The authors remark that Freud's grandson was outside the cot, not inside it, so that he was throwing the cotton reel into the cot and using the string to pull it back out again. As well as representing the baby's mother, therefore, the reel that vanishes into the cot and re-emerges represents the baby as well. The infant is trying to deal not only with his mother's disappearance but with the consequent psychic disorganisation in himself, the loss of his capacity for self-representation that follows on the loss of the object-representation of his mother. 'The representations "mummy" and "child" thus come together in . . . a common double negativity.' This passage may be linked to a discussion in the book's final chapter of primal scene fantasies. When the baby loses the object-representation of the mother, and therefore its ability to represent itself as well, this is a terrifying negative. It can be turned into a positive, however, by the third term, which constitutes the reason for the mother's absence. This is the father. The terrifying 'neither mummy nor baby' becomes 'mummy not there because daddy' (p. 175). This shift does not produce pleasure for the baby, but it is a relief because the negative has become representable and so accessible to thought and feeling.

Sexuality can be an area of mutual incomprehension across the Channel. French analysts may feel that sexuality is underemphasised in British analysis, while British analysts are sometimes baffled by a French ability to discern sexuality even in the most abstract conceptualisations. This illuminating discussion shows how César and Sára Botella conclude that sexuality is what allows us to transcend the unthinkable and makes available the figurative power of the psyche, protecting us against the void of the negative.

It has already been emphasised that the analyst's work of figurability 'originates in community with the analysand's psychic functioning' (p. 71). This leads the authors to say that the analyst works 'as a double' with the patient. The notion of the double, rooted as it is in Freud (1919), is another idea to which the French analytic tradition has paid particular attention (e.g. Green, 1986a: 311–30). In *The Work of Psychic Figurability* the double appears in three guises.

If a primary object cannot achieve a psychic representation of the baby, the traumatic effect may be that the baby cannot then achieve its own representation of itself. The mother needs to be a mirror to the baby, so that the baby may discover itself reflected in the mother's gaze. The Botellas call the mother the infant's first double, saying 'the infant will experience in her what he already potentially has in himself' (p. 63).

The double can also play a role in the development of intellectual creativity (pp. 67–71). First Fliess and then Jung functioned as a double for Freud. But he could not use either one creatively, to see what of himself he might discover reflected in the other, because for some time these relationships were caught up in a homosexual transference. When Freud worked this through in his self-analysis, the external relationship broke down. In the process, however, Freud took a step towards internalising the double and his creativity became freer. Later in his career, the authors suggest, the figure of Moses and the French philosopher and pacifist Romain Rolland functioned in a similar way, prompting in Freud the self-analysis that freed him from a passive homosexual position towards the father and allowed him finally to establish a relationship with the internal double he needed.

In the clinical situation the analyst's work as a double to the patient is analogous to this (pp. 71–85). The analyst, by opening his or her own psyche to a regressive movement, from verbal articulation and object-representation towards non-verbal experience and a quasi-hallucinatory kind of perception, reflects the predicament of the patient's psyche. Because this is inevitably disturbing and 'uncanny' for the analyst, there is a constant temptation to escape from the mirroring between analyst and patient by converting the 'working as a double' into some other more reassuringly familiar and transferentially manageable mode of analytic relating. The task for analysts is to avoid this and give themselves over to the work of figurability as doubles for their patients. Then, like the mother for the infant, or like Freud's doubles as he eventually managed to make use of them, analysts may help their patients to discover their own sense of identity, reflected in the analyst, and a capacity for this psychic work on their own account. What has been irrepresentable and unthinkable can then become representable and intelligible.

The notion of 'the hallucinatory' plays an important part in this scenario. Among a group of interlocking ideas that run through the book, the category of psychic functioning that the authors call 'the hallucinatory' may be the least familiar to an English reader. The following account draws on comments and statements from various parts of the book, to help readers orientate themselves with regard to this concept.

The hallucinatory can be approached by considering how object-representations are arrived at. To begin with there is the bare perception of sensory experience. Chronologically, this belongs to earliest infancy. Formally it belongs, in Freud's terms, to the system *Pcpt*. If the object disappears, the infant responds to its absence by a wishful hallucination that the object is still present. When the hallucinatory satisfaction fails, a word-presentation of the object may emerge, allowing the object to be thought about in its absence. At this point the object is no longer simply there or not there, perceptible or not perceptible. It is now possible to put into words what it means for the object to be there or not and to reflect on whatever multiple layers of significance for the person the object may have. An object-relationship can develop because the object has become internally representable. This highlights once again the crucial distinction between representation and perception. They lie at opposite ends of an axis, so that there is both a continuity and a gap between them. The case of Jasmine (pp. 100ff.) shows what happens when this axis collapses in on itself and the gap disappears.

The psychic functioning that analysts are most used to dealing with, in their patients and in themselves, is based on the interplay of representations. There is the condensation of representations as in dream work, displacement of meaning along a chain of representations and the repression of representations in response to conflict. This is what analysts are used to listening for and they do so by opening themselves free associatively to the same sort of displacement and condensation of their own representations. César and Sára Botella, how-ever, regard free association as only a minimum of necessary modification in the analyst's thinking. This purely representational axis is intersected by the axis 'representation–perception'. (This is another description of the axis 'representability/non-representability' and is related to the progression 'drive, object-representation, thought', both mentioned earlier.) A central theme of this book, as has already been implied, is the need for the analyst not only to deal with the interplay of representations, but also to shift back and forth along this other axis as well.

The work of figurability requires analysts to accept modifications in their thinking that go well beyond a necessary minimum. It involves a formal regression along the axis of representation–perception. Freud calls this an 'alteration in the normal psychical procedure which makes possible the cathexis of the system *Pcpt* in the reverse direction, starting from thoughts, to the pitch of complete sensory vividness', as in dreams when 'an idea is turned back into the sensory image from which it was originally derived' (Freud, 1900: 543). Dreams at night are an example of the hallucinatory at work and they highlight the fact that hallucinatory psychic activity is not to be equated with having hallucinations. In psychotic hallucination, the subject has no sense of his own participation. His psychic reality is negated. The dreamer, by contrast, 'hallucinates a psychic reality in which he can see himself taking part, just as he forms an integral part of the psychical scene in daytime' (p. 127). This comparison is not simply a comment in passing. Fundamental to the Botellas' thinking is the hypothesis that the psyche has a normal aptitude for hallucinatory functioning. This expresses itself in nocturnal dreaming, while in waking mental activity it is usually inhibited in the interests of reality testing. In the particular state of mind, however, that an analytic session calls forth, analysts can allow themselves to regress along the axis representation–perception so as to actualise the hallucinatory in their psychic functioning. This shift towards a more primal form of intelligibility takes place as a response in the analyst to sensing that the patient, in his or her own mind, is in contact with the irrepresentable. The session with Florian (pp. 71ff.), already mentioned, amounted to a waking nightmare for the analyst and it shows how disturbing this unmediated perception of the irrepresentable can feel, precisely because of its hallucinatory quality. This doubling of the patient's experience, however, if the analyst can tolerate and observe it without being engulfed by it, is the essence of the work of figurability.

TRANSLATOR'S ACKNOWLEDGEMENTS

I would like to thank Monique Zerbib warmly for all the help she has given me with this translation, and also Dr Botella for his assistance at the end in finalising the text.

Andrew Weller
Paris, September 2003

AUTHORS' INTRODUCTION TO THE ENGLISH EDITION

> Understanding means translating.
> Georges Steiner, *After Babel*

On the necessity of using the term 'figurability'

For a few decades now, notably thanks to the work of Steiner (1976) and of Antoine Berman (1984, 1985) and Paul Ricoeur (2003) in France, translation has become a discipline of the greatest importance and of particular interest for the psychoanalyst. He cannot fail to ask himself if his writing, like translation, is also, as Ricoeur puts it: 'a creative betrayal of the original, but an equally creative appropriation by the language of reception'. That is to say, of what is unconscious in his patient, of what the analyst says to him about it, including the theoretical elaboration of his interpretation via writing; then, of the reader's understanding of his text in the same language; and, finally, of what becomes of the original text translated into another language. By multiplying so many 'creative betrayals of the original', what remains of the analyst's initial intuition that is inseparable from the setting, and of the highly particular psychic state that is produced in an analytic session?

Taking this complexity into account, and having given the matter much thought, we have finally concluded that, notwithstanding its character as a neologism, introducing the term *figurability* into the English psychoanalytic terminology to name what we call in French *figurabilité* was unavoidable. It is a notion that we have been developing since 1983 on the basis of Freud's use, throughout his work and in an identical manner, of the term *Darstellbarkeit*. He does this notably in *The Interpretation of Dreams* (1900: *S.E.* V, 339) in the formulation *Rücksicht auf Darstellbarkeit*,[1] the title of the sub-chapter D of chapter

1

VI, the French translation of which has been modified three times. The one that has lasted the longest is *La prise en considération de la figurabilité*.

Unlike in French, the translation into English of *Darstellbarkeit* has, to the best of our knowledge, not posed the slightest problem, there having been a general consensus from the outset in favour of the term *representability* (*Considerations of Representability*), employed in 1953 by the translator of Freud's complete works, James Strachey. The purpose of this introduction is, then, to explain why we have not opted for *representability*. Especially as our translator, Andrew Weller, had warned us from the outset that the term *figurability* might be rather off-putting for English readers. Everything encouraged us then, initially, to stick to the existing term *representability*. And yet this did not seem possible, as we would have run the risk of distorting the meaning of the notion of *figurabilité*. The main aim of this introduction was thus initially to explain the grounds for our decision. But as we set about writing it, we noticed that the problem of translation presented us with the opportunity of deepening our knowledge of the notion of *figurabilité*. Quite clearly, the problem had become a much larger one than an issue of language, thus confirming that although it was based on, and closely linked with, *Darstellbarkeit*, the notion of *figurabilité* is not identical with it; the two notions are not entirely overlapping.

Every creation of a neologism doubtless requires sufficient reasons to justify it. Particularly as, in the present case, it is a matter of psychoanalytic vocabulary and we know how much our discipline suffers from what psychoanalysts today denounce as the 'psychoanalytic Babel'. Nevertheless, we had no choice; for, although the use of representability is perhaps adequate as a translation of *Darstellbarkeit*, the same cannot be said for our notion of *figurabilité*: its epistemological field and metapsychological parameters are not identical to those of *Darstellbarkeit*; as we have just said, they cannot be superimposed.

It is worth noting that, unlike in English, the translation of *figurabilité* has posed not the slightest difficulty for Spanish and Italian translations of our book; or for the Portuguese translation of an earlier book, *Au-delà de la représentation*, where there was already mention of *figurabilité*. In fact, the use in each of these three languages, Spanish, Italian and Portuguese, of the term corresponding to the French term *figurabilité*, met with no obstacle: *figurabilidad*, in Spanish; *figurabilidade* in Portuguese; and *raffigurabilità* in Italian (Botella, C. and S., 1997b, 2002, 2003, 2004). And this in spite of the fact that in Spanish, for example, *figurabilidad* was a real neologism and in the two other languages, as far as we have been able to ascertain, it was a term little used or not in use at all. Such an immediate and spontaneous adoption in each of the three languages, as if the new term had always been part of analytic terminology, was probably facilitated by the existence of terms close to it and in current usage such as, for instance, *figura*, or again the popular expression *figúrate* to say 'imagine' in Spanish.

As for history of the successive translations of *Darstellbarkeit* into French, it seems possible to detect a real quest for meaning that is inseparable from the underlying issue that goes beyond the usual complexity of passing from one language to another.

In the first French version of *Die Traumdeutung*, in 1926, its translator Ignace Meyerson, a doctor and psychologist, used the term *figuration* to translate *Darstellbarkeit*. It was thus only later, in the revision made in 1967 by Denise Berger, that the term *figurabilité* was preferred. Whether by coincidence or agreement, Laplanche and Pontalis made the same terminological choice in the *Language of Psychoanalysis*, which also appeared in 1967.

In the French language, the term *figurabilité* is not a real neologism, as we had thought until quite recently, and still thought at the time when the French edition of our book was published in 2001, as the reader can see in Chapter 5. In reality, it is a term in French that is not in common use, which, to the best of our knowledge, only figures currently in one dictionary, albeit one of reference, *Le Littré*. Unusual until 1967, the word *figurabilité* has since become commonly used in our analytic milieu.

This rapid integration seems to prove that Berger, Laplanche and Pontalis were right. Their translation defined the meaning of *Darstellbarkeit* differently and this seemed to suit psychoanalysts. Especially as Merson's translation put the accent on 'the action of representing', on the act of 'giving form', as in that of 'representing through painting'.[2] What is involved here is an action carried out by a subject who appropriates an object for the purpose of transposing it on to a passive support (canvas, paper, film), under the subject's control, on which the representation will appear. A parallel could thus be made, up to a certain point, between a dream and a painting, particularly when the painter strives to represent on the canvas an affect, a mood or alternatively a content, an idea. However, the 'externalisation' of a wish or an idea, which the painting implies, the fact that the latter is designed to be shown and sheltered from time, that it is generally governed by an aesthetic quest, places the painter's work at the opposite pole from the dreamer who is confined within the intimacy of sleep and confronted by the ephemeral nature of his dream. Unlike the painting, the dream is self-sufficient; it has no need of others to fulfil its function. Abandoning *figuration* in favour of *figurabilité* thus seemed perfectly justified.

In the first edition of the *Littré* in 1880, as in the latest edition of 2003, *figurabilité* is defined as follows: 'didactic term; property of all bodies of having or being given a shape (*une figure*)'.[3] Contrary to *figuration*, then, the term *figurabilité* emphasises the idea that it is the object itself that possesses in its nature, intrinsically, a 'property' named *figurabilité* that makes it capable of 'being given a shape'. This intrinsic power can thus be understood not as one of 'transposing' but of being at once the support and the object to be represented, the agent of the act and the act itself.[4] Such a definition involving relations that are quasi-irrepresentable for waking thought and its secondary processes grasps something essential about the world of dreams. In this respect, *figurabilité* is an inescapable notion for analytic theory. And, what is more, our hypothesis is not only that it

3

forms the basis of the metapsychology of the dream-work but also that it is at the centre of general psychic functioning. The translation of *Darstellbarkeit* by *figurabilité* seemed to have become a solid and definitive acquisition.

How surprised we were, then, to learn that a new translation of *Darstellbarkeit* had since been proposed. In the very recent French translation of *Die Traumdeutung* which appeared in January 2003 as part of the *Oeuvres Complètes de Freud* currently being published in France, Laplanche and his imposing team of translators have abandoned *figurabilité* and opted for *présentabilité*.

Why this change? The reasons for it are not made very explicit. Already in 1989, in a special volume aimed at familiarising the reader with the principles of translation, Bourguignon, Cotet, Laplanche and Robert (principally responsible for the *Oeuvres Complètes de Freud (O.C.F.)*) indicate, by way of justifying their terminological choices, that they give pride of place to the term *darstellen*, whose classical translation in French, they tell us, hesitates between the two terms *présenter* and *figurer*. Then, considering that *darstellen* involves 'an activity with an objective or objectivizing connotation', they opt for its translation by *présenter*. Following this line of reasoning, they add that '*présentation* doubtless occurs in dreams generally in a pictural (*bildlich*) form'.

Although the pictural mode of presentation has priority in the process in which the dreamer becomes conscious of his dream, the explanation given by the new translators seems insufficient to justify the reduction of the semantic field of *Darstellbarkeit* to *darstellen* or the priority given to the objectivising visual dimension. The researches of Martine Lussier (2001) confirm this. Freud, she writes, 'does not reduce *figurabilité* to the visual modality since he qualifies it regularly by an adverb ['usually', 'generally']. And when Freud wants to speak of "*figurabilité visuelle*", he qualifies it by an adjective [*bildlich* = pictural, *plastische, anschaulich* = visual]; he speaks of *sinnliche Darstellbarkeit* [Freud, 1905d: *S.E.* VIII, 163] [in English, the term 'sensory form' was preferred], which indicates that *figurabilité* can arise from any sort of sensible quality whatsoever . . . it is the non-limitation to the visual quality which is the basis for the extension of *figurabilité* to the situation of the cure.' This is important for it saves us from getting lost by confusing *figurabilité* and *figure*. There is indeed a risk of assimilating *figurabilité* with the medieval meaning that *figura* takes on in Christian culture with its connotation relative to mystery, to the divine and to its use in the religious domain (the 'quarrel of images'). This would be to disregard the early Latin origins of *figura*. *Figura* comes from the Latin verb *fingere*, to knead, model. 'It is used to describe the work of a potter or baker: space, tactile quality, olfactory quality are thus evoked; finally, it is useful to know that, applied to the abstract, the same verb has the meaning of fiction', concludes Martine Lussier. *Modelling* (like a potter) or *mixing* skilfully (like a baker) or again *fiction* are all fine metaphors for *figurabilité* and for the dream-work.

The same cannot be said for *présentabilité*, which does not evoke movement but, on the contrary, the objectivising immobility of the image. To this one can add that the best argument for the inadequacy of the term *présentabilité* has been given by the translators themselves. *Présentabilité* is said not to be specific to dreams: '[I]n other cases, it can be abstract or again discursive, when it is a question of exposing ideas or theses. Likewise, descriptions of clinical cases are regularly qualified as *Darstellungen: presentations.*' In the same vein, we could add 'show', 'exhibit' (whence the use by Kant of *Exhibitio* instead of *Darstellung*). Or, and it is also religious, the term *presentation at the temple*; or again, with its reference to the social domain, that of *being presentable. Exhibitio, presentation, presentability* are all terms that contain the idea of 'facing'. Consequently, it seems to us that by employing *presentability* to name one of the factors of the dream-work, there is a risk of trivialising or occulting the specificity of the dream, of pushing it in the direction of secondary processes, hence of attributing it with the characteristics of waking thought and no longer taking sufficient account of the differences, the particularities of the psyche functioning during the highly singular state of sleep. The *Darstellbarkeit* of the dream-work then loses its own specificity linking it with the world of dreams and is reduced to the action of '*présenter*' specific to waking consciousness.

Let us note a common point between the two terms. Although *présenter* is a word in common use in French, by contrast its derivative *présentabilité* does not appear in dictionaries we have consulted (the *Grand Robert* and the *Littré*).

As for *figurability*, once again something is pushing translators to use a neologism or at least a term that is not in common use. But what then is this difficulty in finding the right term? What is this sense of dissatisfaction permeating the successive translations of *Darstellbarkeit*, three in about 75 years? Do they not bear witness – this would be our hypothesis – to the fact that when it is a question of naming an unconscious process, especially when this process is the work of the nocturnal psyche, any word-presentation proves to be barely adequate for identifying the process in question? In the last analysis we see this as being the real difficulty with which the successive translators of *Darstellbarkeit* have been confronted. Getting involved in a terminological quarrel here would simply be to avoid this difficulty. Analysts themselves find that putting the intelligibility of the night-time world into words, as Freud tried to do with *Darstellbarkeit*, is such a challenge that, in order to get round it, there is a great temptation to cling onto one of the terms of the different translators, to seek the familiarity of a position already stated, at the risk of reducing the implicit dimension of the original text. Whether one invests the idea of *figure* through Meyerson's *figuration* or stresses objectivisation by opting for the visual dimension of *présentabilité*, it seems to us that there is a risk of missing the point that even in Freud's work *Darstellbarkeit* is but an approximation, an attempt to say something about the intelligibility of the unconscious dream world.

The translation of certain notions of our discipline requires an approach that takes into account more than just the language and the social and cultural context of the epoch, as is the case for literary and scientific translations. Its

5

specificity stems from the fact that the term or the notion to be transposed from one language into another is itself already the product of a 'translation'. Moreover, we would say – paraphrasing Ricoeur – that it is the product of a 'creative translation of the original' carried out by the psychoanalyst/author as he endeavours to put into words and integrate into psychoanalytic theory what, beyond the realm of words and secondary processes, he has implicitly already understood owing to his daily experience of the intimacy of the relations existing between his own psychic activities during the night and his analytic practice.

Accounting for unconscious processes by means of word-presentations is by definition an act of approximation, if not of distortion, given the extent to which the *Ucs.* eludes conscious thought and is of such a different nature. When it is a question of unconscious processes, the author/analyst, writing in the language he usually speaks, is the first 'translator'. This being so, every translation of analytic texts meets with a twofold difficulty. The translator cannot take into account the linguistic problem alone; he must equally endeavour, if not more so, to grasp in each notion the 'creative translation' already effected by the author in his effort to circumscribe the unconscious processes in question. The hesitations concerning the translation of *Darstellbarkeit*, its three translations, are evidence of this difficulty.

Finally, after a certain time of perplexity – impregnated, it has to be admitted, with irritation – we thank the new translators for having obliged us to turn our attention to the problem. This has allowed us to clarify, beyond the linguistic issue, what makes us stick to the term *figurabilité*. No doubt the latter has to be related to the linguistic translation of *Darstellbarkeit*, on condition, however, that one appreciates in the German term its value as a 'creative translation' promising a new concept still in an implicit state of thought in Freud. This shows that, owing to the character of the difficulties that it engenders, and beyond the appearance of being a work, as it is said, of *traditore*, the very process of translating can prove to be that of an *éclaireur* in the double sense of 'clarifying' and of 'sending out on reconnaissance' to explore an unknown terrain. Thus understood, the translator, in fortunate cases, can become an *éclaireur* of the author's thought.

On the notion of 'figurability'

Our hypothesis is thus that the hesitations of successive translators are evidence that, in addition to the linguistic difficulty in designating what Freud calls *Darstellbarkeit*, there exists a difficulty of another order. Concerning the source of the dream-work, Freud may be said to have had an intuition that was never developed – one cannot know to what extent it was conscious – of which only implicit traces subsist. Was it that he did not have time or was it that he did not want to make them more explicit for fear of lessening the impact of his discovery of wish-fulfilment as the paradigmatic objective of the dream?

6

On the subject of the use of the term *Darstellbarkeit*, two remarks may be made: the first is that this term only appears in Freud's work 19 times in all, and each time in reference to dreams; whereas the other factors involved in the dream-work, displacement, condensation and secondary elaboration, can be found frequently in Freud's descriptions apropos different psychic activities. The second remark is that the term *Darstellbarkeit*, to the best of our knowledge, is not in common use in German. It is listed neither in the Sachs-Villatte German–French dictionary of 1905 nor in the Langenscheidt dictionary of 1976 edited in Vienna. The same is true of the Wahrig German dictionary (1974). One finds the adjective *darstellbar*, but its nominalisation is absent; whereas for another term that, as we shall see, is complementary, namely, the adjective *wirklich* (real), its nominalisation, *Wirklichkeit* (reality, in the sense of effective reality), *is* listed.

We can suppose, then, that Freud, like his French translators subsequently, introduced a new term; or at least made use of an unusual term in an endeavour to designate in the domain of dreams a specific action whose existence had hitherto not been suspected and even less recognised.

In the total absence of definition, of description, we thus felt obliged to detach ourselves from linguistic concerns in order to give ourselves a chance of apprehending what Freud transmitted to us implicitly by his choice and by his exclusive and repetitive use in an identical way of the term *Darstellbarkeit*. A close reading of *The Interpretation of Dreams* and the passages concerning the use of *Darstellbarkeit* in the rest of Freud's work allows us to put forward the following hypothesis: the specificity of what Freud discovered in the formation of the dream resides not in what is apparent – the final outcome, *Darstellen, image, figuration or présentabilité* – but in what is imposed by the suffix *bar*, the 'possibility of action'.

When Lacan translated *Rücksicht auf Darstellbarkeit* in 'L'instance de la lettre dans l'inconscient' in 1957, he took account of this in the following way: focusing on the meaning of *bar*, on the meaning it adds, *darstellbar* thus being understood as close to *representable* in the theatrical sense of 'performable' (*jouable*), he translated *Rücksicht auf Darstellbarkeit* by 'considerations of the means of "*dramatization*" (*mise en scène*)' (our italics).[5] Unlike *figuration* and *présentabilité*, the Lacanian formulation '*mise en scène*' – even if in certain respects such a free translation proves to be somewhat forced – seems to us to be a laudable attempt to say something of the 'possibility of action' that *Darstellbarkeit* implies. In effect, by thus privileging the idea of action, inherent to *bar*, Lacan suggests in an insistent way on the existence of a *dramaturgy*, of an 'art of composition' as being the determining phenomenon of the dream. We have seen that, six years thereafter, Berger, on the one hand, and Laplanche and Pontalis, on the other, did not take this into account. As far as we are concerned, while we recognise the interest of the Lacanian translation as an opening in comparison with the earlier term *figuration*, we cannot follow Lacan; for his formulation *mise en scène* poses the idea of a stage manager who is not the dramatist creating the scenario, whereas the action proper to the Freudian *Darstellbarkeit* of the dream refers us to a psychic work implying in one and the same psychic action of the dream: dramatist, stage manager, actors and spectator.

The metaphor of a 'scene' for describing the organisation of an activity, a psychic work, is not exceptional in Freudian texts. For example, on several occasions, each time in the *Interpretation of Dreams*, Freud makes a comparison between memory and dream. They have two points in common: both result in a scenario 'and they were seen like hallucinations'; and he adds: 'a dream might be described as *a substitute for an infantile scene modified by being transferred on to a recent experience*' (Freud's italics). Which confirms what we were saying earlier about the action implied by *Darstellbarkeit* of being at once the support and the object to be represented, the agent of the act and the act itself. (Equally one understands here how important it is for analytic theory to interest itself in this hallucinatory, infantile scene that has never been 'written', that is without a dramatist and yet is the source of dreams and memory – a hallucinatory action which comes into operation each time the conditions are favourable. Dream and memory, reverie and phantasy, are all psychic formations that emanate from 'the capacity for hallucination' (Freud, 1912a: *S.E.* XII, 108) of the unconscious and that 'lost that character only in the process of being reported' (Freud, 1900: *S.E.* V, 546).)

We have perhaps made progress thanks to the idea of the space of psychic action as a scene of hallucinatory quality producing these two formations, dream and memory, both pillars of mental functioning. But, we are still a long way from the import of Freud's implicit thought that we believed we had detected, notably in Chapter VI of *The Interpretation of Dreams*. We may be able to get nearer to it by examining the use Freud makes of the term *Darstellung*, close to *Darstellbarkeit*, in one of his texts written shortly after the book on dreams, 'Fragment of an analysis of a case of hysteria' (1905b). Although this text was only published in 1905, it was written in the first two weeks of January 1901. During the preceding months – since the month of September 1900 – Freud had seen on his couch a young woman of 18, Dora, whose analysis was suddenly broken off by the patient herself on 31 December, 1900. In this text, Freud takes the trouble to define the term *Darstellung*, 'bedeutet ein Symptom die *Darstellung – Realisierung* – einer Phantasie'. (Freud, 1905a: *G. W.* V, 206), translated into English as 'a symptom signifies *the representation – the realization* – of a phantasy' (Freud, 1905b: *S.E.* VII, 47). Why did Freud feel it was necessary to specify that, in the case of a symptom, *the representation* must be understood as *a realisation*? A wishful *realisation* as in dreams? Freud seems to have wanted to reunite symptoms and dreams; he seems once again to have encountered, at the level of the symptom too, something of the specificity of dreams. But how is one to conceive of a representation endowed with a capacity to render real, effective?

At this same period, one finds another formulation that may help us see further. In *The Interpretation of Dreams*, in a paragraph that he added in 1914, very probably at the same time as he was writing up his analysis of the 'Wolf Man' (1910–14), Freud employs a term used in close relation with the dream, namely '*Wirklichkeitsgefühl*' (Freud, 1900: *S.E.* V, 372). This is another curious term that Freud was only to use in his work five times (*The Interpretation of Dreams*; 'From the History of an Infantile Neurosis') and, each time, like *Darstellbarkeit*, solely in relation to the dream. In his text on the 'Wolf Man', as well as in *The Interpretation of Dreams*, the term *Wirklichkeitsgefühl* designates a psychic state that is manifested openly in young children; a qualitative experience in which the content of the dream reality persists after waking and inhabits waking life with its characters for a certain period of time. 'I took quite a long while before I was convinced that it had only been a dream; I had had such a clear and life-like picture of the window opening and the wolves sitting on the tree' (Freud, 1914–18: *S.E.* XVII, 29), said Serguei.

Wirklichkeitsgefühl was to be translated as 'feeling of reality', a formulation that, in our opinion, does not render the full force of the German, even if one considers that here 'feeling' is used in the sense of effectivity, of a real act. However, although 'feeling', like the French translation *sentiment*, its equivalent, seem to be perfect translations, from the standpoint of the practising psychoanalyst, they remain unsatisfactory for they do not reflect the dazzling speed, the force of what is at stake psychically in grasping reality. Would it not have been better to use, in English, as well as in French, the term 'sensation'? This term, identical in the three languages, would have the advantage of being closer to the corporeity and immediateness of an actualisation, of reflecting better the very particular moment in sleep in which psychic reality coincides with material reality.

These three Freudian formulations *Darstellbarkeit*, *Darstellung–Realisierung* and *Wirklichkeitsgefühl*, may be seen as sharing the same idea – that is, the astonishing capacity, proper to psychic reality, for creating the sensation of reality in order to fulfil a wish with the value of a material realisation, either in the suffering of an affect in the case of a symptom or through the hallucinatory quality of the dream; and then, against a hallucinatory background, after waking. This leads us to think that the hallucinatory capacity is a fundamental property in the creation of all normal or pathological sensation feeling. Freud's study of the transference in 1912 would enable him to go more deeply into what is to be understood by this property of making real. During the analytic treatment 'the reactions which we bring about reveal . . . some of the characteristics we have come to know from the study of dreams . . . Just as happens in dreams, the patient regards the products of the awakening of his unconscious impulses as *contemporaneous and real* . . . in accordance with the timelessness of the unconscious and its capacity for hallucination' (Freud, 1912a: *S.E.* XII, 108) (our italics). Then, Freud made a decisive step in the *Introductory Lectures on Psycho-Analysis* (1916–17). He generalised his intuition and launched into a new idea and a new notion: '[T]he regression of the dream-work is not only a *formal* but also a *material*

9

one.' He then asked: 'What is it that forces psychical activity during sleep to make this regression . . . what is the point of reviving as well the old mental impulses . . . of making use of *material regression* in addition to the *formal* kind' (Freud, 1916–17: *S.E.* XV, 211, 212) (our italics). It is a question that remains unanswered. And what is more, in the rest of his work, the notion of material regression was never employed again, any more than were those of *Darstellbarkeit Darstellung–Realisierung* and *Wirklichkeitsgefühl*.

How are we to interpret this absence of response? How are all these erasures to be understood? What does this succession of particular terms – the *Darstellbarkeit* of dreams, the hallucinatory quality of memory, the *Darstellung– Realisierung* of symptoms, the *Wirklichkeitsgefühl*, the *contemporaneous and real* nature of the transference (all terms linked to contexts whose background seems to be the *material regression* and 'the capacity for hallucination of the unconscious') induce us to think? It seems to us that the answer to this question requires a closer examination of the idea of the existence of a capacity of the psyche to create a sensorial quality from a singular and complex unconscious process. It may be said to be an instinctual process, potentially permanently active, whose effects, in certain regressive–retrogressive conditions, provoke a coincidence between outside and inside, a sensation of reality (*Wirklichkeitsgefühl*) triggered endoperceptively, a *brilliant forgery* that renders the original so well that it makes us believe, for instance, during a dream, that we are in material reality. Based on the formulation of *The Interpretation of Dreams*, '*a psychical impulse . . . an impulse of this kind is what we call a wish (Regung) . . . that is in which wishing ended in hallucinating*' (Freud, 1900: *S.E.* V, 566) the model of this *qualitative experience* is a process of 'primordial binding', 'one of the earliest and most important functions of the mental apparatus' (Freud, 1920: *S.E.* XVIII, 62) 'determined, according to our hypothesis, by virtue of the tendency to make all the stimuli of the moment, internal and external, converge into a hallucinatory perceptive coherence. *It is this convergent perceptive-hallucinatory intelligibility of primordial processual quality which we call "figurability"*'.

On the notion of 'psychic quality'

Although the idea of instinctual process poses no particular theoretical problem, in that this formulation essentially defines the movement and impulsion (*Regung*) characterising the basic psychic constituents, drive, wish and affect (*Triebregung, Wunschregung* and *Affectregung*), it is, by the same token, necessary to give some thought to what may be understood in psychoanalysis by *quality*.

Freud dealt explicitly with the question of *quality* right at the beginning of his work, in 1895, in the 'Project for a scientific psychology'. Thereafter there is little mention of it until the end of his writings, until *An Outline of Psychoanalysis*, written in 1938, a text which has the value of a testament. The point in common between these two texts separated by 43 years is that the notion of *quality* is closely linked in both with that of consciousness and figures in the title of a chapter. Apart from that, the way in which it is envisaged is very different. In 1895, the chapter is entitled 'The problem of quality' and the notion of quality is inseparable there from that of consciousness. It comprises two main ideas, each of which refers to the other: first, consciousness is a momentary quality; and second, the qualities are furnished by the conscious state. On the contrary, in 1938, the preoccupation is no longer with defining or localising the *qualities*. The chapter announces the theme under the formulation 'Psychical qualities'. Although the point of departure is still its link with consciousness, the existence of a quality no longer depends on an agency. Moreover, in 1938, the very term of consciousness designates a phenomenon that is only evident in appearance: 'If anyone speaks of consciousness, we know immediately from our most personal experience what is meant by it.' But this evidence is misleading; for, in reality, consciousness is 'a fact without parallel, which defies all explanations, all descriptions' (Freud, 1938b: *S.E.* XXIII, 157).

Detached from consciousness, the notion of quality, thus generalised, was to become in the *Outline* the instrument that enabled Freud to envisage the psychical topography under a new dynamic angle, namely, as a process. Without preparing the reader, and perhaps without really realising that he was unifying the two topographies, which represent a modification of the theory and analytic practice, Freud wrote: 'which we describe as psychical qualities . . . Thus we have attributed three qualities to psychical processes: they are either conscious, preconscious or unconscious' (Freud, 1938b: *S.E.* XXIII, 159–60). However, Freud must have had a certain awareness of the possibility of an upheaval when he affirmed: '*The theory of the three qualities* of what is psychical . . . seems likely to be a source of limitless confusion rather than a help towards qualification' (Freud, 1938b: *S.E.* XXIII, 161).

This chapter generalising the notion of quality as a permanent property of movement capable of becoming an effective process ('effective sensation of reality': *Wirklichkeitsgefühl*) at any point whatsoever in the psychical topographies was the culmination of a long evolution of Freudian thought. Following the discovery, in the aftermath of the 1914–18 war, of the existence of neuroses without the participation of the agency *Ucs.*, of traumatic neuroses caused by external events, Freud found himself obliged to undertake a profound revision that resulted in the introduction of the death drive in 1920 and then in the creation of the second topography in 1923. With the new topography, he conceived of a modality of psychic functioning that now took account of the external world. Unlike the conception of the first topography, the new agencies, the ego, id and superego, are described with hazy contours, as if they were inter-weaving. One and the same quality can be propagated and have simultaneous effects on the three agencies, just as it can present itself selectively under the aegis now of this, now of that agency. Furthermore, the psyche can no longer be envisaged as an apparatus governed exclusively by the principles of pleasure and reality. It must also have a function of binding, of elaboration and integration of disturbing elements, external and internal, by virtue of a *work of transformation*. This being so, the reason for the existence of dreams becomes more complex; to the dream's function of wish-fulfilment must be added that of elaborating and integrating traumatic traces (1932).

Compared with the principal stages of the evolution of the theory of the drive itself (sexual instinct, self-preservative instinct; life instinct, death instinct), those concerning the generalisation of the processual quality of instinctual life appear very discreetly and are part of the implicit ideas in Freud's work that remain to be explored, representing a vast field for psychoanalytic research. Among others we are thinking of the texts *The Ego and the Id* (1923a), *Inhibitions, Symptoms and Anxiety* (1925a), 'A disturbance of memory on the Acropolis' (1936), 'Constructions in analysis' (1937a) and *An Outline of Psychoanalysis* (1938b). The clarification of such a line of thinking, even if implicit, renewing the theory, must obviously involve the examination of the successive changes that have taken place within psychoanalytic practice.

Within the limits of this introduction, we can say that the analyst of today has every interest in taking account of the fact that the activities of the ego, the id and the superego are made more complex by the *qualities*, conscious, preconscious, and unconscious, and owing to their simultaneous power of actualisation. Every content implies all three possible statuses: that of *representation* (conscious, preconscious, unconscious); that of *perception* (conscious, partial, disavowed); and that of the *hallucinatory* (endoperceptive, exoperceptive [hallucination]). Taking account both of the topographical conflicts and the processual qualities of a content – whether the latter presents itself to consciousness in the register of *representation, perception,* or again of *hallucination* is of incontestable value for evaluating the economic and dynamic moment of a treatment and measuring the changes that have occurred. The reader will find in the text of the book clarifications concerning this dynamic: representation–perception–hallucination and its interest for analytic practice.

For a definition of 'figurability'

To conclude this introduction to the English edition of our book we must now return to what we understand by *figurabilité*, which we propose to translate by *figurability*. In the definition of the notion *figurabilité*, we are endeavouring to take account of its *processual quality*, which, capable of becoming *real effective* in regressive-retrogressive states, is, however, not representation, perception or hallucination, but a fourth form of intelligibility implying and implicated in the three others. *Figurability* is a psychic property determined by a tendency towards convergence, the actualisation of which triggers a process of binding all the constituents, all the external and internal stimuli. If this develops fully, for instance, in dreams, it will culminate in a perceptive hallucinatory coherence, while being neither perception nor hallucination, for there is no participation of the sense organs. And what is particularly strange for our rational thinking is that, unlike a hallucination, *figurability* must be envisaged as 'material' quality; and, unlike representations and perceptions, which belong to permanent orders (at a later stage in the book we speak of the permanence of a *symmetry representation–perception*), *figurability* has a vocation of transience, of instantaneity, of a dazzling speed of accomplishment, as in dreams.

Figurability is to be considered as an instinctual process whose quality derives from a property of intrapsychic movement of convergence and hallucinatory intelligibility, the dream being its most successful manifestation. At a lesser degree, *figurability* is equally at work during other retrogressive moments of psychic life. For example, in the form of phantasy of unconscious origin whose sudden emergence surprises the ego; or, with the participation of the latter, in the form of *rêverie*; or again, *figurability* is at work in the analyst during the session when a particular retrogressive phenomenon occurs in him, often of decisive importance for the treatment, which we call an 'accident of thought'.

César Botella
Sára Botella
Paris, December 2003

PART ONE

The work of figurability and the negative

1

THE LIMITS OF THOUGHT:
PARIS–LONDON BACK AND FORTH

In his *Letters on England*,[1] Voltaire wrote:

> A Frenchman arriving in London finds things very different, in natural science as in everything else. He has left the world full, he finds it empty. In Paris . . . for your Cartesians everything is moved by an impulsion you don't really understand, for Mr Newton it is by gravitation, the cause of which is hardly better known . . . There you have some appalling clashes . . . Finally, the better to settle if possible every difficulty, he proves, or at least makes it highly probable . . . that a plenum cannot possibly exist, and he brings back the vacuum, which Aristotle and Descartes had banished from the universe.

In this opposition, Descartes' Paris is a world full of dependent relations, leaving no place for the vacuum, a world where clarity and understanding impose on things their notion of what is evident – one only sees what one understands – and Newton's London is a world with a spirit emptied of dependent relations, determined to see, even if it costs the extinction of its lanterns, confronting what seems uncertain, doubtful or strange. For psycho-analysts, the contradiction between the worlds of Paris and London forms the limits of one and the same path – namely, the limits of the functioning of our thought. Thinking, it could be said, is an incessant journey back and forth between Paris and London.

The Newtonian conception is more the product of a powerful work of 'figurability', akin to that of the dream, than a process of rational thought: the universe is an infinite vacuum of which only an infinitely small part is filled by objects – objects that move across this limitless and bottomless void. Nonetheless, the identity and reciprocity between terrestrial and cosmic bodies, between apple and planet, is absolute – each body stands in relation to all the other bodies and is united with them.

It is understandable that this fine figurability was disconcerting for the scientific mind of the epoch for which any notion of the existence of a connection between distant bodies raised the fear of animism. Newton's intuition implies the boldness and subtlety of a movement of thought, transforming all the data of the moment into one single unity, bridling the immensity of the irrepresentable vacuum. It is a work of figuration that is independent of reason, just as it is independent of its direct prehension. This induced René Thom (1993) to say: 'But if one looks at the birth of the great scientific theories, one can say that imagination, conceptual construction, have in general preceded the facts of experience.'

In Newton's universe, 'the clock implies the clockmaker' remarked Voltaire; a formula that captures both the qualities of Newton's figurability, which can seem mysterious and worrying, and his need to render his intuition familiar by making God the basis of the reality of gravitation.

The respective particularities of Newton's and Descartes' thought, insofar as it is pushed to the maximum of its potential, indicate the limits, the two extremes, of all thinking. Faced with the unknown of the void, Newton finds a solution by retrogressing towards a hallucinatory figurability, while clinging to the familiarity of his idea of God; whereas Descartes, thanks to the materiality of ideas, clings to his secondary thought processes, thereby avoiding the hallucinatory void.

For his part, Freud, confronted with the unknown, resorts neither to God nor to reason; the epigraph of *The Interpretation of Dreams* applicable to his whole work, speaks volumes in this respect:

> Flectere si nequeo superos, Acheronta movebo [If I cannot bend the Higher Powers, I will move the Infernal Regions].
>
> Freud, 1900: 608

Nevertheless, Freud remained attached to the positivism of the scientific thinking of his time. Like Darwin, faced with nature, he understood the functioning of the unconscious as a mechanism that is at once blind and formidably efficient. In this resolutely positivist spirit, Freud bridled the vertiginous unknown of the unconscious, while clinging to his belief in the materiality of the force of the drives, that is to say, in quantity, cathexis, facilitation, resistance; in the reality of a psychic mechanism. His solution, faced with the unknown, lies on the side of neither London nor of Paris, but in their common denominator: the concrete nature of the theory of the drive is 'our mythology'. As Michel Neyraut (1997) has said, 'one of the first paradoxes is that the irrational runs behind reason in order to defend it'.

Nevertheless, Freudian drive theory, taken literally, is present at the heart of a topographical conception of the psyche that cannot be separated from the model of an apparatus closed in on itself by the superposition of the poles perception–consciousness. Thus envisaged, the topographical conception requires a 'progressive' theory of thinking, a detour via word cathexes; it precludes retrogressive movement, oscillations between the two poles of perception and hallucinatory experience, journeys back and forth between Paris and London. It has no answer to the capacity of thinking to achieve, even in the waking state, a state of perceptual identity, an opening up of the pole of perception to the hallucinatory.[1]

If the psychoanalyst is satisfied with a reading of Freud's thought exclusively in the light of its rational order, once confronted with the unknown of the session, he or she will have the tendency to cling to the cohesion of ready-made concepts, to analytic knowledge. In this respect, he resembles the post-Newtonians. He overestimates the efficacy of a mechanism, at the risk of misappreciating the scope and range of Freud's thought. Spontaneously, he will be reluctant to engage in any reflection outside the two Freudian topographies, at the risk of carrying out a mutilating reduction of the enormous complexity of the analytic session. It is as though any approach 'extra-muros' in relation to the edifice of the world of concepts ran the risk of endangering thought, of rendering ideas confused and unintelligible. With the psychoanalyst, as with any man, thought loathes a vacuum.

However, while it is true that Freudian thought is fundamentally a theory centred on representation, it is no less true that it is open to perspectives enlarging its scope and range beyond representation.

One of these is the idea that thought in the form of word-presentations is not the only form of thought that exists; there is also 'unconscious thought', just as there is hallucinatory 'visual thought' in the form of the dream. For thought is not only an instrument for grasping reality; in the last resort, it is 'a substitute for a hallucinatory wish' (Freud, 1900: 567).

From this point of view, an attentive reading reveals a long path of negativity in Freud's work. Not only with the rather noisy introduction of the death drive, albeit in continuity with the dialectical principle of the theory of the drive; but also, after 1914, in a discreet vein but one fraught with consequences, with the 'Wolf Man' (1914–18) and the 'Metapsychological supplement to the theory of dreams' (1917a [1915]), in which Freud was concerned with hallucination, including negative hallucination. Then, with *Mourning and Melancholia* (1917b), the texts on 'Neurosis and psychosis' (1924c), 'Negation' (1925b), 'Fetishism' (1927a), 'A disturbance of memory on the Acropolis' (1936), one can follow the thread of the path of negativity leading to 'Splitting of the ego in the process of defence' (1940 [1938]) and the notion of 'negative reactions to the trauma' in *Moses and Monotheism* in (1937b). The key notions, then, are less the usual ones of drive–repression–phantasy, limiting the theory to one axe *Unc.–Pcs.–Cs.*, than those of object–reality–disavowal, forming a metapsychological complement, a new paradigmatic axis: drive–negativity–thought.

(In fact, the upheaval introduced by the death drive – the turning point of 1920 – does not reside so much in the notion of death working on us from within, as in the notion of a death drive, an indispensable precondition for being able to think about a realm beyond primary and secondary processes.)This was the way Freud found of taking the first steps towards conceptualising negativity.

But how, then, are we to conceive of a metapsychology, capable of oscillating back and forth between two poles, which would embrace the negative, by definition irrepresentable, the immediateness of figurability and the detours and torments of the world of representations? Such a theory would stand in need of appropriate concepts, commensurate with certain retrogressive movements of thought in the session bordering at times on the traumatic perception of the void, disturbances, 'accidents' of thought, the irruption of an enigmatic figurability, giving rise to changes of direction in the course of the analyst's thinking.

2

THE NEGATIVE DUALITY OF THE PSYCHE

On duality

Classically, the Freudian topographies – *Cs.*, *Pcs.*, *Ucs.* or ego, superego, id – are thought of as proceeding from the most superficial to the deepest strata and there will be no difficulty in agreeing that the corresponding graph would comprise a vertical axis along which the circulating element does not undergo a transformation – representation remaining representation. It is the topography that qualifies representation sometimes as conscious, sometimes as preconscious or unconscious. These were the foundations of the metapsychology of 1915. While we understand the cardinal role of this axis for Freudian thought, if we want to envisage the study of the oscillations and changes of a qualitative order, notably during the regressive states that do not fail to occur during analytic work, then it is necessary to add to this vertical axis one where the elements constituting it would not be differentiated in terms of their displacement, their greater or lesser distance from consciousness, but in terms of a qualitative order, independent of their topography. The same content will have a different status depending on the quality of the investment (*S.E.* 'cathexis'):[1] representation, perception or hallucination – the qualities of investment depending on the complex dynamic of the modes of intelligibility, in their relations with reality testing.

A theory that favours the vertical axis will lay emphasis on psychic places, resulting in a conception of psychic functioning based on the psychoneurotic model of organisation – a model in which the vision of an essentially autarchic psyche dominates. This is true of the psychical apparatus of the first topography. But, for a theory that is primarily concerned with transformations, a model cannot so easily be found in Freud; for verticality is present even in the second topography. However, in the aftermath of 1920, Freud's thought moved away from the model of the dream as wish-fulfilment in favour of an openness towards the world. The principal reason for this was the discovery of a neurosis with an exclusively external aetiology, without topographies, representations, or repressed infantile wishes playing the slightest role – namely, traumatic neurosis, where hallucinatory repetition is identical to traumatic perception. From this point on, it proved indispensable for Freud to take into account the principles governing the vertical axis as much as those pointing up the distinction between representation and perception. On the vertical axis, characterised by displacement, a content is defined by its localisation in one place alone, whereas, on the new axis, the same content can find itself in two distinct places, but endowed with different qualities, for instance, those of representation and perception. This view of reality presupposes that the intrapsychic and the world, representation and perception, are not, in the last analysis, the autonomous identities they would seem to be.

A graph with two axes, where the vertical axis has an intrapsychic tendency and the horizontal axis accords priority to the role of reality and the object, would be better equipped for studying certain notions and limit concepts, as well as for conducting the analysis of borderline patients for whom one of the major difficulties is their inability to distinguish between what belongs specifically to them and what comes from the object. The mechanisms of Freudian projection, Kleinian projective identification and Lacanian foreclosure could then be envisaged from a wider perspective and not just in terms of their relation to what is repressed or disavowed.

The interdependence of representation and perception is not, as Freud sometimes asserts, just a matter of reproduction. Our theoretical hypothesis on this is akin to the notion of duality as it is currently envisaged in quantum physics – as far as we have understood it, at any rate, while not having any special knowledge of it:[2] the disconcerting property, as much of matter as of energy, of being able to present itself under the double nature of corpuscle and wave. In quantum physics, depending on the conditions of observation, it has become possible to have two contradictory definitions of the same object. The problem raised by quantum objects is that their nature is nothing other than what is revealed by the method of observation and thus it depends closely on the conditions of observation – that is to say, what is revealed of the object is the fruit of the conjunction between its nature and the procedure of observation employed. The dual relationship between the microscopic object, invisible and undetectable by our sense organs, and the macroscopic instrument of observation, confined to temporo-spatiality, requires that a certain rational mode of thinking be challenged, or even abandoned, in favour of other forms of logic that elude our preconscious organisation. Only a considerable effort of abstraction, a *primordial abstraction* (see Chapter 4), makes it possible to distance ourselves from the immediate experience of our sense organs, to the point that quantum physicists are tempted to define reality, that is, their own quantum reality, by parameters which they describe more as 'mental' than 'material', the latter no longer having any real meaning for them. Thus, the acceptance by the scientific community of the existence in the same object of study, the particle, of a corpuscle–wave duality representing a radical breach between the object and its representation, obliges us to reconsider what our instrument of observation, our sense organs, propose as being identical with the familiar sense we have that something is self-evident. Let us recall, though, that Freud had already warned us of this in a succinct way at the end of his work in *An Outline of Psychoanalysis* (1938b): 'Reality will always remain "unknowable"' (p. 196). As early as *The Interpretation of Dreams* (1900), he had asserted that reality could in no case simply be raw material emanating from the sense organs:

> Our waking (preconscious) thinking behaves towards any perceptual material with which it meets in just the same way in which the function we are considering [i.e. secondary revision] behaves towards the content of dreams. It is the nature of our waking thought to establish order in material of that kind, to set up relations in it and to make it conform to our expectations of an intelligible whole.
>
> S.E.V, 499

To the extent, he would add in 1912 that, 'if, as a result of special circumstances, it is unable to establish a true connection, it does not hesitate to fabricate a false one' (*S.E.* XIII, 95). How, then, can we avoid the necessity of rethinking the notions we take as most self-evident, perception and representation, and in particular the notion of object-representation?[3]

This loss of the unity of representation, implied by the astonishing corpuscle–wave duality, evokes, for the analyst, a duality of quite another order. With all due caution, we are not far here from the child's capacity for thinking, evoked by Freud (1900) in connection with a child in mourning, which it would be wrong to reduce to mechanisms of splitting and denial: 'I know father's dead, but what I can't understand is why he doesn't come home to supper' (p. 254). This is a quality of the child's way of thinking, not a deficiency. Here we are in the register of animistic thinking, specific to the young child, who, confronted with the object's absence, and following the failure of the purely hallucinatory solution, will resort to such a dual mode of thinking 'there . . . not there', resulting in an evolution towards the symbolic form (the wooden reel game described by Freud in *Beyond the Pleasure Principle* (1920).

Moreover, as in quantum thinking, there is no possibility of linking the two statements rationally. While not wishing to distort our comparison by an excess of analogy, let us simply point out that in both cases – in quantum and animistic thought – a duality is sustained by a negative – namely, the lost perception of a strongly invested object: the father for the child, the macroscopic object for the physicist. It is necessary to be able to continue to think when our sense organs and our usual temporo-spatial means fail us. It is also worth pointing out that the notion of duality is not employed here as a binary relation or conflictual duality, but as the duality of one and the same object. This possibility has led Catherine Chevalley (1990) to say of the corpuscle–wave duality: 'there would no doubt be some advantage to be gained from considering, within the long tradition of philosophy, the question that arises once again here of knowing how to treat two contradictory statements concerning the "same object" '.

Hegel and the addâd

In a day and age when science had totally disinvested the notion of the Newtonian void, the young Hegel was already complaining about the rationalism fragmenting the world and separating ideas such as sacred and profane, faith and knowledge, mind and nature, individual and community. He saw in these 'polar oppositions' the cause of an unfortunate 'split' (*Entzweiung*) between 'absolute subjectivity' and 'absolute objectivity', the cause of the rigidity, the 'solidification' of thought. This said, let us just note that in his works *Logic* (1804–1805), the *Phenomenology of Mind* (1807) and *The Science of Logic* (1812–16), the issue is above all one of recognising that 'within one and the same relation a thing both exists-in-itself while, at the same time, being its own lack or negative'; that the 'principle of identity says nothing'; that 'there exists above it, as above contradiction, an even more elevated sphere which is its negative unity, its ground.' 'Identity is nothing but non-being, whereas the negative is the root of all movement, of all vitality.' The negative 'must be both self-subsistent, thus the negative self-relation, being-for-self; but, as pure and simple negative, it must have this self-relation which is its own, its positive, only in the Other'. And finally, the 'prodigious power of the negative' – which unites and separates, abolishes and conserves (*aufheben*) – leads us to question the immediate evidence of our sense organs. In fact, Hegel's conception concerning the possibility of transforming an apparent separation into a *negative superior unity*, brings us closer to the Newtonian conception of the void, as well as to the corpuscle–wave duality of quantum physics, helping us to understand the unity of the psyche better. Especially when he recognises in the term *aufheben*, reuniting union and separation, abolition and conservation, 'the speculative spirit of our language, which goes beyond the simple "either–or" characteristic of understanding'.

Every psychoanalyst is bound to think here of Freud passing from the German language to the language of dreams:

[T]he alternative 'either–or' cannot be expressed in dreams in any way whatever. Both of the alternatives are usually inserted in the text of the dream as though they were equally valid. [He then continues] . . . the way in which dreams treat the category of contraries and contradictories is highly remarkable. It is simply disregarded. 'No' seems not to exist so far as dreams are concerned. They show a particular preference for combining contraries into a unity or for representing them as one and the same thing. Dreams feel themselves at liberty, moreover, to represent any element by its wishful contrary; so that there is no way of deciding at a first glance whether any element that admits of a contrary is present in the dream-thoughts as a positive or as a negative.

Freud, 1900: S.E. V, 427–30

The dream is a 'language without grammar', Freud said when taking interest, in 1910 (Freud, 1910a: *S.E.* XI, 155), in a study by Karl Abel in 1884 on the contrary meanings of primal words. The author studied them particularly in the old Egyptian language, where they can be found in a relatively large number; then in the Indo-European languages where Abel believed he had found examples of what he interpreted as primitive testimonies of language. Notwith-standing the severe critique by Benveniste (1956) who considers such a stage in a language as 'pure fancy', Sami Ali (1977) endeavours to show that these examples abound in the Arab language, with a recent survey fixing their number in the region of 300. These are the *addâd*, words with antithetical meanings, a few examples of which we will now cite from Sami Ali's book: *sârim* (night and day), *siwâ* (other and same), *sara* (unite and disunite), *aswad* (black and white), *sakeb* (near and far), *warâ* (in front and behind); or again, containing double contradictions like *dûn* (high and low; in front and behind). They are evidence, Sami Ali, 'not of a deficiency, but of a semantic richness'; their fundamental quality being that they attempt to 'communicate the uncommunicable' (see Chapter 12), owing to the very fact, we would say, of having been able to preserve the relation to their negative duality. This gives them the capacity of being the avenue, par excellence, of Sufi mystical practice, which, unlike Christian mysticism, does not need to be practised in the *via negativa* of renunciation. Owing to their nature, the *addâd* can easily destabilise preconscious formations and give rise to a withdrawal of investment from the realm of representation, a psychic state that may be likened to the narcissistic regression of sleep in the sense that, as for the latter, word-presentations are erased, making way for hallucinatory tendencies.

The negative of the analytic setting

Freud invented the analytic setting, which includes the virtual disappearance of all perception, in particular that of the analyst who removes himself from the analysand's view. These conditions imposed by the setting are at the origin of specific psychic movements for which an analytic theory oriented exclusively by positivist concerns only has partial answers. It is not enough to explain the analyst's withdrawal as Freud's solution to the need to protect himself against the affective assaults of his analysands – such as Breuer taking flight with his wife in face of Anna O's solicitation. By the same token, the hypothesis can be framed of the existence of an initial intuition on Freud's part – namely, the need to establish a setting *negativising* perception, as an indispensable means of approaching the psyche. It is by virtue of the analyst's withdrawal that his regressive omnipresence in the analysand's psychic space occurs, that the traumas of childhood are awakened, that infantile sexuality resurfaces and that an authentic transference neurosis, an actualisation of the infantile neurosis, can be established. Such a regressive state, peculiar to the mind during the session, can certainly be explained in terms of a psychoanalytic conception that favours the mechanics of a reversible linear movement regression–progression and of its connected systems of representation in which contents and memory predominate. This is the metapsychology of 1915, a theory of interpretation and, more widely, of analytic work, based essentially on the model of interpretation of the dream narrative. It is capable of explaining the dynamics of the transference, the mechanism of repression and the return of the repressed, the necessity of recapturing forgotten memories and the efficacy of interpretation. But we cannot be satisfied with this; for the negativising conditions of the setting generate other regressive processes that cannot be understood in terms of the topographies, conflicts or memory. Just as the dream process cannot return to the conditions that gave rise to it, its orientation towards the hallucinatory solution being irrevocable, the irreversible retrogressive processes of the session cannot rediscover their origins or undergo a change in their orientation (see Part Four; Botella, C. and S., 1997a). Unlike reversible processes, such as symptoms and the transference, they do not correspond to the idea of a past that is represented, conserved in the form of repressed memory. In fact, the understanding of these irreversible processes requires analytic theory to be open towards the pole *Pcs.–Cs.*, to hallucinatory perceptual processes. Freud had already sensed this in 1915, as can be seen from two articles written simultaneously (according to the *Standard Edition* between 23 April and 4 May 1915): 'A metapsychological supplement to the theory of dreams' and *Mourning and Melancholia*.

The negative duality object-representation: self-representation

Analytic practice has confirmed for us the ideas advanced in *Mourning and Melancholia*; namely, the traumatic quality of the object's absence is experienced as an extreme anxiety that does not concern the subject's integrity but the subject in his entirety. The permanent solution against distress can never be to cathect or invest the object's presence, or again, to have auto-erotic recourse to a part of the body as its substitute – these are merely palliative measures. The only genuine solution lies in the mind's capacity to represent (*figurer*), to invest the object-representation, whether it be the primitive ego or the constituted psyche that is concerned. Only, as we shall see in the next chapter, investing the representation, like hallucinatory wish-fulfilment, has its limits.

Although the term investment of the object-representation carries with it certain misunderstandings – and on this point we would refer the reader to the *Language of Psychoanalysis* (Laplanche and Pontalis, 1967) – analytic theory cannot do without it. The main difficulty is that, generally speaking, one understands by 'object-representation' a single investment, a simple and delimited psychical entity, whereas it is the outcome of multiple investments marked by at least two tendencies: one, 'anti-narcissistic', in Francis Pasche's sense, the centrifugal tendency of a wishful impulse in its inexhaustible quest for the object; the other, the auto-erotic return to oneself – a movement of return where general links are formed at the heart of what, in the last analysis, proves to be a primordial binding object–body–psyche is made up of reflections and projections between the endopsychic perception of the erotogenic body ego and that of the external object coming from the sense organs. In reality, this subject–object relation constitutes one and the same movement, which is underpinned by traumatic and disorganising forces emanating both from the arepresented 'chaos' of the id and from the aperception of the sense organs. It is underpinned, then, by both the drive and by the object's absence.

Notwithstanding a few passages in Freud that are coloured by a certain psychologism, no analytic theory which claims to be rigorous can conceive of the notion of 'object-representation' either as the duplication of a perception, or even as a repeatable and stable figure, but rather as a complex formation, a network of ego investments following the unifying tendency that is proper to it, a sort of reservoir of infantile sexuality that polarises the object and narcissistic infantile bindings as a whole, thereby guaranteeing the constancy, the permanence of our psychic functioning. As a genuine pole of attraction for all the other representations, the object-representation invested by the ego pertains rather to a processual order and, no less than the dream-work, to the unifying power of narcissistic regression, to its tendency to bring together the different forces at play. To this is to be added a supplementary terminological difficulty, in the measure that the 'object-presentation' is to be considered as being inseparable from that of the subject. The best illustration of the object-representation–self-representation duality is the wooden reel game described by Freud in *Beyond the Pleasure Principle* (1920). Like other authors, we will dwell on it briefly, as Freud's description remains such a fertile source of ideas on the constitution of the psyche.

Curiously enough, none of the numerous authors who have taken interest in the description of the wooden reel game has stressed the fact that Freud says that his grandson is outside his cot and not inside it, as one naturally tends to imagine. And furthermore, that it is from his position outside it that he throws the wooden reel over the edge of the curtained cot; then, by pulling on the string he draws it back out of the cot again. Although the wooden reel certainly represents the mother, it must, if only because it enters and comes out of the cot, equally represent the baby himself. The child is striving, then, not only to master the absence of the invested object, but also its consequences, his own disarray, the exhaustion of his psychic capacities to maintain the object-representation, the risk of the loss of his own representation (see following chapter). The representations 'mummy' and 'child' thus come together in the absence, in a common double negativity.

Freud may not be far from such a hypothesis when he relates in a footnote (Freud, 1920: *S.E.* XVIII, 15) another of his grandson's games at the same period, complementary to the one just mentioned: during his mother's absences 'the child had found a method of *making himself disappear*. He had discovered his reflection in a full-length mirror which did not quite reach to the ground' (our italics). By replacing the wooden reel with his own reflection in the mirror, the child now amused himself, by crouching down and standing up again; by making his reflection in the mirror disappear and reappear. He repeated the same onomatopoeia that he uttered with the wooden reel: '*o-o-o-o/da*' (gone/there), but now added when his reflection disappeared in the mirror: '*baby/o-o-o-o!*' (baby/gone); and probably, but Freud does not say this, '*baby/da*' (baby/there) when his reflection reappeared in the mirror.

We notice, then, that in the formative process of object-representation, the subject's specular absence is just as important as the object's real absence; and further, that the subject–object link is sustained by the negativity common to the two representations. In fact, the notion 'object-representation' could be replaced by the formulation of Hegelian inspiration: '*negative duality object-representation/self-representation*', by the idea of a 'negative higher unity' that would nuance any subject–object separation and contradict any reduction of the notion of 'object-representation' to mere memory images of the real object.

28

3

NON-REPRESENTATION

The object of this chapter (which is a revised and corrected version of Botella, C. and S., 1983a) is to study the dynamic and economic value of 'figurability', the 'sensory strength' of the image – Freud's expression – and the analyst's use of it in the treatment. We shall present here the earliest stages of our research into figurability, at a time when we were treating children, some of whom were severely ill.

Our experience as child psychoanalysts confronted us with the phenomenon of autistic children sleeping with their eyes open. Their gaze, which traversed us during the day, continued during the night to fade into a remote background of nothingness. Once the first signs of an object-relation emerge in their treatment, these children begin to scream with terror in their sleep. Initially, as the initial investment of the perceptions and object-representations is still fragile and fluctuating, without there being any real distinction between what is perceived of the object and what is represented, the object's absence is in danger of being the equivalent of the loss of its representation. And, more than the loss of the object, it is the danger of the loss of its representation, the heir of hallucinatory wish-fulfilment, which is a synonym for distress.

Instead of a hypothetical genetic succession from the pleasure ego to the reality ego, we find it more heuristic to envisage their early simultaneity and a psychical functioning that already has contradictory interests. Contradictory, and not conflictual, which makes us refrain from speaking of a very early splitting of the ego, the notion of splitting being linked to that of a defence mechanism in the face of a conflict. Let us say that the ego has a double origin. Freud affirms in 1915 in *Instincts and their Vicissitudes*:

> At the very beginning, it seems, the external world, objects, and what is hated are identical. If later on an object turns out to be a source of pleasure, it is loved, but it is also incorporated into the ego; so that for the purified pleasure-ego once again objects coincide with what is extraneous and hated.
>
> *S.E.* XIV, 136

To put it in another way, perception is hated by the pleasure ego, and condemned to be persecuting, the residue of the pleasure ego; on the contrary, for the reality ego, equally governed by the pleasure principle, perception is its raison d'être. In 'Negation' (1925b), Freud maintains the theoretical positions he advanced in 1915 and adds that:

> The first and immediate aim, therefore, of reality testing is, not to *find* an object in real perception which corresponds to the one presented, but to *refind* such an object, to convince oneself that it is still there.
>
> *S.E.* XIX, 237

✶ As long as the reality ego cannot confirm sufficiently that the object presented still exists, and also in reality, the perception remains persecuting for the pleasure ego. Moreover, the object's absence cannot be recognised and will be traumatic as long as the object-representation is maintained by the pleasure ego. *Indeed, in our view, it is not the loss of the object but the danger of the loss of its representation and, by extension, the risk of non-representation, which denotes distress.*

The danger of the loss of the representation provokes a real void with an implosive effect, precipitating the hated perception in the psyche. Being the shadowy equivalent of the representation that has disappeared, the persecuting perception invades the scene. In the shadow of the lack of satisfaction awakened by the absence of the invested object, more than the signal anxiety aroused by the risk of losing the object, it is the automatic fright of implosion that is called on to become a signal warning of the danger of losing the representation of this same object. The use of the effect of the implosion of perception by the emerging ego, in the figurative depictions of a nightmare, is a violent defence against the risk of non-representation; the 'sensory strength' of the hallucination of the nightmare is a performance necessary for the survival of the psyche.

It seems that the small child who wakes up terrified, with a wild expression in his eyes, has only been able to preserve his investments of object-representations, his desire, thanks to the nightmare. His nightmare may be said to have preserved him from the gaze that burrows its way towards infinite indifference. Likewise, when the child has difficulty in going to sleep, just when he should be withdrawing investment from the perception of his objects, letting himself be carried along by the flow of narcissistic regression, more than regretting or refusing to let go of the external world, is he not afraid, rather, of drowning the representation of his objects in the effusion offered by sleep? And are not all of us, each night, threatened by this primordial conflict re-actualised by the narcissistic regression of sleep, threatened by the ghost, the shadow of the object that has haunted us since the cradle in order to preserve us from the worst, from the loss of representation, a question of psychic life and death?

Thomas and the wolf

Drawing on clinical situations, we have suggested since the beginning of our writings that, within the framework of the theory of representation, a conceptual role should be accorded to the experience of the absence of representation (Botella, C. and S., 1983a). At the time, any reference to negativity was subject to lively debate, notwithstanding the English publications of Winnicott and Bion, and, in France, of André Green.

Thomas was a little 4-year-old boy who, up till the age of 20 months, had undergone numerous hospitalisations and surgical operations (his sub-clavicular artery was badly implanted; he choked and had difficulty breathing; moreover, he had a malformation of his urethra). His whole development was slow. When one of us saw him, when he was 4, Thomas could only utter a few, barely intelligible words. Although his parents described him as presenting autistic traits, Thomas had never really lost his appetite for the object, his elan towards the other. He certainly sought contact but was incapable of maintaining a relationship; and he behaved like an affectionate child who quickly drops adults, taking refuge in a quiet corner from where, neither timid nor absent, he contemplates the world. As for the new situation, the new object, that therapy represents for any child, Thomas threw himself into it wholeheartedly. With the ardour of fresh hope, he ran off with a pot of glue, the contents of which he breathed in passionately, like a drug addict, giving one the impression of an extraordinary reunion occurring. At other times, seeking some rays of sunlight, he would lie down on the desk and absorb them with his eyes open, without even blinking. Then, for a long time, his favourite activity was throwing and banging solid objects against the hard surfaces of the room. What interested him was making noise. He would go: 'grrrr . . . grrrr!'

It is not difficult to guess the sort of construction the analyst made on the basis of these elements – the smell, the light, and the noise – probably sensory traces, perhaps marks left by an early object. In his formulations, the analyst tried to introduce a large quantity of affect: 'When you were in the hospital where the smell was very strong and the light was very bright, it was difficult to breathe . . . it was as if everything was going to go "grrrr . . . grrrr . . .!"'.

At the end of the sessions, Thomas manifested depersonalising anxieties. Interpretations about separation brought him no relief. And yet the analyst was trying to find the right level of interpretation. They all failed, whether they concerned the whole object or the part object; the Oedipal level or destructive envy of the breast or the nipple, hate or depression. Thomas' state of distress was such that, for his immobilised and absent ego, the word-presentations coming from the analyst had no import; whatever their content, the child was unable to hear them. He was beyond the reach of all usual communication. What was one to do? A mother would take the child in her arms, thereby communicating what words cannot transmit. But the psychoanalyst? Faced with the repeated and bitter failure of his interpretations, was he simply to resign himself, to content himself with taking the child back to his mother in the waiting room, even though he could not help noticing just how destitute the child seemed? Faced with this pale, immobile, haggard-looking child, the very picture of terror, the analyst himself had, as it were, a nightmare. He then said to Thomas: 'Grrrr . . . grrrr! Are you afraid of the wolf?' And without thinking about it, he spontaneously imitated the nasty beast that bites and claws. Terror stricken, Thomas signalled to him to stop, but his disarray disappeared and he was able to leave. The time after, when the moment came to separate, the analyst repeated the episode of the wolf. Thomas was no longer depersonalised; he propelled himself into the corridor and, wanting to frighten everybody, yelled out: 'Grrrr . . . grrrr . . . the wolf!'

What had the analyst done with this child? Was his first intervention, the 'hospital', a construction of a historic past with 'fragments of truth', as Freud says?

In effect, we believe bits of material reality existed – the smell, the burst of light, the noise of breathing – but we strongly doubt that they had attained the quality of psychic representation. In all probability they remained pure sensory elements. And although there was an attempt at elaboration in the game of making the noise 'grrrr . . . grrrr' or in the fact of becoming intoxicated by breathing in deeply the emanations from the glue or in dazzling himself by exposing himself to the rays of light, these are above all autistic forms of behaviour in search of sensations of dizziness bordering on losing consciousness. Nevertheless, one may wonder if there were an initial stage of psychic representation of these first experiences at the hospital, which was quickly dislocated into the form of their sensory elements. We shall never know. Contrariwise, we do know how disorganising the effect on the child's psyche is of such non-represented sensory elements, just as we know how unfailingly beneficial the effect is when the analyst can take up these elements in a construction composed of pictorial forms, such as a recollection. This work gives the very ill child the feeling that he exists, that he endures; thanks to this, his suffering will be linked up with the past, his emotions will come together in the form of memory, 'just as a fountain basin collects water', to use Freud's beautiful image (Freud, 1900). And, if Freud says that 'dreaming is remembering', might it be said that in cases like that of Thomas, remembering is dreaming, that the past cannot become memory without a dream-work furnished by the analyst?

The second intervention, the 'wolf', was not a story in images or a psycho-dramatic enactment, but a flash of the analyst, a work of figurability giving a meaning to Thomas' disarray and relieving the analyst of the sense of torment and disappointment resulting from the failure of his usual analytic methods. But, then, why did he evoke this single, terrifying figure? When Thomas remained terror stricken by the separation, it was not, in our view, a state triggered by a precise problem, for instance, oral. The traumatising power of separation, and Thomas' limited possibilities for elaboration, meant that once his protective shield was broken, his whole system of representation, which was already precarious, was completely swept away. By naming and mimicking the wolf, the analyst was not evoking the meaning of a phantasy in the face of loss, but was soliciting in the child a psychic work comparable to his own, the double, as it were, of the evocative force of his own work of figurability; Thomas used the wolf as a real representation weapon against the distress of *non-representation*. At that moment, the effect of the image 'wolf', had, above all, the function of containing distress that had not been represented and was provoked by the menace of losing the object and less that of a specific content, for instance, oral, i.e. of being devoured. If, nonetheless, one really wants to refer to a content, one might consider that the image 'wolf', for the analyst, makes use of autistic elements present in the sessions, that is, the fixed gaze of the child absorbing, without blinking, the sunlight; the importance of smell, the child inhaling noisily, the child yelling and so on. The question now arises: what was it that mobilised the analyst's psyche, without his knowing it, in the direction of such a psychical work? Would it be directly those sensory elements characteristic of Thomas or the effect that these elements had on him, a worry, a sense of uncanniness appealing to a universal reference, to typical dream images and to children's fairytales? In any case, it was only later, after the event, that the representation of the wolf would make it possible, if necessary, to make customary interpretations such as, 'When you have to leave me, you are so angry that you would like to claw me, to eat me like a wolf' and so on.

In fact, the analyst did not formulate a latent content that he had discovered behind a manifest content, but in the absence of both he advanced preconscious formations susceptible of attracting, one day, other representations, of serving as manifest content. A sort of analytic process in reverse in which the analyst promotes the child's preconscious. Under the effects of the captivating power of the analyst's figurability, we see emerging in the child the rough outline of a world of representations.

But, then, why does the child analyst's so often produce a work of figurability akin to a nightmare? We think that the functioning of sick children such as Thomas subjects the analyst's mind to severe ordeals. Not only is the analyst deprived of his setting and his tool, interpretation, but, in addition, he feels uneasy owing to the vagueness of the representations that the child awakens in him, until he is himself menaced by the worst, that is, the absence of any representation. Thus tested and weakened – just as the sleeper's ego can be weakened by the narcissistic regression of sleep – and menaced by *non-representation*, the analyst's ego will react. Of course, in order to defend himself, he could cease to invest his function, or worse, the child, or alternatively, over-invest his capacities for intellectualisation, for theorisation, concluding, in an assured tone of voice: 'He is autistic!' We think that in Thomas' case, the analyst's ego, 'sapped' by the failures of his habitual interventions, found the solution in the figurative images of a nightmare. Thus, if the hypothesis we have put forward concerning the function of the nightmare is sound, there are grounds for thinking that an affect, signalling the danger of *non-representation* that was almost awakened in the analyst, immediately 'created found' a figure, an adequate representation. The formal regression and the fluidity of the analyst's libido enabled him to come up with the figurative image of a ferocious beast relating to his own infantile sexuality. His psychic work continued by adopting a mode adapted to his special relationship with the child; the analyst then introduced his 'nightmare' in a form charged with the pleasure of a game.

Once the figurability nightmare had been expressed in gestures and words, the 'wolf' became, as René Diatkine has suggested, a fairytale. Indeed, experience has taught us that, with young children, the dynamism of this type of intervention is comparable to that exerted by the telling of fairytales: in a tender context, the adult evokes representations, highly charged with instinctual drive activity, situated elsewhere and in the past of a 'real' story, since it can be evoked at will. The representations thus conveyed awaken the child's own capacity for figurability and diminish the disorganising pressure of the pre-represented instinctual contingent. In the communication between the child and the adult, the fairytale forms a real bridge, leading the intensity of the child's unstable, fleeting experience, which cannot easily be represented in a relationship with his real objects, towards the universe of the stable and representable relations of a story. From the terror of the nightmare to the marvellous world of the fairytale, the fundamental distress of *non-representation* is demolished.

Thérèse

Thérèse, a little 8-year-old girl, was regarded as 'bizarre' by the nuns at the convent where she had been since she was 3, the date of the sudden death of her father, who had brought her up until then, her mother being unable to take care of her. During the first meeting, Thérèse approached the analyst as if she were having an hallucination of him instead of looking at him. Light footed, she glided towards him, enveloping him with her beautiful, sombre and feverish expression. She said to him: 'Do you know that the earth is round? . . . The sky is everywhere . . . my dad is dead . . . he talks all day long to God.' 'What do they say', the analyst asked her. 'Poor Thérèse, she is all alone . . . I would like to be very nice so that I can go to heaven quickly.' Following this encounter, session after session, Thérèse would say: 'Tell me about the first time!' And each time, the analyst would repeat for her the tale of their first encounter. For Thérèse, there was no question of breaking the continuity of her work of figurability. Settled into the universe of her images, with time suspended, within the confines of the perception–consciousness already open towards hallucination, she blocked out, by means of constant illuminations, the image of the pain of her loss. The economic exigency for hallucinatory continuity meant that Thérèse was unable to allow room for representations, for discontinuity, the recognition of differences: presence/absence, present/past, penis/no penis, boy/girl.

During one session, when she was playing at being at school, Thérèse cried out : 'Girls after the boys, boys after the girls!' Between boys and girls, she weaves infinite links. By blocking out the horror of the reality of the lack of her object, Thérèse was alienating her consciousness. By over-investing the only thing within her reach that was permanent, the figurability of things and the sensoriality of words, she avoided the affects of a process of mourning that would overwhelm her protective shield. The analyst's use of the child's hallucination in the form of a repeatable tale integrated the child's hallucinatory solution within a new context, that of the recent libidinal investment of the object-analyst. Thanks to this, the process of mourning could develop and Thérèse was able to cry for the first time over her father's death.

Theoretical and practical considerations

From the beginning of his work, Freud noted that the inability to mourn a loved one can lead to an inhibition of the painful affect. By disavowing the perception of the lack, there appears in waking life a hallucination of the dead person in place of the painful affect. In 1932, while studying the dream-work again, Freud established a parallel between the disappearance of the affects of the dream thoughts and the 'sensory strength' of the dream pictures. He writes: 'the importance of the ideas that have been stripped of their affect returns in the dream as sensory strength in the dream-pictures' (Freud, 1932b: [1933]: *S.E.* XXII, 21). This displacement of the energy of the affects towards figurability confirms what we thought previously about Thomas: whether it is the terror of *non-representation* or of the pain of mourning, the retrogressive movement of thought is a means of transforming the force of the affects into the 'sensory strength' of a visual image. Moreover, in Thérèse's daytime functioning, it is remarkable that formal regression, the hallucinatory character of her thinking, avoids a splitting of the ego and it is sufficient to give fresh impetus to the movement in the reverse direction – by means of a new investment followed by the story of its past in the form of a fairy tale – to transform the hallucination into the simple figurability of a recollection, to give mourning its right to exist. (This also reminds us of 'I know father's dead, but what I can't understand is why he doesn't come home to supper', a remark reported by Freud in *The Interpretation of Dreams* and uttered by a boy after the sudden death of his father (*S.E.* IV, 254).) Pain, which had been masked by the 'sensory strength' of hallucination, will reappear, attenuated by the figurability of the past shared with the analyst, initiating a process of mourning.

35

In another context where mourning was impossible, a small 4-year-old boy was unaware that he had been adopted when he was just a few weeks old and remained so until he was 3, when his mother had her first unexpected, unhoped-for pregnancy. One day, when out walking, his mother suddenly decided to tell him about the adoption: 'You know, you were not in my tummy.' The child stopped in his tracks, petrified. Suddenly, he brightened up and declared triumphantly: 'But, of course, I was in my daddy's tummy!' Then, when his mother said this was not so, he replied with conviction: 'But yes, yes, I know it's true, I have seen the photo!' For a long time, no one in the world could take his 'truth' away from him, for it protected him from the trauma of losing his mother. Thanks to the emergence of an infantile theory, the strangeness, the pain of the loss were avoided, the child's love for his mother was preserved, the 'hole' of the withdrawal of investment from the representation of the mother was immediately filled by the sensory strength of the sight of the pregnant father; the work of figurability, the photo, triumphed over the void.

When a child, on seeing a newborn baby, asks himself the question, 'But where has he come from?', when he is faced with the 'vital exigency' (*Lebensnot*) and moved by his immediate libidinal demands, he responds to the 'question-riddle' by a mental work, by a formidable surge in his capacity to represent. In fact, whether the situation is one of a birth or of 'the very incomplete perception of parental relations', in such circumstances, the child is always faced with a withdrawal of investment on the part of his parents and, consequently, is also confronted with his own tendency to disinvest his parents. On noticing the difference between the sexes or on being faced with the threat of castration, the result is the same, in the measure that the child will tend, at this particular moment, to disinvest the mother, an individual without a penis, the penis being 'the primordial erotic object' at this particular moment. The true motive force behind the creation of the sexual theories is the risk that the child will disinvest the parental objects. And just as when he was confronted with the object's absence in the past, or during the narcissistic regression of sleep, this tendency to disinvest objects plays the role of an alarm signalling the danger of losing their representation. The only way forward is to represent. Without discussing the possible origins of the primitive scene in perception and/or in phylogenetic phantasies, we consider that it should be considered first and foremost as a sexual theory, perhaps the first sexual theory that the child is obliged to create. Even if populated with monsters, it is a lesser evil, like the nightmare.

The 'sensory strength' of the figurative means of successive sexual theories thwarts the torments of perception, such as that of the distinction between the sexes and the child will have the strength of hallucinatory conviction: 'But yes, mummy and daddy's widdlers are the same . . . I've seen them.' The figurative means employed in the sexual theories of children are 'analogous with the attempts of adults, which are looked at as strokes of genius, at solving' – on the basis of 'fragments of real truth' – 'the problems of the universe which are too hard for human comprehension' (Freud, 1908: *S.E.* IX, 205–26). Both arouse the same conviction as hallucinatory regression in dreams and delusions.

We think that, at certain moments, when the analyst is obliged to ask himself of his analysand: 'But how is he made, how does he function?', he is not far from the child's mode of thinking when faced with the 'questions-riddles' culminating in the creation of the sexual infantile theories and, like the child he used to be, the analyst is also condemned to have a 'stroke of genius' to represent these theories for himself.

In extreme situations, the work of figurability allows the analyst to maintain his analysand's investment and to preserve his own capacities for representation. Whether his expression remains at the level of perceptual identity or reaches the elaborative level of a fairytale, it will certainly always have the advantage of the 'sensory strength' of visual images, but it will also have the particularity of being able to provoke a contrary effect to that of an interpretation. Once put into words, the image succeeds admirably in becoming, for the analysand, a formation equivalent to the manifest content of a dream or a screen memory. Denise Braunschweig and Michel Fain (1981b) rightly denounce the screen memory as a truly anti-analytic work and show the ease with which the analysand will attempt to make use of the most adequate interpretation in order to construct a screen memory. Our view is that this is a particular effect that the analyst can try to achieve in certain cases with a view to consolidating the coherence of the analysand's ego, as he did with Thomas and Thérèse. And, more generally, in the course of all analytic work, the analyst's work of figurability is part of the analytic process and represents a precious tool for its progression or even the sole means of reaching certain areas of the analysand's psychic life.

The analyst's work of figurability with two children led to interventions whose form is akin to that of children's fairytales: 'Once upon a time . . .' This is astonishly reminiscent of the intervention described by Freud (1937a):

> Up to your nth year you regarded yourself as the sole and unlimited possessor of your mother; then came another baby and brought you grave disillusionment. Your mother left you for some time, and even after her reappearance she was never again devoted to you exclusively. Your feelings towards your mother became ambivalent, your father gained a new importance for you.
>
> *S.E.* XXIII, 261

This was the example given by Freud at the end of his work to illustrate the construction interpretation whose value, for the analysand's evolution, does not reside so much, as he admits himself, in the recollections it can evoke or in its historical reality as in the degree of conviction that arouses in the analysand. At bottom, we wonder where the limits are – the conjunction and disjunction between the interpretation construction and the intervention fairytale resulting in what we would qualify as an analytic process in reverse. Without going any further here into the search for this rapprochement, we wish to say that a story impregnated with visual images has the force of impact of perception. It obliges the mind to believe – to believe in the 'wolf' – 'in the baby at the hospital'. It is said, is it not, that 'seeing is believing'? The stamp of the analyst's work of figurability on the interpretation awakens a sense of proof, of authenticity in the analysand. Here, it is as though the 'truth' were visible.

4

THE GEOMETER AND THE PSYCHOANALYST

On the occasion of the homage paid to René Thom in Gif sur Yvette on his 70th birthday, we had the honour of being asked to make a psychoanalytic contribution.

One of René Thom's fields of research is the elucidation, starting with notions of continuity and discontinuity, of what 'might constitute an *a priori* ultimate kernel of the biological individual, *constituting* his psyche'. Such research supposes an inevitable confrontation between Thom's thought and Freud's theory, something Michèle Porte (1994) had already attempted with pertinence in *La dynamique qualitative en psychanalyse*, an in-depth study of Thom's thinking. As far as we are concerned, we have found that we are in agreement with Thom's thinking on an unexpected issue, namely, the role of the negative in the constitution of the human psyche.

Our concern, then, has not been so much to establish a comparison between Thom and Freud as between Thom and contemporary psychoanalytic theory, in that it attaches major importance to the notion of the negative.

Let us take as our starting point the study carried out by Michèle Porte. She quite rightly points out that any attempt to establish a comparison between Freud and Thom must take into account the fact that Freud created an exceptional framework for thinking about psychic processes, whereas Thom, with his ontology of *Prégnances et Saillances* (Thom, 1988), created a conceptual framework which enables one to think about the events of reality and their psychic meaning. And it is precisely this articulation between psychic processes and events of reality that is at the centre of contemporary analytic theory, the latter being the fruit of an evolution in the Freudian conception, essentially intrapsychic, whereby its horizons have been broadened to take into account the role of the primary object and the environment in the development of the mind. In this general context, we are particularly interested in Thom's idea concerning the experiences of the infant, that 'salience (*saillance*) is linked . . . to the perception of a qualitative discontinuity'; and, in his description of pregnancy (*prégnance*) as a well of potential charged with 'negative intensities' capable, in the case of human beings, of 'becoming distorted in the course of time', of 'bifurcating into several minima'. It is this negative potential, then, that makes the first psychic organisations possible; these are its 'unoccupied minima' that will be filled by the 'infant's infantile experiences'. What is involved here, according to Thom, is the phenomenon of the imprint, 'a component that could be called "cultural"'. From there, he is led on to Pavlovian conditioning and to the idea that this represents an ideal system for explaining how the mind is constituted.

For the psychoanalyst, in addition to the primordial experience that Thom calls the mother's 'imprint'– her physical presence, toilet training, a series of concrete realities – must be added, and with just as much primordial importance, the failures of these experiences. In Freud's thought, especially after he wrote the article 'Formulations on the two principles of mental functioning' (1911a), it is in the encounter between the 'imprint' and the work imposed by negative experiences that the human psyche is constituted: for instance, the experience of the absence of food which triggers the hallucinatory satisfaction of the need. It will be the ensemble formed by the concreteness of the satisfaction, the experience of its absence and the hallucinatory solution, and then its failure, which will have a fundamental role for the constitution of the psyche. The effectiveness of the procedure resides in the fact of a non-distinction between sensory and motor perception and the hallucinatory solution.[1] But maintaining the hallucinatory solution, beyond the necessary recognition of the state of need, signals the existence of a severe pathological entity.

If we are so attached to the role of the negative, it is because it seems to us that a theory which only takes account of the investments of the *salient* forms by a *prégnance*, or – to employ Freud's formulation, inspired by Hegel and Frazer – the sole presence of the 'higher unity of contact' (Freud, 1912b: *S.E.* XIII, 85), would reduce the psyche to a totalising type of functioning with relations of identity between psychic reality and material reality. The duality *representation–perception*, which is a determining factor for the thought of man, emerges in the projection on to the absence, the void, left by the object. This is the case, whether it be the creation, in primitive man, of the body–soul duality originating in the projection concerning the death of what is not his own body; or alternatively, of the creation in the child of the object-representation in the face of the mother's absence. The dimension of a 'higher unity of the negative' works on the psyche just as much as contact impregnates it.

'My basic belief,' says Thom, 'is in the continuous character of the universe and phenomena, and of the substratum of phenomena' (Thom, 1993: 62). Then he adds: 'Primitive experience . . . is linked to the sensation, or the perception, of a qualitative discontinuity.' We could affirm with him that 'in the beginning' a hallucinatory continuity emerges from the impact of the 'negative intensity', of the lack, of the absence, transforming biological needs into a state of psychic quality. And it is only when faced with the persistence of biological needs, and thus following the failure of the hallucinatory solution, that the psychical apparatus 'had to decide to form a conception of the real circumstances in the external world' (Freud, 1911a: *S.E.* XII, 219), to recognise hallucinatory perception as qualitatively different from that of the sense organs, by experiencing the internal world as distinct from the external world. Resulting from this failure of hallucinatory experience, the distinction outside–inside is constituted by a '*discretisation*'[2] of hallucinatory continuity into sensory discontinuity.

But psychic *discretisation* is not limited to that. Concerning *pregnance* fear, Thom raises the problem that in addition to the simplicity of the emission of a cry of alarm by the animal on watch when it perceives the predator, the perception is not of the enemy itself but only of signs of it. The cry, then, has to modulate a difference between announcing the existence of the traces of a predator that may be close but is not visible and announcing a predator that is immediately visible. Thom imagines that if the cry signalling the presence of the enemy is compared with a formulation such as, 'there is the animal', in the case where there are only traces, one should add, in order to translate the modulation of the cry: 'Yes, but it isn't there.' That Thom conceives the increased complexity of the communication in terms of the expression of a contradiction that may be summed up as 'there is the animal . . . it is not there', bears a quite unexpected proximity to the position we have arrived at along very different paths. In order to understand what is essential in the communication of the infant, the problem obviously has to be posed not in relation with a *pregnance* fear but with a *pregnance* love, not with a predator but with the desired object, not with a feared presence but with a feared absence. The words 'there is mummy . . . she isn't there' are a 'cry of love' as much a 'cry of alarm'. Word-presentation emerges from the absence of the invested object and sets up, in place of the hallucinatory content, the object-representation experienced within, doubled by that of the recognition of its absence without, in perception. This fundamental duality between representation and perception cannot, it seems to us, be superposed on the sensory discontinuity outside–inside.

Thanks to the treatments of so-called borderline personalities, we have understood that, in psychoanalysis, the notions outside–inside cannot be reduced, as Freud believed, to a separation based simply on the sensory foundation of bodily limits. The distinction outside–inside is not the consequence, as far as the outside is concerned, of the impossibility of distancing it by means of a motor act. The stability of the discontinuity outside–inside is the product of a permanent psychical work in the waking state, a test of reality that is organised according to the contradiction constitutive of the discontinuity representation–perception that we express by the contradictory formulation: the object is '*Only inside–Also outside*' (see Chapter 8). Such a paradoxical discontinuity – a

41

discontinuous continuity, one could say – defining the duality representation–perception impregnates qualitatively the sensory outside–inside and has, as a consequence, the great theoretical difficulty of conceptualising the relation in man between his psychic processes and the events of reality. We shall return to this in connection with animistic thinking and the dynamic of the double.

Added to this is the fact that even sensory experience is not, in the last analysis, as simple as it seems to be. Thus to avoid reducing unjustifiably the notion of perception to the immediateness offered by the sense organs and to give a sense of its great complexity from the viewpoint of psychoanalytic theory, we like to evoke a story as curious as that of the tic related by René Thom. It concerns one of the complications of nature surpassing man's imagination and defying all logic, mentioned by Rémy Chauvin (1992) in *La biologie de l'esprit*. It is the strange sexual encounter between a flower, the orchid, and a particular species of wasp, the Gorytes (see Chapter 4).

(In fact, what is perceived by the sense organs, in an apparently simple and immediate way, is the final product of a work involving a complex process with its roots both in the loss of the *object of hallucinatory satisfaction*, working for perception, and in the absence of the invested object, working for representation. The negative duality of this whole process forms the basis of the symmetry *representation–perception* (see Chapter 2).)

We now come to what seems to us to be the most significant aspect of the encounter between Thom's thought and psychoanalysis today. It involves the importance given to intelligibility either, for Thom, in the form of a 'geometrised thinking', or, for psychoanalysis, in the form of figurability, an intelligibility that is accessible not only in the narcissistic regression during sleep and dreaming, but also during sessions in the moments when the psychoanalyst's thinking regresses.[3]

From 1932 (*New Introductory Lectures on Psychoanalysis*), one can assert with Freud that *the primary foundation of dreaming is not so much the fulfilment of a wish, even if this remains the dream's objective and defines its content, but hallucinatory activity itself, the need to represent.* The same may be said of the foundation of the general functioning of the psyche; this is noticeable at the level of the analyst's work at certain traumatic, or simply regressive moments of his thought. From this point of view, the *first task of the psyche consists in a work of figurability, with a view to rendering intelligible what occurs in it.* We have already pointed out, accordingly, that in the 'Project' (1895) and throughout his work, Freud continually maintained that the task of the system 'consists in contrivances for transforming an external quantity into a quality' (Freud, 1895: *S.E.* I, 309). This becomes clear during regressive states of thinking – obviously, during night dreams, but also during the analyst's work in the session. We will consider this point in the following chapter. Let us say that a 'figurability' occurs in the analyst that often reveals the existence of something irrepresentable in the analysand – irrepresentable in that it is the existence of a sort of trace, of a perceptual order, that has never gained access to the level of a representation and can finally present itself and become intelligible, thanks to its being integrated through the analyst's work of figurability. Here, the analyst does not associate ideas, times, objects; he does not interpret strictly speaking, does not reveal a repressed idea, already there, which is his usual work, but he creates/finds (in Winnicott's sense) on the spot, that which, in the analysand, should have been represented but has not been. He gives intelligibility to a trace that is irrepresentable, 'untranslatable' into word-presentations.

Thom considers that what is required for elementary intelligibility is a type of thinking that can be located in experience: 'an elementary experience which is entirely determined by the totality of its projections on to qualitative spaces of sensory origin'. This formulation is perfectly suited for defining figurability.

The psychoanalyst and the geometer are thus agreed on the importance accorded to the mind's capacity for figurability. In the retrogressive direction, in a state sometimes experienced as traumatic, the resurgence of the perceiving subject in search for *the lost object of hallucinatory satisfaction* provokes, in a hallucinatory or quasi-hallucinatory mode, the intelligibility of the representable links, whether it be a question of a concretisation in new psychic links or in the geometer's lines.

'Geometrising thought', Thom likes to say. *Geometrising, we would say, is in the nature of retrogressive thought.*

What is involved is the formation of a retrogressive movement of coherence, which is original in each case, a primordial psychic activity, *a primordial abstraction*. In addition to the presence of an image, a content, a conceptual abstraction, the presentability of the *primordial abstraction* is a movement of thought with a global tendency, which traces unitary links, without any distinction made between what produces and what is produced; the dancer and the dance are the same. *Primordial abstraction*, cut off from secondary links and the sense organs, an 'accident' of thought, as it were, returns to the hallucinatory dimension of satisfaction, creating its own perceptive coherence of the moment.

Let us note, with respect to the term abstraction, that psychoanalysts are influenced by a certain pejorative connotation, stemming both from the confusion between the abstract and the general, in the sense of a distancing from the sensible, the concrete and the localisable, and by modern semantics, which treats the problem of abstraction from a purely formal standpoint. *Primordial abstraction*, as we conceive of it, depends not on mathematical forms as Bion and Lacan thought, but on the immediate experience of a hallucinatory movement, a generalised psychic impulsion, whose effects are commensurate with the reality of the moment as a whole. To reduce it to a system, to a structure pertaining to secondary thinking, would be to deny its perceptual, lived character, closely linked to its hallucinatory nature.

Accordingly, we distinguish *primordial abstraction* from secondary abstraction. The latter is a mode of thinking capable of distinguishing and isolating a set of elements and examining all the associative links that it contains; it works on minimal secondary links, formal elements, with a view to discovering the formations of systems, of structures. In secondary abstraction, links are not created but decoded.

As far as *primordial abstraction* is concerned, one of the finest examples is that of Newton, of which we have already spoken. Alexandre Koyré's *Etudes Newtoniennes* (1968) grasps this in a remarkable way: it enables Newton to oppose and unite at the same time the discontinuity of matter and the continuity of the void. Gravitation and the intelligibility of the universe are born, he said, of points and lines traced in the space of an absolute void by the geometer's hands, guided and oriented by God. The links that Newton grasped are devoid of all reference, causality; they do not presuppose any specific link with things, neither are they subject to the uncertainties of experimentation or the lability of matter. It is through these links set up as laws that things exist and are revealed. This is why Newton declined to explain them. He had the deep intuition that any mechanical interpretation of attraction would limit the significance of his conception of the void. Which is exactly what was to happen with the post-Newtonians.

5

FIGURABILITY AND THE WORK
OF FIGURABILITY

Figurability, the work of figurability and the attempt to conceptualise them, have constituted our main line of interest since our first article on them in 1983. Taking into account our reflections since then, we discussed them again recently (2001) in our Report to the Congress of French-Speaking Psychoanalysts, in somewhat similar terms to those we are employing here.

Freud's interest for dreams remained centred on their interpretation. This might explain, at least in part, why he accorded little space in his theory dreams, or more broadly of psychic functioning, to the notion of 'figurability' itself.

In the French edition of Chapter VI of *The Interpretation of Dreams* (1900) 'figurability' (*S.E.* 'representability') is defined as a specific method employed at the heart of the dream-work, on an equal footing with the three others: displacement, condensation and secondary revision. These last three were developed at length and were to reappear constantly in Freud's work, acquiring the nobility of basic concepts to the point of being considered as the primordial procedures of the unconscious system and, as a result, permanently present in psychic life; whereas 'figurability', on the rare occasions when it is mentioned, was the object of few commentaries and remained confined to the domain of dreams.

It is equally surprising to note that, even initially, Freud was not concerned to define the notion of 'figurability', as if the formulation employed in the title of section D of Chapter VI – in French, *prise en considération de la figurabilité* (*S.E.* 'Considerations of representability'; G. *Die Rücksicht auf Darstellbarkeit*) were sufficient. He was not any more explicit in his work as a whole. Thus, in 'Metapsychological supplement to the theory of dreams' (1917a [1915]: *S.E.* XIV, 228), the formulation is identical to that of 1900. And in spite of the fact that in his *Introductory Lectures on Psycho-Analysis* (1916–17), 'figurability' is said to be 'psychologically the most interesting (. . .), the most regular one' (*S.E.* XV,

175) of the four factors comprising the dream-work, its study remains very succinct. By the same token, when, in 1932, in his *New Introductory Lectures on Psychoanalysis* (Lesson XXIX, p. 20), he refers to the dream as a *'primitive language without any grammar'*, Freud remains equally evasive about the notion of figurability. Except, however, for the fact – and this opens up new prospects – that he adds that figurability facilitates condensation and the creation of *'new unities'* (p. 20): an idea that was already present in 1900, then in *Totem and Taboo* (1912b) and in *An Outline of Psychoanalysis* (1938b). We shall return to the cardinal importance of this idea of 'new unities'.

This absence of definition and study of figurability might explain its almost complete absence in post-Freudian theories, notwithstanding the fact that, from the perspective of the metapsychology of 1900, figurability is a fundamental and permanent psychical requirement that should be taken into account in every analysis.

The French term *figurabilité* is a neologism, which the translator of *Die Traumdeutung*, Denise Berger, introduced as a translation of *Darstellbarkeit* in the French edition of 1967, a revised version of Meyerson's translation. Why did she resort to this neologism when she had translated the term used in the title of the precedent sub-section C (*Darstellungsmittel; S.E.* 'The means of representation'), as *'modes de figuration'*? It is a pity that she did not allude to it either in her foreword or in the footnotes; for, by using the term *figurabilité*, Berger was already, perhaps without realising it, touching on the problem of *presentation*, a subject of study of contemporary psychoanalysis.

The closest term that we have found in French dictionaries is *figurable*, for which *Le Robert* gives the following definition: *'Qui peut être figuré, représenté'* (i.e. that which can be depicted, represented). In other languages, the expression *Darstellbarkeit* was translated by 'representability' in English and *representabilidad* in Spanish. To the best of our knowledge, in the dictionaries of these two languages no term currently exists corresponding to the French term *figurabilité*.

That it is absent from French language dictionaries may come as a surprise for the analyst, but what is most surprising is that none of the dictionaries of psychoanalysis (Roudinesco-Plon; Chemama-Vandermersch), with the exceptions of Laplanche and Pontalis (1967) and de Mijolla (2000), gives it any space. It is even absent from the exhaustive (853 concepts and notions) *Sigmund Freud, Index thématique* by Alain Delrieu (1997). Laplanche and Pontalis situate the term *figurabilité* in the context of the notions of perceptual identity and thought identity but, like Freud, they stay with the formulation *'prise en considération'* ('considerations of'), although when dealing with other notions in *The Language of Psychoanalysis*, they always develop a thorough and historical study of very high level. As far as we know, the only dictionary to study this notion is not psychoanalytic. In the *Encyclopédie Philosophique Universelle* (Jacob, 1990), the term, freed from the formulation *'prise en considération'*, is presented by Monique David-Ménard who, drawing on Lacan, and Lyotard (1985: 248–60)

– despite the fact that Lyotard criticised Lacan severely with regard to the notion of what is representable (*ce qui est figurable*) – underlines the radical difference between the plastic arts, which are thoroughly visual, and the speaking arts, and relates the notion of *figurabilité* to the desire that hallucinates its object.

Unless we are mistaken, it is only in France that the notion of 'figurability' has aroused a certain interest among psychoanalysts. Michel Fain was the first person we heard speaking about it outside the context of the dream. If we have understood him correctly, he has a conception of figurability that refers less to the transformation of thoughts into images – for this, he makes use rather of the notion of formal regression – than to a formation between self-image and feeling, or even to a bodily attitude influenced by the ideal ego. Between sense of self, image and attitude, the examples he uses – which have now become classics – are 'the swaggerer' or 'the speaker who adopts a bombastic style'.

Jean Guillaumin (1979: 59, 114) was the first to insist on the vagueness of Freud's definition of figurability (*Darstellbarkeit*). He suggests that such imprecision is perhaps due to the fact that: 'The problem of the image confronts us directly with that of passivity (. . .) and that Freud kept himself somewhat at a distance from what might have led him to make a radical analysis of the passive moment.' Could such a relation between figurability and passivity be generalised and extended in the analytic milieu? Could it be one of the reasons for the 'reserved' attitude of psychoanalysts towards figurability, towards the difficulty of assuming these unexpected and surprising moments that the analyst's thinking is 'subjected' to in the course of his work? The general tendency is to forget them immediately.

Thereafter, apart from Porret (1997) who develops certain points in common with ours, analysts have not made figurability a central subject of study.

Nevertheless, certain authors, even if they have not been directly interested in it, have been led, in their conceptions, to take figurability into account. Thus Didier Anzieu (1994), in his general theory of 'thinking', employs the term *figurativité*, referring to thing-presentations. This is also the case of Piera Aulagnier (1975) when she described the notions of *pictogram* and *pictorial language*. In her conception, as the 'pictogram' is a thing-image, a 'sensory image', a 'mode of representation specific to the primary', 'between the impulse to see and the epistemological impulse', figurability has its place as a means of access to 'nomination'. In short, the notion of figurability in Aulagnier's work is limited to two uses: one rendering it identical to the 'thing-image'; the other integrating it within a genetic development where 'the visual precedes the acoustic, sight precedes knowledge whose possibility of nomination, the sensory image, is the first referent of the representation that it makes possible' (Aulagnier, 1975: 130). As for the role of figurability in analysis, Aulagnier declares: 'The essence of figurability becomes the most drastic injunction of our practice.' Her approach goes 'from the interpretable to the "representable"' (*figurable*); '*one must find the words which make the thing-presentations "representable"* [our italics] for both partners'; this is 'the most arduous task of the interpreter' (Aulagnier, 1986: 338). In spite of the proximity of our concerns with respect to practice, her conception of figurability seems to us to be contrary to that of the dream-work, and thus to ours. Arising from the constraints and difficulties to which the analyst's thinking is subjected in the work with psychotic analysands, the notion of figurability, for Piera Aulagnier, bears the mark of a theory erected essentially on the basis of this experience and the study of the particular psychic organisation of psychosis.

As for authors of Kleinian inspiration, only Bion has taken interest in it, although his notion of 'maternal reverie' differs from Freud's conception of figurability (*Darstellbarkeit*) (see, in this connection, Botella, C. and S., 2001).

As far as we are concerned, the notion of figurability under the formulation of '*formal regression of thought*' has become a source of research occupying a central place in our reflections. At the outset, as for Piera Aulagnier, it was the therapies of psychotics – in our case, of very young psychotic children – which led us to grasp the importance of figurability, to see that what is involved is nothing less than a question of psychic survival. But while these treatments enabled us to understand its vital importance, it was owing to the analytic treatments of neurotic and borderline adults that we became aware of its metapsychological status, whether in respect of the range of its effects on all the forms of psychic expression or of the immediateness of its effects on traumatic situations. And it was above all as a result of being confronted with certain traumatic aspects of the analyst's thinking during the session that we progressively understood that the notion of figurability cannot be reduced to the image and that it is the product of a complex daytime work akin to that of night dreams.

Starting with the difference that Freud establishes between the dream proper, with its manifest content and its latent content, 'a particular form of thinking', and what he considers as being 'its essence', the 'dream-work which creates this form', we have theorised a distinction between figurability itself and the *work of figurability*.

As a primordial means of binding, 'one of the earliest functions' (Freud, 1920: 62) of mental life, the work of figurability is a founding psychical process, which, pursuing the backward, retrogressive course, is assumed to be determined by the tendency to make all the data of the moment, internal and external stimuli, converge into a single intelligible unity aimed at binding all the heterogeneous elements that are present into an atemporal simultaneity in the form of a hallucinatory actualisation, of which the most rudimentary primal form is a work of figurability. Whether it leads to the 'figurable' dream thought based on the primary processes or, by means of a 'detour' due to their inhibition and to the action of secondary processes, to thought in the form of word-presentations, whether during the night or day, the work of figurability represents the 'royal road' of all intelligibility. This retrogressive process is propelled by 'a function in us which demands unity, connection and intelligibility' (Freud,

1912b: 95), by what we define as a principle of convergence–coherence (Botella, C. and S., 1992a, 1996). In its capacity for transformation (in Bion's sense) and integration (in Winnicott's sense), it plays the role of reorganising psychic life as a whole. This is why it has an undeniable 'anti-traumatic' value in the treatment; it is the only means of gaining access to, and of revealing, the negative of the trauma.

When in borderline situations, quite unexpectedly and involuntarily, the analyst's thinking regresses beyond the state of floating attention and his word-presentations tend to be disinvested, an *accident of thought* may occur, a rupture with the world of representations. Equivalent to the traumatic state of non-representation, the 'accident' supposes a retrogressive movement of convergence–coherence, tracing new links in the simultaneity of the varied and multiple fields of the session: the patient's discourse or acting out, the transference/counter-transference, as well as a whole variety of 'actual perceptual material' ranging from sensory perception and momentary bodily impressions to the 'sensory remains' of earlier sessions. It is the psychic capacity of such a movement that we call *figurability* and its accomplishment, *work of figurability*. Its result is 'a "figure" common to representation and perception' (Green, 1993). The retrogressive movement of the analyst's thought opens the session to an intelligibility of the relation between two psyches functioning in a regressive state. The outcome of this *mode of working as a double (travail en double)*, so to speak, reveals that which already exists in the analysand in an irrepresentable state, as a negative of the trauma, and can at last have access to the quality of representation. We shall return to this later.

PART TWO

The dynamic of the double

6

ON THE AUTO-EROTIC DEFICIENCY OF THE PARANOIAC

> [T]he weak spot in their development is to be looked for
> somewhere between the stages of auto-erotism,
> narcissism and homosexuality.
>
> Freud, 1911b: 62

The following brief comments concerning the case of Freud's female paranoiac analysand ('A case of paranoia running counter to the psycho-analytic theory of the disease') (Freud, 1915a: *S.E.* XIV, 263) represent, in broad outline, some of the aspects of what we will call the auto-erotic weak spot of the paranoiac.

'Lying partly undressed on the sofa beside her lover . . . a most attractive and handsome girl was "admired", without any sexual act having taken place and perhaps even any contact.'

In this sequence, one can discern the very nature of the trauma suffered by the analysand; it contains, in a condensed form, the circumstances and reasons for the onset of her delusion. For this young paranoiac woman, finding herself in the arms of a man is already a traumatic situation, owing to the loss of the homosexual tie with a more or less desexualised object,[1] namely, 'her elderly mother' doubled by 'an elderly lady'. To this loss, which is a frequent motive for decompensation in paranoiacs, entailing a true rupture in the permanence of their sense of identity closely linked to the homosexual double, is added here the absence of heterosexual fulfilment. This situation, difficult for any woman, became insurmountable in her case; feeling frustrated, she could not make up for it through the pleasure 'of being admired'; for, according to the hypothesis that we shall be developing in this work, the paranoiac does not have an eroto-genic body susceptible of being exhibited. Without the bulwark of a truly erotogenic body that this analysand had been unable to constitute, the gaze of the young man, fascinated by his sexual, and perhaps uninhabited object, was intolerable. If the other person did not speak to her or touch her, or if his words and his acts were simply extensions of his gaze, the young woman, fascinated herself, with her identity adrift, and without an invested body, risked falling into the psychotic abyss, experiencing the terror of the non-object absolute distress.

The absence of a genuinely Oedipal context, the loss of the homosexual investment of the maternal image, the lack of an erotogenic body, meant that the day after the first hour of disastrous love, in a desperate attempt to maintain an object, a link, a look – even if negative – the image of the mother was transformed into 'the hostile and malevolent watcher and persecutor' (Freud, 1923b: *S.E.* XVIII, 268). Being persecuted is better than losing object relationships altogether. During the second encounter, the repeated trauma had an even greater effect. Although initially she felt petrified and psychically dead, the young girl recovered by means of certain perceptions: a ticking noise, the sight of two men. And it was only through the effort of projection involved in creating a scenario that the unrepresentable and inexpressible terror of the non-object would acquire a meaning: the lover's traumatising look would be transformed into spying, into cameras. Her delusion saved her from the most catastrophic decompensation. In reality, the fictive harm caused by the photos hid an authentic affliction, from which every paranoiac suffers: the photos 'taken' of her represented the loss, the dispossession of a part of herself being taken away by the double.

As we move on from the article of 1915, we wonder why, after demonstrating so brilliantly the connection between homosexuality and paranoia in 1911, in the case of President Schreber (Freud, 1911b: *S.E.* XII, 3), Freud felt the need to return to it four years later. It is true that he wanted to show that homosexual tendencies underlay the apparently heterosexual factors giving rise to the delusion; but was not the real novelty – and perhaps the deeper motive that led Freud to write the article – that of relating homosexuality, both feminine and masculine, not so much to the sexual double as to what he calls in this text 'the earliest image of the mother' (*Urzeitlich*)? This need to introduce the term *Urzeitlich*, as well as that of *Urphantasien* a few lines later, shows Freud's desire to find the ultimate explanation – a desire that was already present in his first writings under the guise of the term *Urszenen;* then under that of *Urverdrängung* (primal repression) in 1911, in the text on Schreber.

All the reflections that we shall be developing here are situated along the axis of 'the earliest image of the mother' and will be confined to this train of thought, although it will not be possible to go into all the ways in which this 'earliest image of the mother' is bound up with homosexuality in paranoiacs.

Concerning Schreber

When Freud (1911b) shows in his 'Psycho-Analytic notes on an autobiographical account of a case of paranoia' that homosexual fears and desires underlie paranoid delusion, we are very far removed from the description of homosexuality in the publication on Leonardo da Vinci (letters to Abraham, 24 February, 5 June and 8 December 1910: Abraham and Freud, 1965; Jones, 1955), even though it was only written a few months before:

> In all our male homosexual cases the subjects had had a very intense erotic attachment to a female person, as a rule their mother, during the first period of childhood . . . The boy represses his love for his mother: he puts himself in her place, identifies himself with her, and takes his own person as a model in whose likeness he chooses the new objects of his love.
>
> Freud, 1910b: *S.E.* XI, 99–100

Freud took up this conception again in 1922 ('Some Neurotic Mechanisms in Jealousy, Paranoia and Homosexuality'). For Schreber, the issue was not one of identifying with a mother who desired a man; his drama did not involve repressing a dynamic and constituted homosexuality, but rather the impossibility of gaining full access to it.

Freud considered Schreber's sun to be God in person and, consequently, as a 'sublimated symbol of the father'. However, he pointed out at the same time that in German the word for sun is feminine in gender and that Schreber referred to it as the sun-prostitute. In fact, the description of this sun god with its anterior realm (*vestibulum – Vorhof –* vagina) and its active posterior realm, a symbol of virility, inclines us to regard it as bisexual. Moreover, in 'Leonardo da Vinci and a memory of his childhood', Freud notes that 'only a combination of male and female elements can give a worthy representation of divine perfection' (*S.E.* XI, 94).[2]

Schreber's sun does not seem to have developed into an exclusive representation of an ideal father; it fell short of this, sometimes being bisexual, and sometimes a vehicle of the horror of castration (Medusa) (see 'Le bouclier de Persée ou psychose et realité', in Pasche, 1988). When Schreber boasts of being able to gaze at the sun-Medusa directly with his own eyes, and when he has no need of Perseus' shield mirror, what power does he have against the horror of castration? How is it that, having been continually threatened with emasculation during his delusion, he did not need, like Perseus, to make use of the mirror reflection (Botella, C. and S. and Haag, 1977)?

Freud thought the solution to President Schreber's conflict was to be found in accepting castration. However, it seems that, in his enthusiasm for establishing the homosexual origins of paranoia, he failed to take certain details into account. His citations from the *Memoirs of My Nervous Illness* (1955) on the importance of 'reconciliation' as an element in the process of recovery, are taken from chapter XIII, a detailed reading of which shows that it is not really a matter of 'reconciliation' with mankind, but only of a 'reasonable compromise' consisting in making mankind perish 'in its actual form' and in transforming the 'human shapes' that Schreber was still able to perceive as 'fleeting and improvised men'. It is only at the price of this disappearance of the human species that Schreber can advocate, when describing his conflicts of 1895, the solution of emasculation. On reading further, one notices that in reality, this is only a temporary solution. In Chapter XXII (p. 212), the last of the *Memoirs* written in September 1900, this solution was being replaced by another, this time definitive:

> But whether . . . unmanning can really be completed I dare not predict; it is even more difficult to predict the future since I have had to correct my earlier view that mankind had perished. It is therefore possible, indeed probable, that to the end of my days there will be strong indications of femaleness, but that I shall die as a man.

Schreber kept his penis; his emasculation and transformation into a woman did not occur. His final and definitive solution was not then to accept castration but to become bisexual, in the image of the sun god. In his regression, he went beyond the difference between the sexes; now that he could no longer be touched by the horror of castration, he would be able to gaze at the sun, his double. Schreber is like the maternal divinities described by Freud (1910b) in 'Leonardo da Vinci and a memory of his childhood':

> In none of them is there a combination of the true genitals of both sexes . . . all that has happened is that the male organ has been added to the breasts which are the mark of the mother, just as it was present in the child's first idea of the mother's body.
>
> *S.E.* XI, 97–8

But is this delusional bisexuality solely a solution for avoiding castration? Such an explanation is insufficient. It was owing to the bisexual representation of himself that Schreber would attain the 'voluptuousness' that he considered as a share of the 'divine bliss' accorded to men. In the penultimate chapter (XXI) he writes: 'I have to imagine myself as man and woman in one person having intercourse with myself' (p. 208). This state of completeness, of bliss, he attributed to his bisexuality, characterised by the words 'I am looking at myself' and 'coitus with myself'. When Schreber attained the desire and delusional phantasy of bisexuality, it was his way of declaring, by insisting on the word 'myself', that the definitive solution to his conflict lay in self-reflection, no more or less than in the practice of auto-erotic activity. With his regression, he abolished all homosexual and heterosexual erotic attraction; there could no longer be any question of castration, of being transformed into a woman or of forced coupling. Delusional bisexuality, a truly auto-erotic stronghold, led to radical narcissistic withdrawal. Now that men were sexually disinvested, they were no longer a source of anxiety and, consequently, Schreber was able to finish his *Memoirs* and write the appeal addressed to the expert in July 1901: 'I have known for a long time now that the people I see before me are not "fleeting-improvised-men" but real human beings' (p. 288).

Auto-erotism, favouring the desexualisation of social relations, opened up a new prospect, namely, the possibility of a splitting of the ego, making the persistence of the delusion and social adaptation compatible.

At this point, another question must be raised. Is it enough to see Schreber's auto-erotism as a purely genital affair? Schreber asserts that this intercourse with himself or achieving a 'certain sexual excitement' does not correspond to 'any idea of masturbation'.

Why should we not regard this formulation, rather than a negation, as the revelation of a certain secret truth? For it is probable, given the eminently oral universe of Schreber's delusion, that genital auto-erotism masked in reality an oral auto-erotism, a sort of oral onanism, which obviously has nothing whatever to do with 'any idea of masturbation or anything like it'.

In an earlier article, we said that, in a newborn baby, the action of sucking a part of the body, the thumb, in general, has the function of appropriating what is soothing in the object-mother; or rather, of appropriating what the object-mother of this period is, that is to say, an indivisible child–mother composite element. Here we are following Freud (1938a) in *Findings, Ideas, Problems*, where he considers that the child thinks of himself as 'I am the breast' and it is only once this has been lost that the notion 'I have the breast', that is to say, 'I am no longer the breast' can occur. The infant's activity of thumb sucking, whereby he cuts himself off and emerges from the child–mother continuity, thereby becoming autonomous, may be considered as an intermediary stage between 'being' and 'having': I have/am the breast, according to André Green's (1976) fine formulation. Owing to the success of this auto-erotism, Schreber's aspiration, and that of every baby, could be realised: 'distinction without separation', 'union without fusion', as Francis Pasche, adopting the Sufi formula of Ibn 'Arabi,[3] liked to say about Schreber. (See also Ali, 1980.)

But, at the level of social relations, thumb sucking beyond an appropriate age is very quickly considered as an object of derision or even as a sign of mental backwardness. One can understand how, for President Schreber, in search of his auto-erotic rampart, and only having his intelligence at his disposal, only his thoughts as a shield, it would have been unbearable to have to admit to himself that the solution to his conflict would be to regress to the level of the 'bliss' of thumb sucking: 'Can there be any prospect more terrible for a human being so highly gifted in such various ways . . . than of losing one's reason and perishing an imbecile', he writes (p. 212). For him, the only acceptable solution in order to imagine 'the bliss' of oral auto-erotism was to translate it, in accordance with his ego, into a more developed sexual language, that of bisexuality and coitus with himself.

Faced with the disorganising threats to his narcissism stemming from his oral desires linked to his auto-erotic quest, Schreber found relief in his thoughts, in the creation of a delusion. It is as if the creation of the delusion, just as much as the activity of delusional thought, represented for him a successful auto-erotic act with an economic value similar to that of the auto-erotism that is heir to the continuity of the relation between mother and child.

In order to surmount 'the unhappiness of his erotic life', Leonardo da Vinci created androgynous figures in his paintings with smiles of ecstatic bliss, 'representing the wishes of the boy, infatuated with his mother, as fulfilled in this blissful union of the male and female natures' (Freud, 1910b: *S.E.* XI, 118). Whereas President Schreber, without the aura of such a mystery, without triumphalism, and probably without the same happiness, could only resort to thinking, to thinking about nothing but himself, by throwing himself into a tormented quest for something of the 'blessed fusion' of the light of a mother's gaze, of the arms which would cradle him.

Now that we have concluded our observations on the case of President Schreber, we conclude this section with the following remark: a fundamental weakness in the erotic organisation of the oral universe is, in our view, an important aspect of paranoid structure. In order to clarify this idea, we are going to set out our position on the notion of oral auto-erotism, its economic value and its influence in the constitution and functioning of psychic life. Although we mistrust the fascination exerted by the archaic universe – René Diatkine (1974, 1979) has quite rightly denounced this fact on several occasions – we opt for a genetic perspective. Why? Analytic experience, with children or adults does not grant access to a reconstruction of the past through the transference relationship; 'fragments of historical truth' are sometimes simply suggested to us by certain states or certain actions. This being the case, if we want to advance our knowledge of the foundations of psychic functioning, we are obliged, at a given moment, to introduce temporality into the elaboration of our intuitions. This approach, leading to a theoretical reconstitution of origins in itself is debatable, can be more easily accepted if we do not delude ourselves by forgetting that, in any case, the genetic perspective is only a means, a tool to help us approach unknown zones of the psyche. The permanent confrontation between the genetic perspective and clinical psychoanalysis must be its guide, its compass.

Forms of primary and secondary auto-erotism

It was the treatments of very young children and therapeutic interventions with infant–mother couples (Botella, C. and S., 1978) that led us to accord the greatest importance to auto-erotic activities and, in particular, to thumb sucking in the infant–mother relationship.

The first object is formed by sensations aroused by the light of the mother's face, the contrast between her skin and hair, the shine in her eyes . . . by her smell, her voice and also by contact, pressing against the mother's body . . . by the nipple in the mouth, the effects of food in the digestive apparatus . . . by care for the skin and other erotogenic zones . . . by the way of being held, carried and so on. The first sensations, that is, when what belongs to the mother or to the child cannot be differentiated as far as the latter is concerned. The infant is as much the sensation awakened by his own mouth as that awakened by the breast, as much his own tongue as the nipple or the light of the mother's face. He is as much his mother's arms and hands providing care as his own members.

These different sensations, which are initially independent of each other, are brought into relationship, and linked up by virtue of the mother's investment, without which they are in danger of remaining unconnected, dispersed. These sensations, at times more or less gathered, and at others dispersed, become increasingly concentrated around the experience of maternal care, in particular, of breastfeeding. Let us note that they do not have the character of psychic representation, at least in the full sense of the word, and do not involve a true recognition of the object. Neither can one speak of fusion or confusion, relatively late mechanisms indicating a wish to keep the object undifferentiated, requiring, paradoxically, a certain awareness of a self that is separate from the other.

Economic upheavals progressively undermine this balance. Faced with the pain of waiting, the infant defends itself by means of wishful hallucinatory satisfaction, reproducing the continuous universe of the experience of satisfaction. Following its failure, 'the psychical apparatus had to decide to form a conception of the real circumstances in the external world' (Freud, 1911a: *S.E.* XII, 219) and it is in the stage between these two forms of mental functioning – one that has become insufficient, the other that is not quite operative as yet – that thumb sucking acquires all its importance. What was merely a reproduction during the experience of hallucinatory satisfaction, will now, by this means, acquire the character of an 'appropriation'. [Through his repeating 'at will', which is independent of the state of need, the infant appropriates the oral pleasure with his thumb in place of the breast; by directing his own gaze inwards, he takes in his mother's gaze with it. All the other sensations of the experience of satisfaction will come together around this axis. It is by reproducing what the object contributes that auto-erotism represents the first conquest, the first experience of autonomy, as Fain and Marty have pointed out. Thus, by sucking his thumb, the infant, who is thereby trying to maintain the continuous relationship, undermined by states of distress, paradoxically facilitates the advent of the object and, consequently, completes the separation] Freud (1916–17) expresses this in masterly fashion:

> [T]he erotic component, which is satisfied simultaneously during the [nutritive] sucking, makes itself independent with the act of *sensual* sucking; it gives up the outside object and replaces it by an area of the subject's own body. The oral instinct becomes auto-erotic.
>
> *S.E.* XVI, 329

In normal development, the first encounters between hand and mouth, fortuitous to begin with and probably mechanical, will soon acquire the value of an 'appropriation'. If the activity of thumb sucking persists, it may become associated, as things develop, with a real phantasy activity; but, in the final analysis, it will still represent a pre-representational substitute of the primitive child–mother relationship. Its aim will vary according to the child's age, circumstances and psychic structure; for instance, sucking can have the function of evacuating the representation, of 'not thinking', as one 5-year-old child said who was in therapy with one of us. In certain cases, sucking will remain a purely mechanical act without having the value of appropriating the mother's care and without any accompanying phantasy activity.

In our work with Geneviève Haag on the stage prior to sucking, we have tried to show how the child whose object has lacked adequate qualities or who has suffered the ravages of catastrophes and, consequently, whose early auto-erotic activities were not sufficiently unified at the heart of a relationship, will only be able to use the dispersed auto-erotic elements of its organs without bringing them together into an act of sucking. Such a child will over-invest the erotogenic zones themselves: the eyes instead of looking, the muscular sensations of his members instead of their functions, intestinal noises and movements, dizziness and so on; each of them acting in its own interests. Instead of having his thumb in his mouth, with an inward-looking expression, one will observe, for instance, at a given moment, a finger scratching something; at another, the child's gaze will be fixed on a spot of light or he will be clicking his tongue and so on. These features can all be found in autistic children. One still has to determine the part played by these dispersed forms of auto-erotism, their degree of persistence in normal development, as well as the possibility of a return to this mode of functioning, once it has been 'surmounted' (Freud, 1919) and replaced by a unified auto-erotism.

In other words, we are outlining *two types of auto-erotism that can be qualified as primary or dispersed and secondary or unified without this necessarily implying a temporal succession*. Here primary and secondary emphasise the quality of the object-relationship, in the same way that Freud used them for narcissism and primary and secondary masochism. Secondary modes of auto-erotism, for which the model is thumb sucking, imply that the continuous relationship has been appropriated. They are constituted according to a spectrum defined at one extreme by a violent appropriation of that which forms the continuous relationship; and, at the other, by the 'passive impregnation' described by Luquet (1961). The more the child has been enriched by the stamp of the qualities of the earliest relationship – its rhythm, its high and low moments, its moments of fullness and emptiness – the more it has been cemented with satisfactions, the richer the child's secondary modes of auto-erotism will be. In normal development auto-erotic modes of functioning are secondary from the outset; the fate of primary auto-erotic modes of functioning is to be gathered together in the earliest relationship and to be taken over by the child in the guise of secondary auto-erotism. Unlike the latter, which has the capacity of retaining excitation, primary forms of auto-erotism are, above all, over-investments of discharge itself, for its own sake, until it is exhausted. Nevertheless, they are the source of a certain auto-erotic satisfaction and represent a minimal organisation of the libido; for instance, in the form of erotogenic masochism (Freud, 1924a: *S.E.* XIX, 157), such as the auto-erotic banging activities of the autistic child. This is an extreme attempt by the child, who is not adequately contained within a relationship, to organise himself instead around his own body (Kerstemberg, E. and J., 1965).

Just as thumb sucking represents the appropriation by the child of the child–mother universe, notably that of feeding, equally the progressive recognition of other elements of the continuous relationship as belonging to him, represents acts of appropriation. The erotogenic body is truly constituted from the moment the infant is able to experience, as a source that is entirely at his disposal, the same pleasure that he once obtained from the continuous relationship. It is this appropriation of the pleasure experienced in the continuous relationship that is the basis of secondary auto-erotism, a vast movement including, among others, the auto-erotic 'looking at oneself', which is of particular interest for us in understanding paranoia.

Looking, being looked at, looking at oneself

We think of the organisation of the auto-erotic activity of 'looking at oneself' in terms of the complex interplay of activity and passivity inherent to the constitution of all secondary auto-erotism: in an active movement, the infant's eyes catch the mother's gaze looking at the child who is letting himself be looked at passively. However, we should not delude ourselves; this is more a metaphor than a description. The issue here is not so much one of incorporating or introjecting at the psychic level the gaze in his mother's eyes, but of the child's capacity to reproduce, by gathering together his sensations at the sensory motor level, what he feels when his mother is looking at him. In fact, when we speak of 'looking at oneself' we mean by that the auto-erotic reproduction, independently of the object, of the first experience of 'being looked at'. The very early transformation of this experience of 'being looked at' into an auto-erotic activity of 'looking at oneself', is a fundamental qualitative leap. Just as, later on, making use of this auto-erotic 'looking at oneself' in the capacity for self-observation will also be a decisive step. The importance of this can be verified by looking at the failures, at this level, of the paranoiac.

In this same year of 1915, during which Freud wrote up the case of the 'admired, watched, photographed' patient, he defended, in *Instincts and their Vicissitudes*, his ideas on the instinct of looking. We can find there the following striking assertion: the starting point for the scopophilic instinct is not activity directed towards an extraneous object. A preliminary stage is assumed to exist where the object is part of the subject's own body: 'For the beginning of its activity the scopophilic instinct is auto-erotic', he writes (*S.E.* XIV, 130). If, at this stage, 'seeing' is more a question of 'feeling', if the first movements of 'looking' are constituted by reproducing the sensation of being looked at by the mother, before the subject cuts himself off from her so as to be able to look at her, in the full sense of the word, then indeed we can say with Freud that, at the outset, 'looking' is auto-erotic.

Everyone knows that a harmonious distribution in the libidinal economy of the three currents of the scopophilic instinct (looking, being looked at and looking at oneself) is indispensable to the satisfactory functioning of each individual. Freud's analysand, who was 'admired' by her lover for 'her charms which were now partly revealed', said that she was being watched, photographed with malicious intentions. Someone else's gaze, however benevolent it is, is always experienced by the paranoiac as dangerous; for 'being looked at' puts him or her in a position of unbearable passivity. Indeed, it seems to us that in paranoia, the distribution of the three modalities of 'looking' is a mark of the specific characteristics of this affection. The active form 'looking' is exercised with ease and the passive form 'being looked at' is fundamentally unacceptable; but it is in the reflexive in-between stage of 'looking at oneself', in the mixture of activity and passivity, being both the subject who is looking and the object that is being looked at, that the roots of paranoia are probably to be found.

With Schreber, we came to the conclusion that the paranoiac suffers from a deficiency in the constitution of his oral auto-erotism. Now we are putting forward the idea that this deficiency extends to the non-organisation of the auto-erotic stage of 'looking at oneself'. In order to explain ourselves, we must examine the intricate relations between 'looking at oneself', 'being looked at' and the perception of the object.

From the point of view we are adopting here, the first object-mother can be interpreted as the inscription of these repeated satisfactions in the form of secondary auto-erotism. 'Repeated situations of satisfaction have created an object out of the mother', Freud wrote (Freud, 1925a: *S.E.* XX, 130). If this object-mother is born in the experience of satisfaction, contrariwise, the perception and the representation of the mother are born in the shadow of the absence of satisfaction. The infant's eyes will only open definitively in frustration, in hate. 'Seeing' will have the task of filling the void, of avoiding the state of distress; 'the image' will emerge and relieve the experience of terror by giving form to affect. With the loss of the object-satisfaction, 'not-seeing', hitherto synonymous with the pleasure of the continuous relationship, will be associated with distress; the state prior to seeing will forever after become the equivalent of *Hilflosigkeit*.

At this point in the process, since the perception and representation of the object have the same economic value, the infant, faced with the pain of loss, would become absolutely dependent on the mother's perception, '*would cling*' as much to the sight of her as to the representation of her, if his auto-erotic tendencies did not come into play at the same time. With the auto-erotic modality of 'looking', the distinction between 'here' and 'there' is formed, providing the basis for the early ideas of inside–outside.)

The composite primitive double

Under normal conditions, 'the mother's body is the first mirror' (Pasche, 1988), in that this body is invested by the infant as the first model. The infant will succeed in gathering up these 'disjecta membra' by imitating the model of the mother, by being her reflection; as he has appropriated the breast and the gaze, he will appropriate his own members. The infant will consider everything that cannot be appropriated as being external to him. We do not follow Tausk's (1919a) description of a stage in normal development during which the infant considers his own body as being external to him. For us, the issue is one of a weakness in the primitive continuous relationship. The next stage in Tausk's genetic schema – 'identification with one's own body'– seems to us to be the ultimate solution of the infant (future schizophrenic?) allowing him to gather his own body together, in place of the mother's body and gaze.

The mother as a mirror makes us think of the notion of the double. To say that the mother is the first mirror comes down to assuming that she is the first double; that is, the infant will experience in her what he already has potentially in himself; his erotogenic body will be reflected on the mother's body. At the same time, it would be fair to suppose that the infant can only exist at the outset by being the mother's double, in the sense that his experience of himself will depend on what he receives from her. In fact, this double already exerts itself at the heart of the continuous relationship where 'being looked at', erotogenic body, and perception of the double are closely interdependent and constitute the basis of the auto-erotic activity of 'looking at oneself'. The appropriation of the *composite primitive double*,[4] has the value of an early outline of identity, a highly complex process to which we shall return in the following chapters. For the moment, let us return to the *Introductory Lectures on Psycho-Analysis* (1916–17) where the previous citation from Freud continues as follows:

Further development [i.e. of auto-erotic activity] has two aims: firstly, the abandonment of auto-erotism, the replacement of the subject's own body once more by an outside object, and secondly, the unification of the various objects of the separate instincts and their replacement by a single object. This can, of course, only be achieved, if the object is again a whole body, similar to the subject's own.

S.E. XV, 329

63

One of our female analysands who was in face-to-face therapy was a paranoiac who experienced moments of delusion. Her bodily attitude would remain fixed through all the sessions, on the watch for the analyst's slightest move. In the street, she felt she was being observed, watched. Once the therapy was sufficiently advanced, the treatment was continued in the lying position. The analysand very often needed to turn round in order to look at and control the analyst, until the following primitive maternal relationship was established: she was convinced that the analyst was looking at her continuously, that a mother was admiring her. This investment of the analyst as a primitive mother contemplating her child with wonder seems of paramount importance. Racamier points out (1980) how the paranoiac defence aims above all at protecting the subject against his passive desires directed primarily towards the mother. Our analysand leads us to think that the paranoiac's passive desires tend to be condensed in the form of 'being looked at' by the mother. In her treatment, a simultaneous movement of investing the analyst's 'gaze' as well as her own body letting itself be looked at progressively transformed this body, hitherto immobilised, into a unified erotogenic body – which is missing, as we have said, in every paranoiac. In fact, the paranoiac's proud bodily attitude must not be equated too hastily to a real libidinal investment of his body; on the contrary, the haughty attitude is an artifice, nourished by megalomania, which the paranoiac uses to gather together a body which is not sufficiently libidinally invested, lacking erotogeneity.

At this stage of the investment, by the analysand, of the object–mother–analyst's 'admiring gaze', a dream appeared whose interpretation revealed her wish to walk in the street completely naked so that her body might be admired. Although she had previously been terrified of other people looking at her, she now began to dress in a way that is aimed at attracting looks. She learnt to swim so that she could sport herself in swimming pools. With a certain surprise, she found herself being drawn into a sexual liaison with a couple. The analyst discovered that the sexual attraction was secondary, even absent, in this relationship; the fundamental wish being to have her body admired by the couple, to be looked at by the parental representatives. Our analysand, like Freud's, was struggling with issues related to the primitive scene, but here the delusion of being watched, observed, was replaced by the wish to be admired. What is astonishing is that the unfolding of exhibitionism in our analysand coincided with a reduction in her sense of being persecuted. 'The hostile and malevolent watcher and persecutor', described by Freud, disappeared in favour of the mother's admiring gaze; that is, from the moment the paranoiac has access to an erotogenic body that he can show and exhibit, the paranoia loses ground. Thus the following formula may be employed: *exhibition is the antidote to paranoia*.[5]

Paranoiac clinging to the real object

In 1922, Freud described paranoiacs as people who 'expect from all strangers something like love' (Freud, 1922b: *S.E.* XVIII, 226). Among other authors, Racamier has shown (1966) how the paranoiac has a permanent need to cling to a real external object, on the condition that he is able to keep it both 'within reach and at a distance'. We share these points of view entirely. It is certain that, ultimately, the paranoiac's true mode of relating, beyond projection, is a sort of *clinging* to the external object; but this great need for the external object is unbearable for him and he hates it.[6] With the same insistence and permanence as this 'clinging', the paranoiac exerts a contrary force, which, while conserving a close bond with the external object, makes this submission acceptable in his eyes. The principal mechanism that he uses to this end is projection: 'He hates me; he persecutes me', instead of 'I need his love'.

The treatment of our analysand illustrates this problem of the paranoiac well. Before investing the analyst's gaze, when she sensed the slightest risk of closeness, she resorted automatically to procedures that were guaranteed to distance the analyst. For instance, she would evoke a memory of something she detested about him. By this means, she transformed him into a 'bad beast', to use her expression, and thus succeeded in making the sense of 'closeness' disappear, which she experienced as a danger of subjection. Once some distance had been created again, she would recover her serenity. At other moments, with the help of her projections, she would seek out a bad, persecuting object, other than the analyst, ensuring that the latter was thereby distanced. Hypochondriacal preoccupations about a part of her body represented a manoeuvre with the same aim.

With our analysand, the change linked to investing the analyst's 'gaze' gradually made these mechanisms unnecessary and marked a turning point in her development. Her body, which had now become erotogenic, provided a protective barrier against the excessively strong impulse propelling her towards the object. The acquisition of a bodily erotogeneity now formed a link with the object, while at the same time guaranteeing a certain distance from it. However, although it is true that she is now able to do without an external persecuting object, she still has just as much need to cling to the external object and, more precisely, she needs his 'gaze'. We think that she will remain in this state of dependency as long as she is unable to acquire the capacity of looking at herself auto-erotically.

To conclude, on the basis of these clinical observations and our genetic elaboration set out earlier, two questions emerge: beyond projection and the homosexual complications, is the essential mode of paranoiac functioning what we call *paranoiac clinging*? and does this clinging of the paranoiac have a direct link with that of the small child who fails to achieve a truly secondary auto-erotic movement? While awaiting more certainty on this, one could put forward the hypothesis that it is at the price of *clinging* to the external object, to his gaze, that the paranoiac achieves his unity; and that it is at the price of projection that he tolerates the *clinging*. While abhorring his absolute dependence, he chains himself to his object so as to avoid ever again sinking into the dark regions of the non-object or into the madness of dispersed auto-erotic activities. Deprived of a truly erotogenic body, the primary source of a sense of identity, he is condemned to search for a figure that will reflect this body and so will look for a double. It will obviously be a double of the same sex – less by homosexual attraction than in the hope of finding his identity, on the model of the primitive mirror relationship with his mother. The persecutor, the eminently narcissistic external object, his double to whom he has always been clinging, is perhaps that aspect of the composite primitive double that he has been unable to appropriate; that is to say, this double represents a part of the continuous relation that has been lost and that he has been unable to make his own. The injustice the paranoiac believes he is the victim of could lie therein: a fragment of his identity, of his narcissism, has escaped him with the double. As long as he does not have an erotogenic body, the paranoiac will remain paranoiac, that is, he will continue to cling to his persecutor; and as long as he does not succeed in looking at himself auto-erotically, he will cling to the external object.)Let us listen to Freud: 'Since Fliess's case . . . a piece of homosexual investment has been withdrawn and utilized for the enlargement of my own ego. I have succeeded where the paranoiac fails' (see Brabant, Falzeder and Giampieri-Deutsch, 1993–2000).

WORKING AS A DOUBLE[1]

Psyche is extended; knows nothing about it.
Freud, 1938a

We do not doubt the importance of the close relationship between transference and counter-transference forming the central axis of the analysis in any treatment. However, in this chapter, we will primarily be concerned with elucidating the existence of certain psychic processes that are covered over most of the time by the transference/counter-transference dynamic. We shall also be trying to identify situations where a shared complicity – frequently an unconscious homosexual complicity – between the two protagonists of the session, impedes the emergence of a certain mode of relating that, owing to its unusual or strange nature, is experienced as disturbing or even disorganising. A feature of this mode of relating is that an area of the psyche of which the subject was hitherto unaware strives to find its way into consciousness. In the first place, our intuition will be based on an idea halfway between scientific hypothesis and fiction, concerning the evolution of Freud's thought and his successive transferences on to Fliess, Jung, then Romain Rolland, and finally Moses, at the end of his life.

The orientation of our research into the notion of homosexual investment may be compared with the attitude Freud (1900) recommended to analysts in a footnote of 1925 in relation to the dream:

I used at one time to find it extraordinarily difficult to accustom readers to the distinction between the manifest content of dreams and the latent dream-thoughts . . . The need to interpret it would be ignored. But now that analysts at least have become reconciled to replacing the manifest dream by the meaning revealed by its interpretation, many of them have become guilty of falling into another confusion which they cling to with equal obstinacy. They seek to find the essence of dreams in their latent content and in so doing they overlook the distinction between the latent dream-thoughts and the dream-work . . . It is the *dream-work* which creates that form, and it alone is the essence of dreaming – the explanation of its peculiar nature.

Freud, 1900: *S.E.* V, 506

More than the content, manifest or latent, it is the 'work of homosexual transference' that is of interest to us here.

The evolution of Freud's thought and the double

Let us tackle this 'work of homosexual transference' at work in every treatment by drawing the now classic parallel between Freud's homosexual transference onto Fliess and the discovery of psychoanalysis. Notwithstanding Jones' different point of view, we imagine that Fliess loved more the man Freud than his ideas, that he loved him above all with an erotic investment and that his ideas represented for Fliess an elegant finery rather than the fundamental reason for his friendship. Having said that, Freud's homosexual investment of Fliess was more than an end in itself, a means of making Fliess a double in the service of the blossoming of his thought. Fliess' libidinal gaze, the response of the double nourishing Freud's narcissism, enabled the latter to throw himself headlong, without fear, into the auto-erotic movement inherent to all original thought. It may be said that Fliess represented a sort of detour via reality, a reality test, a materiality enabling Freud to overcome the fear of vertigo, the fear of the auto-erotic madness of unbridled thought. And yet original thought requires a rupture.

Indeed, the development of Freud's thinking seems to have been a long journey oscillating between gaining reassurance from his investments in 'material' doubles and the need to free himself from them so as to be able to continue to create. Freud knew this very well: 'It seems certain that homosexual love is far more compatible with group ties, even when it takes the shape of uninhibited sexual impulses – a remarkable fact, the explanation of which might carry us far' (Freud, 1921a: *S.E.* XVIII, 141). This is a complex matter, for although the 'materialisation' of the double, with the aid of the hook of homosexuality, offers a protection against the vertigo of thought, the price to be paid is the adhesion, the collage of thought to the double, the sacrifice of differences. And it was the transition from the relationship to a 'material' double, to the relationship to an autonomous, internal double, as a result of analysing homosexuality, that would give Freud's thinking all its originality. *The Interpretation of Dreams* was not born of Freud's homosexual transference towards Fliess; on the contrary, it came into being when he surpassed it by beginning his self-analysis in 1897. Before that, there was the 'Project', reflecting Fliess' biologising outlook. Between the two there was a painful rupture.

Our feeling is that Freud's homosexual dream concerning Fliess, which was repeated several nights in a row during the summer of 1904 when they had fallen out definitively, and regarded in *The Interpretation of Dreams* (Freud, 1900: *S.E.* IV, 145, note 1) as a hypocritical dream, for it disguises the wish to break up his friendship with Fliess by feigning the contrary, expresses, through its hypocritical homosexuality, a wish other than that of blocking out aggressivity. It attempts to hide the universe of solitude emerging after the disappearance of the 'material' double, to deny the gaping hole opened up by withdrawing his investment from Fliess and to fend against the insufficiency of the internal double. It was an attempt destined to failure. A few weeks later, Freud suffered a psychical disturbance on the Acropolis, the analysis of which only saw the light of day in 1936 in a letter to Romain Rolland, an echo of his investment of Fliess reverberating in the present.[2]

At the end of the year 1911, as he was once again 'absorbed' by the investment of the double, incarnated now by Jung, Freud complained bitterly about the lack of originality in his thinking: 'I always find it hard to conform completely to another's thoughts . . . I am working hard on the psychogenesis of religion, finding myself on the same track with Jung's "Wandlungen"' (letter to E. Jones, 5 November 1911: Jones, 1955: 394, vol. 2).

Moreover, it was a fresh attempt to free himself from the 'material' double, by continuing with the analysis of his own homosexuality – after fainting in front of Jung in November 1912, an event that was reminiscent of a similar disturbance in front of Fliess in the same place – that would enable Freud to emancipate his thinking. The months that followed saw the birth of a first study of the double ('The "uncanny"') (*S.E.* XVII, ed. note p. 218; letter to Ferenczi, 12 May 1919: Brabant, Falzeder and Giampieri–Deutsch, 1993–2000) not published until much later (1919), the 'Theme of the Three Caskets' (1913), the fourth and final part of *Totem and Taboo* 'which will perhaps hasten my breach with Jung' (letters to E. Jones, 9 April 1913 and Ferenczi, 8 May 1913: Jones, 1955: 396, vol. 2) and the first approach at a study of Moses ('The Moses of Michelangelo', 1914), constituting the ferment of a future crisis. Moreover, as a result of being released from the double Jung/Fliess, Freud was able to go beyond Fliess' biological concept of periodicity in favour of the psychical compulsion to repeat ('Fausse Reconnaissance ("déjà raconté") in Psycho-Analytical Treatment' and 'Remembering, Repeating and Working-Through' and, in October 1913 (Jones, 1955: 116, vol. 2) with a fervour comparable to that of *The Interpretation of Dreams*, to conceive of the complete draft of his text 'On narcissism: an introduction', which represented a radical revision of his theory.

When, at the end of his life, Freud reinvested Moses, he found his thinking was once again impeded. He was assailed by doubt, 'the historical novel won't stand up to my own criticism. I need more certainty', he wrote to Arnold Zweig on 6 November 1934. One month later, on 16 December, he was discouraged: 'Don't say any more about the Moses book. The fact that this, probably my last creative effort, should have come to grief, depresses me enough as it is' (Freud, 1970: 98). The courage and certitude he sought did not come through scientific discoveries but through his relationship with Romain Rolland, the least 'material' of his doubles (they only met once). With regard to the pacifist writer admired for qualities Freud could equally apply to himself – his 'love of truth', his 'courage as a thinker' (1936: *S.E.* XXII, 239) – he was finally able to tackle, 32 years later, the gaping hole opened up by the 'dematerialisation' of the double Fliess and to analyse his disturbance on the Acropolis. The fragment of self-analysis, constituting his open letter to Romain Rolland in January 1936, freed Freud further from his passive homosexual position towards the father and allowed him to escape from the impasse of Moses by transforming the 'founding father' (who had faced him with 'quite special difficulties – internal doubts as well as external obstacles') into an internal double (a text in which the themes of uncanniness and the double appear again).

Freud was then in a position, in the summer of 1936, to rewrite his work on Moses, and to abandon himself at last, without fear, to a relationship with an internal double. His thinking was now able to function through perceptual identity providing the much wished for certitude of the soundness of his views. From the materiality of his homosexuality, Freud had moved on to a sense of assurance in his psychic functioning. A vast work of figurability, on the model of an internal mirror work, with reflected images, led Freud to 'the perception of historical truth', arousing in him the intimate conviction of the historical reality of his intuitions. The 'truth' was no longer only 'external', material, following the logic of reflections governed by secondary processes, but 'internal', intimate, arising from the force of the impact of perception awakened by a work of figurability, the only means of awakening external truth.

We believe that this new relation to Moses, via the intermediary of Romain Rolland, awoke in Freud hitherto relegated – and not 'dried up' – psychical possibilities, and that the culmination in the perception of the 'historical truth', in intimate convictions, released a new dynamic of thought, enlightened Freud, and led him to fresh perspectives on the analyst–analysand relationship. We see evidence of this in the change that occurred in Freud between his two technical writings of 1937. The new relation to Moses enabled Freud, over a period of a few months, an interval during which he finished *Moses* (Freud, 1970; Freud, 1937b) to move from the conception of the biological bedrock, of which the 'repudiation of femininity' (*S.E.* XXIII, 211, 256) is part, limiting the possibilities of the analytic process and the action of the analyst, to that of 'Constructions in analysis' (published in December 1937), where the analyst is no longer a person handicapped by the weight of biology, the limits of secondary processes and the recollection of memories but, on the contrary, by virtue of his psychical functioning alone, can bring the treatment to its resolution. A few months after his text on the impossibility of terminating an analysis, Freud put forward an idea, which, it seems to us, was revolutionary – namely, that the conviction aroused in the analysand by the work of the analyst 'achieves the same therapeutic result as a recaptured memory'. He then added: 'The problem of what the circumstances are in which this occurs and of how it is possible that what appears to be an incomplete substitute should nevertheless produce a complete result – all of this is matter for a later enquiry' (Freud, 1937a: *S.E.* XXIII, 266). From thereon, analysis could no longer be considered simply as a work of remembering.

Freud's thought, then, re-emerged invigorated by a mode of functioning involving an internal double during the study on Moses; a mode of functioning that gave him the certitude that the analyst's intuitions through perceptual identity can contain the psychic 'truth' of the analysand. This is possible – and herein lies our thesis – when this work of the analyst, consisting notably of figurability, originates in community with the analysand's psychic functioning. The conviction, emerging initially in the analyst, in reality belongs to both. *The conviction of today is no longer the suggestion of yesterday, but the product of a common work.*

The analyst's work of thinking, as we imagine its evolution in Freud, oscillates during the analytic encounter between the homosexual transference/counter-transference dynamic, revealing the history of the analysand's infantile neurosis and the dynamic of the double through perceptual identity and is directly in tune not with the analysand's mechanisms and unconscious phantasies – as is customary in analytic work – but with their weak spots, opening up flaws, gaping holes in his functioning. This mode of thinking reveals, in particular, aspects of the analysand's infantile history with which it has not been possible to work; hence its importance, its necessity, in the analyses of borderline cases. As this mode of thinking is obscured most of the time by the unconscious homosexual dynamic and the efforts of the preconscious ego to avoid it because it is a source of feelings of uncanniness, we call it *functioning or working as a double (travail en double)*.

Florian

The following case is an extreme scenario, involving a turbulent and, fortunately, rather rare session, whose analytic understanding requires us to consider a certain number of facts and mental processes operating in the analyst, which are the consequence and reflection of 'flaws', of the absence of any possibility of intelligibility on the analysand's part.

It was an apparently ordinary neurosis that brought Florian into analysis, but at certain moments of the regression, originating in the analytic situation, his system of neurotic defences proved insufficient and he was forced to use means of coping other than those characteristic of neurosis.

At the beginning, as at the end of each session, Florian was constantly observing the analyst, not in a mistrustful way, but, one might say, without sufficient conflict, without any inhibition. His expression was neither curious nor guilty, but seemed to be clinging to his perception of the analyst. Once he was lying down, Florian would cling to the perception of a noise, an object, a light, or whatever and would then construct rational associations and commentaries in connection with them. This was how he accomplished his work in the session while, at the same time, his muscles would tighten up to the point of causing him pain. Rediscovering his muscular tension and clinging to a perception were the mechanisms Florian used less as a defence to avoid a possible emergence of repressed ideas than a means of survival against emptiness, against the disorganising effect of losing his perception of the analyst.

In the session prior to the one we shall be discussing in detail, Florian related a dream, which was a rather rare occurrence. '*We are together . . . you are going to have a shower . . . I don't follow you*', but he did not bring any associations. Being a man, the analyst's associations naturally suggested themes of communal showers between men. He said vaguely to himself something like: Florian is beginning to emerge from a regressive state, from an overly archaic mode of relating; perhaps this dream, with its homosexual content, represents a turning point in his analysis and foreshadows the alleviation of a lateral investment in operation from the beginning. For, the day after the first meeting, Florian had formed a passionate friendship with a man who had some points in common with him, i.e. with a 'material' double.

This dream was the culminating point of a movement in the treatment. And yet the analyst had a barely perceptible, almost intangible feeling, alerting him to the presence in his analysand of another universe sustaining his economy. This was perhaps due to Florian's readiness to relate his dream and to the analyst's satisfaction; or alternatively, it may have been due to the homosexual counter-transference that became manifest slightly too easily, too hastily.

In the next session, Florian did not need to go looking for perceptions; they came to him on a massive scale: 'I saw you this morning . . . You were on the Boulevard Saint-Michel!' (The analyst had indeed been on the Boulevard Saint-Michel that morning, but what Florian had not noted was that the analyst was accompanied by his wife.) A few minutes of silence followed. Then, strangely enough, Florian was seized with doubt: 'It was you that I saw, wasn't it?' With intervals of silence, the sense of doubt continued, becoming more accentuated, accompanied by rising anxiety: 'I thought I saw you . . . I did, didn't I? I'm not sure any more if I saw you . . . You were wearing dark glasses, weren't you?' He was increasingly tense, anxious, then gave up: 'I don't know any more if I saw you or not . . . You were wearing dark glasses, weren't you?'

Meanwhile, the impressions emerging from what Florian had been saying aroused in the analyst an increasingly sustained feeling of 'derealisation'. He was struck by the discrepancy between the embarrassing picture of himself that was being imposed on him as he was listening to the analysand and the pleasant memory that he had of his morning, a sunny morning on which he had been out for a relaxing walk. Surreptitiously, he was infiltrated by an image accompanied by a word that did not come from the analysand and one he did not normally use: 'hieratic'.

His work of figurability could be summed up with the phrase: 'hieratic ego with dark glasses'. Vague thoughts came to him; surprisingly, like the analysand's, they were shrouded in doubt: 'Dark glasses . . . but do we say dark glasses? Don't we say sunglasses? Dark glasses – the glasses used by a blind man . . .? It's strange, dark glasses . . . Ah, glasses for mourning!'

'Hieratic ego? What does hieratic mean? Solemn? Is the image solemn? It's more rigid than solemn. Rigid ego . . . Dead!? . . . A living corpse . . . Ego, menacing and indestructible like the living dead in the film of the same title[3] and, at the same time, on the point of turning me into dust.'

A struggle was going on in the analyst, although he was barely conscious of it: his narcissism held on firmly to his pleasant recollection of the morning, but it was as if there was a force resisting it. Under the influence of what the analysand had told him, a sinister image of the morning forced itself on him, stuck to him like the shadow of his own experience. He was prey to a double self-representation: 'Relaxed-ego, hieratic-ego', the first of which, only, was recognised as belonging to him, as something familiar, whereas if the figuration 'hieratic-ego' had not been controlled by a diurnal ego but produced by the regressed ego of the sleeping state, it would have had all the characteristics of a nightmare. Two representations, then, depicting in fact two parallel modes of work in the same psyche.

The analyst got himself out of this state by means of humour. The terrifying living corpse with dark glasses assumed a peaceful, relaxed appearance, sunbathing like any other holidaymaker. A corpse on vacation! Now he was able to laugh! The analyst's black humour clearly enabled him to recover. It was a triumph for his narcissism trying to save the unity of his identity at that moment, a way of making the incompatible double representation evolve towards a compromise solution, a condensation, in which the pleasant nature of his memory could link up with, and overcome, the horror of the nightmare.

But Florian went on speaking and the analyst's pleasure associated with his note of humour did not last very long. It was as though listening to the analysand was drawing him once again towards a world of terror. And when the analyst heard Florian say again in an intransmissible, flat voice: 'Dark glasses . . . You had dark glasses?' he felt his nightmare welling up again. There followed a heavy silence, longer, more pregnant than usual, which was interrupted by the analyst, practically without his realising it, by a questioning mumble. Erm? 'I don't know any more if I saw you or not . . .' said Florian; and he added the astonishing formula: 'I don't know any more if I saw you . . . I am looking for you in the image and I can't find you any more.'

In other words, the analyst had disappeared in Florian's hallucinatory memory. Can such a withdrawal of investment from the representation of the object be qualified as a negative hallucination? What is certain is that at the same time as this psychical phenomenon took place in Florian, there occurred in the analyst a work of figurability in the form of a nightmare. Are there not grounds for thinking, then, on the basis of this clinical observation, that there is a correspondence between the void of the analyst's disappearance from the analysand's 'image' and the fullness of the means of figuration employed by the analyst's nightmare? Further, that the analyst's nightmare is the counterpart, the complement, the positive of the analysand's negative hallucination? And moreover that the analyst's psyche served as a 'darkroom' revealing what could only be inscribed negatively in the analysand?

Once he had recounted his hallucination of the absence, Florian calmed down a bit and then recalled the dream of the session before. The analyst had forgotten his nightmare; he was only too happy to turn his thoughts to the shower! Florian said to him: 'If I don't follow you into the shower, it is because something prevents me.' And quite naturally, the analyst was on the verge of making an intervention on the subject of homosexuality. Suddenly, as if it was an ordinary session, repression took over again as in the case of a usual negative Oedipal complex. But, simultaneously, and almost imperceptibly, he had a vague feeling he was being baited by his analysand and so he kept silent. Then Florian did not know what more to add on the dream or what to talk about. Perhaps he felt frustrated by the fact that the analyst was not saying anything. 'Shall I tell you about my duty period [he had been on duty at the hospital] . . . Since I have nothing else . . . I had three deaths.' The words came out brutally, bluntly and the forgotten nightmare came back to the analyst equally brutally: three deaths; three weekly sessions. Then Florian spoke about an elderly couple, former deportees; the widow had particularly irritated him because he felt she had been relieved by her husband's death; although, as he had cancer, it was better for him that he had died. 'It was perfectly obvious that she did not want to follow him', commented Florian. The idea immediately sprang to the analyst's mind: 'Ah! The point is that he didn't want to follow me into the shower either . . .into death!' The analyst then had the impression that the whole session was falling into place and acquiring meaning. 'Following me into the shower', the negative hallucination, and 'hieratic-ego' were thus connected by the notion of death. The analyst now understood his intuition that the analysand's homosexual transference was a lure and how his own homosexual counter-transference, denying Florian's destructiveness, suited him. Destructiveness was the kingpin holding together the negative hallucination and the nightmare. Operating against this world of ego disorganisation, of terror, were homosexual investments, in both analysand and analyst, functioning as a lifebelt.

While Florian was speaking about deportation, the idea of death in the shower took on a terrifying dimension for the analyst; and, as Florian, whose infantile history had no connection with the Nazi horror, returned immediately to the dream, the analyst heard himself saying: 'The shower is a gas chamber.'

The analyst's *work as a double* (*travail en double*) ended here. He was finally able to formulate in words what, until then, had only been possible to grasp through affects and images. His words rendered the colour of his nightmare and finally gave Florian's foreclosed affects, and his nightmare that had remained blank, the right to exist. Heavily charged with visual imagery, expressed through perceptual identity, the intervention led to liberating, violent sobbing from Florian, which he was unable to control during the rest of the session and with a great deal of difficulty once he was on his feet again.

This opening up of the containing dyke against affects seemed to be closer to the economic solution of a straightforward discharge than to a symbolic meaning of an hysterical order. And if one accepts the idea that Florian's noisy sobbing was the echo – albeit somewhat out of step – of his own affects, which until then had been foreclosed in him, but which, contrariwise, caused the analyst to have a nightmare, is there not good reason for thinking that two psyches were necessary in order to construct a single psychic object?

Theoretical and clinical commentaries

The latent content of Florian's dream calls for some reflection. Do the words 'I don't follow you' or, to be more precise, the negation of 'I follow you', really represent a repression of homosexuality, or rather, are they a sign, along with the negative hallucination, of the difficulty of homosexual investment, and even ultimately of the difficulty of being able to invest the object in any real way? It is as though Florian were caught between the need to invest the analyst as a narcissistic, homosexual double and his terror of losing his boundaries in doing so, of passing over on to the other side of the mirror. In a later session, he was finally able to express this drama himself in words, to condense it in a succinct phrase: 'Either I take interest in you and forget myself entirely, or I negate you.'

(From the point of view of analytic technique, one may consider that, in the initial period of the session, the absence of any intervention by the analyst concerning the dream was judicious. Not only because the dream represented the return towards the analyst of libido that had hitherto been lost in a lateral movement, in a passionate friendship with a double, but also because it was the first time that homosexuality had appeared clearly in the material of the treatment. By the same token, should he not perhaps have intervened when the analysand began to doubt his memory, to depersonalise himself? Instead of letting himself be carried away by Florian's state, and accompanying him in his regression, instead of identifying with him to the point of becoming his reflection, his complement, instead of functioning as a double, should the analyst not, for instance, when his analysand became depersonalised, have simply recalled the dream of the session before? That is to say, should he not have intervened as closely as possible to the ego by giving, for instance, an interpretation such as: 'If you are hesitating about whether you saw me or not, it may be because the possibility of meeting me outside the session was the equivalent for you of following me into the shower'? He might then have added: 'Just as when you were a child, you both wanted to take a shower with your father, and yet were afraid of doing so.' Or he might have said something about the denial of the primitive scene. Such interpretations were available to the analyst and would certainly have had the virtue of reducing Florian's anxiety. The latter would have disappeared the moment the analyst had named it, had given the disarray a meaning, a content. Such an interpretation would have avoided Florian's distress at the same time as stopping the uncanniness and the retrogressive course of the analyst's thinking; it would have avoided the analysand's negative hallucination as well as the analyst's nightmare. An intervention of this sort would surely have had a soothing effect, but our reproach is that attributing a homosexual meaning would have suffocated the material which led to the association 'shower–gas', revealing a particularity of Florian's structure, of the drama of his impossible homosexual quest. It was the figuration of this world of homosexuality, a disorganised world, a source of terror, which made it possible to get the analytic process moving again at its true conflictual level. In fact, the sudden confrontation in reality with a primitive scene overwhelmed, as a result of its intensity, the precarious interplay of Florian's Oedipal investments. The dark glasses may certainly be seen as representing his castrating wishes towards the analyst and may be likened to the 'widow', representing a coveted Oedipal mother, but the investment of these representations was unable to resist the economic/dynamic situation that had been triggered. The flaw in Florian's secondary auto-erotism, with its repercussions on the constitution of his alterity, meant that his transference desires could not be organised and the analyst could not be invested either as a loved father or as a feared rival, a 'sandman', or one who 'tears out eyes', symbolising castration. Florian was thus subjected to such a disorganising level of tension, to such a destructive experience, that he would try to get out of it, if he could, by decathecting the analyst and the analysis.

Now we can imagine that on seeing his analyst in the street (who, conse-quently was no longer invested with the same narcissistic characteristics in duplicate; he was simply an external object), and while referring to him as he told the story, a sense of danger was awakened in Florian faced with the picture of the analyst who had become too autonomous, too concrete, involving the risk for Florian of being absorbed by it and of forgetting himself in the process. Threatened with the danger of not existing, as much by the presence of the object as by his tendency to disinvest it, Florian came within a hair's breadth of the danger of *non-representation*, hence the extraordinary hallucinatory surge transforming the memory into the sensory power of a negative hallucination. Being obliged both to deny and recognise the object's presence at one and the same time, he succeeded in doing so perfectly with his dazzling negative hallucination.

Nevertheless, alternative possibilities were available to Florian other than this radical solution corresponding to an exceptional economic situation; he could employ the mechanism of negation in a more nuanced fashion, as the dream

76

shows. And although the negative hallucination totally denied the object's presence, the dream, by way of contrast, bore witness to a certain acceptance of its existence. Florian's dream represented, above all, the enactment of his new, recent affirmation: the statement 'I don't follow you' could be understood as a 'I am not you'. By means of the negation of 'I am you', a negation in front of the emergence of the double, Florian marked the beginning of an alterity, a mirror alterity, it is true, but alterity nonetheless; for the animistic continuity – in which the subject is the double of an object that is the double of the subject – was broken.

The dynamic of the double: animistic, auto–erotic, narcissistic

> *The idea of the 'double' does not necessarily disappear*
> *with the passing of primary narcissism, for it can receive fresh meaning*
> *from the later stages of the ego's development.*
>
> S.E. XVII, 235

It is above all in French psychoanalytic publications that the notion of the double has been developed. The authors who have influenced us most in this connection are Christian David (1971) and André Green (1974). (See also Braier, 2000.)

Since the works of Rank and Freud, there has been a tendency, initially, to consider the double as a unitary and invariable notion: a specular image, a hallucinatory projection outside, of a bodily representation of oneself the primitive function of which is an 'energetic denial of the power of death' (Rank, 1914: 235). But beyond this most wide-ranging and representative sense of the double, one can find in contemporary psychoanalytic literature all the complexity of an original dynamic. Freud himself had already had a glimpse of it. Thus, in 'The "uncanny"' (1919) he puts forward the idea, as we recalled in the epigraph, that 'the idea of the "double" does not necessarily disappear with the passing of primary narcissism, for it can receive fresh meaning from the later stages of the ego's development.' Namely, the agency of 'moral conscience' and the fact that man is capable of self-observation that 'renders it possible to invest "the old idea of a double"', Freud adds, 'with a new meaning and to ascribe a number of things to it – above all those things which seem to self-criticism to belong to the old surmounted narcissism of earlier times . . . But it is not only this latter material, offensive as it is to the criticism of the ego, which may be incorporated in the idea of a double. There are also all the unfulfilled but possible futures to which we still cling in phantasy, all the strivings of the ego' (p. 235–6). These avatars of the double, self-observation, ego ideal, moral conscience, constitute an ensemble which later on, in the *New Introductory Lectures on Psychoanalysis* (1932b), Freud includes under the name of superego.

But that is not all. Along with the idea of a double progressively taking on itself a variety of contents, one encounters in Freud descriptions concerning different constitutions and forms of the double. It is not so much a question of this or that stable form as a fundamental organisational mode of inter- and intrapsychic reality, capable of assuming sometimes one form of the double and sometimes another. Indeed, in 'The "uncanny"', the double is defined as 'a creation dating back to a very early mental stage', belonging to an animistic world and considered at that time as having a 'more friendly aspect'. But 'when this stage [of assurance against death] has been surmounted', the double can transform itself into the terrifying image of a 'harbinger of death'. It is in *Totem and Taboo* (1912b) that Freud develops his conception of the animistic character of the double:

> A general overvaluation has thus come about of all mental processes . . . things become less important than the idea of things . . . the reflection of the internal world is bound to blot out the other picture of the world – the one which *we* seem to perceive.
>
> *S.E.* XIII, 85

An animistic world 'which caused us to see copies of our own consciousness all around us' (*S.E.* XIV, 171), 'invented' to use Freud's expression, by primitive man with the help of his animistic capacities in order to struggle against death anxiety. According to our hypothesis, to this creation of the double in phylo-genesis there corresponds an ontogenetic counterpart inherent to the functioning of every psyche; it is inseparable from the traumatic effect of the perception of absence on the 'primary narcissism which dominates the mind and of primitive man' (*S.E.* XVII, 235). The double may be said to emerge in response to the fear of psychic death, in response to the risk of *non-representation*, doubled by a non-perception, whether this occurs in the small child faced with the absence of the object or in the adult each night during the narcissistic regression of sleep arousing the fear of *non-representation*, of *non-perception*; hence the pressure towards a hallucinatory representation of the subject himself (a double) in the dream.

The animistic double

The *animistic double* is thus a mode of thinking in which representation, perception and motility are equivalent and undistinguishable. A product of retro-gressive processes, this animistic double, overflowing with sensory experience, is under the dominance of the perceptual and/or hallucinatory register and is ignorant of alterity. It is a psychic state that only understands the world in terms of what it is itself; the world being simply a mirror for it in which it is reflected through projection.

When Freud describes, in *The Ego and the Id* (1923a), primary identification as 'a direct and immediate identification and takes place earlier than any object-cathexis' (p. 31) one is justified in wondering if, at this level of psychical non-differentiation, Freud's use of the term identification, which by definition, presupposes a relation to a distinct object, is valid. At least if one accepts the existence of a psychic capacity before animism, a *pre-animistic psychic stage* (doctrine of R. R. Marrett (1900), cited by Freud in *Totem and Taboo*, to which we shall return) in which the intrapsychic cannot be differentiated from the non-psychic.

The auto-erotic double

It would seem that the emergence from animism corresponds to the appearance of another modality of the double, the *auto-erotic double*. The psyche, always eager to be reflected and complemented, captures something of this undifferentiated world and internalises its animistic double. For lack of a better term and without claiming any temporal succession, in the last chapter we qualified this movement of 'captation', which is fundamental for psychic growth, as secondary auto-erotism, for it bears the mark of the object even though the latter has not yet been recognised as distinct. Secondary auto-erotism organises the transition from animistic continuity to the auto-erotic double. This means the subject constantly reinvests the erotogenic body, appropriating his own members, his erotogenic zones, which have opened out precisely through contact with the animistic object, whence their quality both of separation and union. The body ego, and one's self-image are dependent on them.

Notwithstanding its narcissistic characteristics, secondary auto-erotism works in favour of maintaining the sense of alterity. During waking life, by virtue of its permanent activity of returning to itself, the auto-erotic double represents an endopsychic mirror which, like Perseus' reflecting shield facing the Gorgon, removes the terror of the danger of *non-representation* and gives support to reality testing. The internal play of reflections of the auto-erotic double, where the subject is both an observed passive object and an observing subject – a miraculous return of the subject to himself – leads Francis Pasche to say in respect of Descartes: 'Thus when I say, "I think, I am", I am split, detached from my thinking self, in order to be able to watch myself thinking' (Pasche, 1981).

The narcissistic 'material' double

But at certain moments this internal mirror can be effaced, making way for a narcissistic regression, which, beyond a certain degree, eclipses the interplay of internal reflections and awakens the terror of an animistic continuity driving the subject to search desperately on the outside for this 'mirror' that he is lacking on the inside and to cling to the perception of a *narcissistic 'material' double.*

The session that we have just analysed is an example of this. The flaw in his secondary auto-erotism reduces Florian to an analytic relation with a narcissistic 'material' double, to functioning in terms of 'psychic life or death': the white of negative hallucination and the black of the terror of *non-representation,* of animistic continuity, projected into dark glasses. If the analyst had manifested himself by giving an essentially Oedipal interpretation relating to homosexuality, as the analysand and his counter-transference wished, so as to blot out a world of terror by 'leaning', so to speak, on the erotogenic body, he would have shortcircuited the possibility of understanding Florian's problem of alterity; the analyst's intuitive representation (*figurabilité*), 'the shower is the gas chamber', evoking both homosexuality and terror, a nightmarish double of 'I don't follow you', would not have occurred. It was this way of *working as a double* that allowed an 'I am me', a body ego, to emerge, a locus of penetration and conservation, of limit and expulsion, making it possible to consolidate the endopsychic, auto-erotic double, a link and separation between the subject and the object cathexis.

As he had hitherto been without any secondary auto-erotic anchoring, Florian had to cling to a 'material' double, to the analyst's perception, in order to avoid the animistic continuity representation–perception; or alternatively to gather, to concentrate himself in his tense muscular attitudes, which, although painful, served to delineate his bodily limits at the price of a certain erotogenic masochism. This was an auto-erotic minimum for the psychic survival of his alterity. However, we cannot deny that Florian longed for a homosexual object investment. The day after the stormy session, he said he felt a weight had been lifted from him and repeated with fascination the intervention 'the shower is the gas chamber', like a child who, in order to be able to go to sleep peacefully at night without having nightmares, needs to be told a horror story inscribing his erotogenic masochism within an object relationship. Likewise, he came back to the dream and said boldly: 'There must be something sexual in it.' By that he meant that he could at last call out desperately for his homosexual, narcissistic double, for he now possessed, in place of an auto-erotic 'I am me', this 'I am not you', the negation we spoke of earlier, the indispensable minimum alterity enabling him to see himself in the analyst without feeling terrified.

State of session

At certain moments, the analyst is brought face to face in his practice with the problem of the regression of his thinking. As early as *The Interpretation of Dreams,* Freud, announcing the fundamental rule, associates free association with a particular state of the psyche in which self-observation is possible: 'a psychical state which bears some analogy to the state before falling asleep' (*S.E.* IV, 20). Thus, the economic and dynamic conditions of the analytic encounter are such that the ego's functioning, which, in principle depends on the mode of activity of the waking ego is at moments akin to the ego's night-time functioning. A complex situation in which the ego of the session that is losing its assets of the waking state – motility, action and perception being in a large measure abandoned as during the sleeping state – does not, like the night-time ego, have the advantages that derive from the opening up of the hallucinatory path; we call this the *state of session* in order to emphasise its temporary, even absurd and monstrous character, halfway between the waking and sleeping state. Moreover the ego, thus disconcerted, has to suffer the libidinal closeness inherent to the session, the re-sexualisation, at the heart of the treatment, of social investments and an increase in instinctual tension owing to frustration; a real instinctual overload whose impossible realisation leads inevitably to an increase in psychic tension, to a plethora. And when the paths of discharge specific to the session – free association, the work of figurability and speech – prove insufficient, this economic ensemble puts the session in an economic situation akin to that of actual neurosis. It may be supposed, then, that just as psychoneurosis admits of a kernel of actual neurosis, there exists in every analytic relationship a certain aspect that is actual. *Just as psychoneurosis tries to elaborate its kernel of actual neurosis, transference neurosis must absorb its actual component inherent to the here-and-now of the session.*

Faced with this problem, the ego in the session, which is neither diurnal nor nocturnal, in order to find a way out, tries to make use of two modes of functioning as best it can. The lesser evil represented by this gymnastics for which the ego is not prepared, has its consequences; for the convergence of the two modes of psychic functioning, daytime and night time, which are normally meant to be separate, raises a state of uncanniness. The state of the session and the proximity of the animistic world that it imposes will entail different adjustments in each partner.

During the session, as thinking proceeds in a progressive direction, one can observe at certain moments, and sometimes continuously in the background, the effects of retrogressive tendency 'which makes possible the cathexis of the system *Pcpt.* in the reverse direction, starting from thoughts, to the pitch of complete sensory vividness' (Freud, 1900: 543) and, as a consequence, 'an idea is turned back into the sensory image from which it was originally derived' (Freud, 1900: 543). The formal regression of thought facilitates the tendency to immediate discharge: the cathexis of the intensity of the ideas overrides the cathexis of the 'connecting paths' (Freud, 1900: 280) and can even result in the predominance of the perceptual quality. In this way, by virtue of its unaccustomed thrust towards hallucinatory figurability, by virtue of its proximity to animistic thought, the formal regression of the session can collaborate in the development of the uncanny, indicating a weakening of the auto-erotic double.

81

One way for the analysand to resorb the state of the session and putting a break on hallucinatory figurability, is to over-invest the object-analyst. We have seen it at work – and above all through its absence – in the guise of a clinging to the perception of an external self-projection, to a 'material' double. Nevertheless, narcissistic though it is, this libidinal investment of the analyst as a double represents, in contradistinction to the animistic double described earlier, a minimum of alterity, a detour via material reality. In fact, the cathexis or investment of the 'material' double is a sure means of eliminating the hallucinatory solution and of maintaining a work via thought identity.

From this perspective, recollection is another means of achieving this, for it can be seen as having a double function: of (a) leading to the resolution of conflicts and to the liquidation of the psychoneuro, and (b) resisting, like a defensive rampart, the continuation of formal regression, of 'bringing regression to a halt so that it does not proceed beyond the mnemic image' (Freud, 1900: 566). In effect, the analysand will spontaneously avoid the risk of the formal regression of his thought by taking refuge in mnemic images, formations capable of inhibiting animistic regression, especially as their vividness, which at times is remarkable, can take charge of the hallucinatory tendency awakened by regression. Thus, remembering (transference being a form of it) reveals the infantile history with its repressed wishes, while setting itself up as a defensive formation against animistic regression by providing the ego with a reassuring sense of *déjà vu*. The complexity of psychical functioning in the analytic situation never ceases to surprise us. Let us add that the point here, in our opinion, is not to relativise remembering and transference; on the contrary, we wish to underline their economic and dynamic weight and the vast field that they cover.

In the light of these considerations, the fact that every transference neurosis involves a homosexual transference could be explained, beyond the dynamic peculiar to infantile object-relations in connection with the auto-erotic double, by the reactivation, at the sexual and narcissistic level, of the animistic tendency originating in the here-and-now of the state of the session; the animistic double will be more or less covered by the narcissistic double, bearing the ideal ego, and by the homosexual object-love, depending on the Oedipal quality of the infantile neurosis. This means that while the *transference and the transference neurosis organise themselves within the upward tendency of the repressed wishes and the infantile neurosis, they are no less facilitated, and even triggered, by the actual neurosis peculiar to the state of the session.* *Grunberger's narcissistic driving face*

Working as a double

If, as we have just seen, the analysand is led along different paths to use his analyst as a narcissistic and/or homosexual double, the analyst, for his part, is not led to invest the analysand in this way. For, owing to his own analysis, as well as to the experience of practising analysis, he is used to coping with formal regression and his animistic tendency; and, depending on the particular economic conditions and moments of the session, he will have at his disposal the possibility of working both via perceptual identity and via thought identity, of functioning as an animistic double and as an auto-erotic double. In effect, if the analyst's thinking can tolerate the movement of regression, without having recourse to defensive solutions such as investing the analysand narcissistically, analytic theories, 'ready-made' ideas, or again, memory, i.e. the reinvestment of his own memory traces culminating in a counter-transference meaning that turns the relationship into something 'already known', he finds himself faced with the formal regression of his thought, with the unknown (see Rosolato, 1978, 1985, 1996, 1999). He is then not very far from the child faced with the traumatic unknown – namely – sexual difference, the arrival of a newborn child, the mother's withdrawal of investment. And, like the child he used to be, the analyst in his regression, will have the tendency to transcend this by means of a work of figurability taking the form that is peculiar to the thought of the infantile sexual theories impregnated with animism. Without the obstacle of the counter-transference and the field of pre-conscious memory, remaining as close as possible to the unknown of the analysand that is a triggering cause of the state of quality of his thinking, interpretations of a particularly intuitive nature can come to the analyst. These interpretations, which are formed along the direct path of regression, give access to unrepresentable areas of the analysand's mind that would otherwise remain unreachable. Under these conditions, the analyst's work of thinking is in continuity with the analysand's psyche and corresponds to the model of the relationship of the dream-work with the day residues and momentary sensory impressions. The analyst's work of figurability, arising from a regressive mode of functioning as an animistic double, has its roots both in the analysand's unconscious and in the analyst's own capacity to tolerate the regressive movement of his thought, making it possible to create new connections, new contents. As a counterpoint to counter-transference elements, the analyst's work of figurability represents both the reflection and the complement of the analysand's psychic functioning.

Just as the counter-transference is the counterpart of the act of transference, that is, a manifestation of the analyst's unconscious along the progressive waking path, the analyst's capacity to pursue, at certain times, the regressive path of animistic thinking is the counterpart of the analysand's regression in dreams. If we follow Freud in his *Papers on Metapsychology* (the chapter on 'The unconscious', where he affirms that, 'unconscious mental activity appears to us . . . as a further expansion of the primitive animism' (*S.E.* XIV, 171), we are bound to admit that analysis can only reach the animistic form of infantile wishes through a hallucinatory-perceptual process, at least where primary repressions are concerned. At certain privileged moments, the transferring analysand, and the analyst in formal regression, are together in a position to approach, or organise, the model of animistic continuity representation–perception constituting the unconscious system. Without this encounter, the analytic process would remain limited; the unconscious, the animistic nature of the repressed aspects of the psychoneurosis, would still remain largely veiled.

This way of *working as a double* thus operates between two psyches. One of them, demonstrating a remarkable degree of momentary plasticity, reflects what is only potential in the other. The need for complementarity is sometimes such that the psychic object is only complete, as Green says, in 'the union of the work of two psyches' (Green, 1974). It is a complex act involving both passiveness and appropriation, revealing and even creating psychic data.

Certainly, this mode of *working as a double* does not often manifest itself openly and most of the time it escapes the analyst's attention; which partly explains the paucity of publications on its role in analytic treatment. Among them, we have been particularly interested in those already cited by Christian David (1971), André Green (1974) and in those that concern paradoxical thought in the work of Michel de M'Uzan (1976).

Let us return now to the session with Florian. The formal regression of the analyst's thought, his *work as a double*, allows him to discern, beyond what is manifest, more than a content, thought or unconscious phantasy, something in the order of a traumatic element, a rupture, in the analysand's representational order. The 'living corpse' was not the translation by the analyst of a murderous unconscious wish of Florian stemming from his infantile neurosis; it arose, on the contrary, in the latter's absence, in the face of the failure of his infantile neurosis, under the effect of a traumatic discontinuity. The analyst's nightmare emerges from this discontinuity and gives a meaning to the analysand's *non-representation*. From this same point of view, the analyst's interpretation 'the shower is the gas chamber', does not correspond either to an unconscious wish of Florian, in spite of the representations 'three dead', 'deportation' and 'widow', which it is tempting to consider as associations that have their origin in the unconscious problematics of the dream. In the session in question, Florian's associations represent, above all, attempts to elaborate his affects of terror arising from the proximity of *non-representation* triggered in the here-and-now of the session and absorbed in part by the flash of the negative hallucination. The figurations 'living corpse' and 'gas chamber' are the echos of this in the analyst. Arising from the regressive functioning of the analyst's thinking, as an animistic double, they bear the mark of what he has been able to pick up of the analysand's terror of non-representation. It is only after they have been evoked in the interpretation offered, that Florian's so precarious auto-erotic continuity is given new impetus, that his internal mirror is reconstituted and that he will be able to form an idea of his distress that hitherto had been unrepresentable. By appropriating the connection between the representation 'shower', coming from his dream, and the representation 'gas chamber' coming from his analyst, he is able to get beyond the fracture caused by his weak narcissism.

The *work as a double* inevitably awakens an effect of uncanniness and the analyst's psyche will have the tendency to defend itself against it, to minimise it or even to forget it immediately. We have read a striking example in which the analyst and the analysand had the same dream on the same night, with a practically identical manifest content. Only the analyst did not want to publish this 'strange' occurrence until 25 years later when the analysand was already dead and he himself was terminally ill, he adds, as if to excuse himself for a misdeed, as if it were shameful to say openly what should remain secret (Rascovsky, 1976). Thus in order to blot out such an event in an analysis, in order to avoid the sense of strangeness, there will be a tendency to consider this mode of *working as double* in ways that are already known, quickly making the uncanny product fit into reassuring pre-established moulds, transforming the strange into the familiar, the sense of uncanniness into its 'positive counterpart', into the *déjà vu*. Sometimes, then, we will be led to think of the notion of counter-transference and as we often, if not always, find a few elements reflecting our own conflicts, we will quickly put the matter aside. Sometimes the phenomenon will be understood as a manifestation of habitual mechanisms; and, depending on each person's theoretical leanings, this mode of functioning as a double will be seen and suffocated under the cover of a hysterical identification, through community or, alternatively, in the form of a projective, or even adhesive, identification, or again as a residue of primary identification. In fact the specificity of this *work as a double* cannot be reduced to a mechanism of identification, even if it is primary identification, although it can be sustained by it; for, in this mode of functioning, identification properly speaking, does not exist; rather, there is an immediate, primitive perceptual capacity, comparable to the figurability, to the endopsychic perception of a dream.

(To conclude, it has to be said that the problem of the distinction between the mechanisms discussed in this chapter and the mode of *working as a double*, which is theoretically evident, is not simple in daily practice, especially as the operative mechanisms depending on each person's structure will occupy the foreground most of the time. The best indicator of its specificity is its hallucinatory character, for this represents the culmination of the formal regression necessary for the expression of a psychical work of this kind.)

8

'ONLY INSIDE–ALSO OUTSIDE'[1]

It might be said that in the last analysis the 'spirit' of persons
or things comes down to their capacity to be remembered
and imagined after perception of them has ceased.

Freud, 1912b: *S.E.* XIII, 94

Like primitive man who accepts the ineluctability of death, acknowledging it
and disavowing it in the same magical act, memory acknowledges and disavows
the reality of loss. And, even when the world is no longer populated with spirits,
in their place memories animate the shadow left by the lost objects. We would
say, then, that remembering is the equivalent of a magic technique.

Similar to Perseus' mirror in front of the Gorgon, memory reflects each new
and thus disturbing encounter on to the reassuring polished surface of the *déjà
vu*, sacrificing the unknown to what is 'already known'. It oscillates between the
two statements, 'Yes, it's true; I can remember it' and, 'No, I have never seen it,
so it's not true.' As a solid shield of reality testing, the work of memory tends to
govern us more than we care to admit, at the risk of distorting our analytic
practice.

Conviction

The discovery of the second topography, discerning at the heart of the
unconscious an id that was no longer comprised of the repressed properly
speaking, a source of infantile amnesia, at once relativised and complicated
the role of memory, to the extent that the last study Freud devoted to it
('Constructions in analysis') (Freud, 1937a),[2] ended by introducing radically new
perspectives. Freud admitted that owing to his preoccupations with the patient's
recollections 'the other portion of the work, the task performed by the analyst,

had been pushed into the background' (p. 258). And not contenting himself either with the already familiar notion of counter-transference or with limiting himself to the notion of construction, Freud drew us into a new and vast field of investigation by inviting us to reflect on 'the link between the two portions of the work of analysis, between his own part [the analyst's] and that of the patient' (p. 259). Most authors have only seen in 'Constructions in analysis' the role of construction and not that of interpretation. In our view, the revolution of this article is not one of 'finding' memories or of 'reconstructing' them, but rather the place accorded to conviction as an inescapable notion in analysis, with a metapsychological value in its own right.

Having been virtually ignored in Freud's texts hitherto, in 1937 it dethroned the previously sacrosanct notion of remembering. Freud now asserted that conviction could achieve the same therapeutic result as a recaptured memory and he opened up a new path of investigation involving the study of the close and dependent relations between conviction, recollection, hallucination and delusion; hence the comparison drawn at the end of the article between hysteria and delusions – namely, that those suffering from them were suffering from their own reminiscences.

Any attempt to approach the psychoanalytic notion of conviction, which has been the object of very little study to date, seems inevitably to involve a double confrontation: with its opposite, doubt, and with memory.

At first sight, it would seem self-evident that remembering engenders conviction. And yet obsessionals, who are champions of remembering, fret with doubt. Freud clearly demonstrated, in 1926, how the obsessional exhausts himself in fighting against the risk of being invaded by animistic thinking that has remained too vivid and against the sense of uncanniness that proceeds from it (Freud, 1925a: S.E. XX). In fact, according to Freud, here, the obsessional's over-investment of doubt – an auto-erotic solution, with anal characteristics rooted in instinctual ambivalence – has the primary aim of mastering the formal regression of thought. And this defensive distancing of animistic thought, resulting in an absence of conviction, may be said to indicate that conviction and animistic thought are inseparable and that their link with remembering is very complex.

In its normal functioning, the mind is capable of making use of its capacities for animistic thinking instead of impeding them or being invaded by them. It is able to transform them – we will say how later – into a process leading to conviction. From this hypothesis there emerges the idea that every analysis necessarily involves the dynamics of the relations between remembering, conviction and animistic thinking.

Freud's attitude to animistic thinking is somewhat disconcerting. Between 1913 and 1919, he approaches the subject with such confidence that we naturally expect it to play an increasingly important role in his work thereafter. On the basis of his description in *Totem and Taboo* (1912b) he asserts in an article as fundamental as 'The unconscious' (1915c) that 'unconscious mental activity appears to us as a further expansion of the primitive animism' (*S.E.* XIV, 171); then, in 'The "uncanny"' (1919): 'When we consider that primitive beliefs are most intimately connected with infantile complexes, and are, in fact, based on them, we shall not be greatly astonished to find that the distinction is often a hazy one' (*S.E.* XVII, 249).

Notwithstanding the significance of these assertions, Freud was to write little more on the subject of animistic thinking, except in *Inhibitions, Symptoms and Anxiety* (Freud, 1925a), with regard to obsessional neurosis; and then, in 1932, in the *New Introductory Lectures on Psychoanalysis.* In neither case are his remarks articulated around the concept of the unconscious; neither do they have the significance that the earlier texts intimated. Should we regard this erasure as the consequence of too much concern on Freud's part to leave a stamp on psychoanalysis of a resolutely positivist, scientific character? The development of his biologising theory of the life and death instincts or, between 1920 and 1922, his decisive position on hypnosis, suggestion and telepathy from which he wanted to distance himself (Freud, 1920, 1921a, 1921b, 1922a), suggest that this was the case. At any rate, the theory of the death instinct (a doubt in 1920 which became a conviction from 1923 onwards) and the notion of desexualisation that it confirms, are, we think, the counterparts of the erasure, at the same period, of an animistic conception of the mind and of the permanent sexualisation that is inherent to it.

That said, the interest Freud accorded to animistic thought in the years 1913–19, had not, however, disappeared; he was working on it behind the scenes. It is discernible, for instance, in the manner in which, from 1923 on, he defined the limits of neurosis and psychosis in relation to the problem of the relation between the internal and external world (Freud, 1924b, 1924c, 1925b, 1927a). It was an implicit conception that would always remain with him. It is operative in his description, in 1926, of Eros which 'desires contact because it strives to make the ego and the loved object one, to abolish all spatial barriers between them', and later on when he advances the idea that there was once a time when the infant 'does not as yet distinguish his ego from the external world' (Freud, 1929: *S.E.* XXI, 66–7, 1938b). In effect, these late considerations represent, we feel, the return of the importance of animistic thinking as it was described before the turning point of 1920:

> A general overvaluation has thus come about of all mental processes . . . Things become less important than ideas of things; . . . the reflection of the internal world is bound to blot out the other picture of the world – the one which we seem to perceive.

> *S.E.* XIII, 85

It was a mode of thinking 'which caused us to see copies of our own consciousness all around us' (Freud, 1912b: *S.E.* XIII, 85, Freud, 1915b: *S.E.* XIV, 171).[2]

Animistic thinking

According to these Freudian approaches, *animistic thinking is a mode of thought in which representation, perception and motor activity become equivalent in the re-emergence of what we have described as the continuous universe.* Dream hallucination, involving both thought and perception, a true relic of animistic functioning, is the most striking example of it (Freud, 1900). This continuity representation–perception, which one finds at night, also tends to occur during the day each time that a sufficient degree of regression occurs. This is sometimes the case during the analytic session.

While apparently being grounded in objective data, it is in the most subjective conditions that conviction is seen to take hold with the most force; that is to say, in the infantile sexual theories, screen memories and delusions.

Having their origin as much in animistic thinking as secondary processes, the infantile sexual theories are based on the hallucinatory dream model and are constituted by a work of figurability. Triumphing over traumatic perception, they carry the conviction of having grasped the truth: 'It's true, I saw it', the child will say. These animistic solutions, created to vanquish what is unfamiliar and disturbing, and to recover a sense of the familiar, similar and intimate, become obsolete under the pressure of the reality principle and succumb to the censorship of repression, leaving a void to be filled at the preconscious level. As conviction in the hallucinatory mode no longer has the right to exist, it is vital for the psyche to create new witnesses, other means of revealing the 'truth', better adapted to the new demands. The screen memories unfold and allow for the return of hallucinatory continuity without compromising the discontinuity representation–perception; they provide the basis for the sense of a present as an extension of a hitherto non-existent past. The adult can exclaim with the same conviction as the child: 'Yes, it's true, I remember.' The phenomenon of the *déjà vu* may be considered as a regressive return of continuity in the place of 'I remember'.

Caught up in the repression of the infantile sexual theories, and pushed aside as memory unfolds, the animistic mode of thinking tends to disappear, to be relegated to unconscious functioning, whereas conviction remains a psychical act of cardinal importance. Should one infer from this psychical necessity of conviction, that infantile sexual theories and screen memories have the purpose, among others, of sustaining conviction; and, that conviction is an indispensable adjustment, a bridge, an intermediate chain or a softening filter between internal and external reality?

Whether it comes in the form of theory, recollection or mere intuition, conviction is marked by the animistic mode of thinking; it is a vehicle both of qualities of affect and of representation without being one or the other. Experienced as a feeling, it is a hallucinatory experience of continuity projected onto the sensory realm, thereby imposing itself like a dream image, the impact of a perception. Thus the hallucinatory power of animistic thinking, intrinsic to all conviction, participates in the evocation of our most ordinary memories.

'Only inside–also outside'

One of the meanings accorded to the term conviction after 1920 refers to castration in the girl and its negation, accompanied by the certainty that she had, has or will have a penis. There is an anti-traumatic alliance, then, between negation and conviction – two aspects of the same process – that has repercussions for the functioning of reality testing. Conviction is at the heart of the relation of the mind to reality.

Being in a position to recognise the reality of this or that thing presupposes that the subject has emerged from what Freud calls the stage when the infant 'cannot as yet distinguish his ego from the external world' – in other words, that the indispensable discontinuity between representation and perception has been constituted. Our hypothesis is that, for this to happen, reality testing has to involve the paradox of disavowing reality. In the animistic world, the perception of the object, a factor facilitating non-distinction, has to be disavowed energetically so that 'belief' can be maintained in its existence simply as a representation; without which, its control is uncertain and the distress of absence, the animistic equivalent of the subject's own disappearance, is a constant threat. With the help of secondary auto-erotism, animistic continuity is interrupted by a negation of the perception of the object, by means of a sort of 'No, it is only in me.' Such a negation of the perception of the object, without a withdrawal of investment from it, could be inserted between the two phases of being and having described by Freud in 1938 (Freud, 1938a: *S.E.* XXIII, 299). Between Freud's first proposition, 'I am the breast', and the second, 'I have it – that is, I am not it', we would interpose, 'No, it is only in me.' This destruction of the object in perception, owing to the omnipotence of auto-erotic thinking, is the only means of protecting the subject against the terror of the object's disappearance in perception, of preserving his capacity to represent, to think. Every act of thought is guilty, in the background, of the murder of the object; this is a very different mechanism from the radical schizophrenic withdrawal of investment from the thing-presentation of the object for which the price that has to be paid is the capacity to think (Freud, 1915c, 1917a).

At the heart of reality testing, the negation of the object in perception, which is neither a disavowal nor a negative hallucination, is simultaneous with belief in its existence. A 'No' concomitant with a 'Yes' allows the object to be refound just when it is being disavowed. This, in our view, is the meaning of the famous passage of Freud in 'Negation' (1925b):

The first and immediate aim, therefore, of reality-testing is *not* to find an object in real perception which corresponds to the one presented but to *refind* such an object, and to convince oneself that it is still there.

S.E. XIX, 237

In spite, we would add, of the energetic negation that we inflict on it. Then, when Freud says: 'What is unreal, merely a presentation and subjective, is only internal; what is real is also there *outside*', he leads us to think that reality testing operates according to a double contradictory conviction – namely, that *the object exists 'Only inside—also outside'*. There is, then, a double psychical movement containing an incompatibility that is nonetheless complementary; an indication of animism that is inconceivable at the level of secondary thinking. It is out of this psychical work, similar to a magic technique, that the sense of existence and of reality will emerge.[3] It corresponds to Freud's conception where perception is envisaged as a 'confirmation' of a presentation, itself a 'reproduction' of the perception. We will be developing this point further on in connection with reality testing (Chapter 11).

The second phase of castration, the sight of the absent penis, is thus less a perception that forces itself on the child as a triumph of a reality principle than a consequence of this complex work burdened by animistic thinking. The capacity to perceive the sexual difference as a lack only comes with the conviction that the object can 'really' carry out the threat, since the child himself has the animistic conviction that the object can, in conformity with reality, 'really' inflict such an act. Castration can exist in perception because it is present in the presentation. The psychic organisation of the castration complex at the heart of the representable world, freed of animism, represents a qualitative leap in which the work of memory, temporal discontinuity, experiences of '*déjà vu . . . entendu*', reveal the causal succession: 'It is missing because . . .' The child will thus believe in the threat of castration more as a result of his belief in his infantile sexual theory than as a result of the continuity of his animistic thinking. When the distinction between the sexes does not attain the value of a conviction, it remains a mere observation. Psychical reality is always the fruit of work: whether the object is perceived and/or represented, it is created/found at the junction of connections between the logical systems of an infantile sexual theory, animism and memory.

The double movement, constitutive of reality testing, of disavowing the perception of the object in order to be able to invest it in the representation, and reproducing it in the presentation in order to refind it in the perception, is nothing other, then, than a memory function based on the castration complex. Remembering is existing. The present exists because it is memory; because it is a permanent 'deferred action' (*après-coup*) based on the past (Fain, 1982).

Thus by virtue of the 'No' and of memory, the double conviction '*Only inside—also outside*' is at the origin of a change of psychic regime.

91

At the point where hallucinatory animism, the actuality of perception, and the *déjà vu* of memory meet, the richness of the preconscious organises itself by taking advantage of the upward surges of the unconscious as much as of the data of perception. The orientation of investments occurs through the function of attention, which, sweeping aside the memory traces, just when it is scrutinising the world of perception, excludes the risk of a traumatic irruption. It anticipates, predicts and recognises any potentially dangerous perception in the *déjà vu* of the memory traces. This permanent confrontation between the memory traces and new sensory qualities colours, animates and enriches the preconscious memory, in particular at certain critical stages of life, such as the readjustments entailed in puberty and old age.

*(When the work of reality testing does not sufficiently guarantee the discontinuity representation–perception, the function of attention will not be able to reach the animistic memory traces and will see itself reduced exclusively to the relations between preconscious representations–perception. Such a preconscious, cut off from the animism of unconscious traces, is impoverished and itself becomes a mechanism of defence, a drastic means of reinforcing discontinuity.)

As for analytic treatment, we have already suggested in connection with the dynamic of the double, that as a regression of thinking in the session approaches, an atmosphere of uncanniness may manifest itself in both partners – a proximity of the animistic world involving different modifications in each. Given that remembering puts limits on the animistic regressive course, the analysand will emerge spontaneously from the risk of regression by taking refuge in mnemic ideas. A reassuring *déjà vu* of the past, and a particular way of remembering, namely, the act of transference, instead of the feared regressive course, will lead the analysand in the progressive direction of realising his unconscious wishes. Consequently, there is naturally a tendency to think that the 'truth' can only emerge through transference and remembering, to the point that our understanding of the analytic process risks being reduced to these processes alone. This, we think, was Freud's error up until 1937; like the tree hiding the forest, remembering obscured for Freud the importance of conviction. Having said that, by relativising remembering, we do not, however, wish to minimise its role in treatment, but rather to come to a better understanding of its nature by studying its connection with conviction.

As we have already developed this point, we will not insist here on the fact that (an alternative means of recourse against formal regression to remembering and the over-investment of preconscious thinking is to make a narcissistic homosexual investment, to apprehend the external object as one's own double. It constitutes another stopping point in regression, ensuring the maintenance of a relation that, however narcissistic it may be, is nonetheless a relationship with an object, that is to say, a barrier against the return of animistic thinking.)

Things being what they are, the analyst's personal analysis has already confronted him with this issue. But once he is in his armchair, his psychic functioning will be faced with new experiences and other problems, on the condition, however, that he is able to let himself yield as much as he can to the regressive, backward course of his thought processes.

The transferring analysand and the analyst in formal regression are together in a position to approach, and even organise, at certain special moments, the model of the continuity representation–perception, constitutive of the unconscious system. It is in this continuity that the conviction, the 'truth', the reality of psychic events can force itself on both of them and 'achieve the same therapeutic result as a recaptured memory'.

Olga[4]

When one of us made Olga's acquaintance, her thinking was still strongly marked by obsessional mechanisms, in spite of a first analysis. The two sessions that we are going to describe took place after a week during which the analyst had been absent.

As she was on her way to the first session after the break, Olga's mind was in a state of turmoil, at odds with all her senses. Was it the right day? Was it the right time? Was she going in the right direction? Was she on the right floor? As she was standing in front of the analyst's door, time seemed to explode for a moment. Although she was standing still, Olga had the impression she was going up and down, up and down, dizzily. This motor hallucination was rapidly cut short by a thought that suddenly came to her, as if it were self-evident: 'Like that, I let Mme B. have a breather between two sessions.' When the door opened, Olga was already smiling and, for the analyst, the session began with this image of her smiling. The analyst only heard the account of this distressing experience a few weeks later.

Let us remark straight away how difficult refinding the object was for this analysand, even after a short period of absence. (See further on 'The smell of fir', in Part 3.) The habitual mechanisms failed and gave way to regression. With motor activity blocked, thinking rushed along its evolving trajectory and, like animistic primitive man, the analyst resorted to a magic technique derived from motor hallucination in which act and hallucination are indissociable. Hallucinating ascents and descents was a way of annulling the absent sessions by magically retracing the path of what had not taken place. It was a realisation that took the form of a violent coitus denounced by the reversal and the reaction formation that followed: 'Like that, I let Mme B. have a breather between two sessions.'

Unlike the dream-wish fulfilment, motor hallucination, as we have understood it in *Totem and Taboo*, while being a wish-fulfilment, is, so to speak, a vital necessity, a defence against the traumatic dangers arising from perception. In Olga's case, the issue was to avoid refinding the object; and more exactly, the risk of being invaded by the intolerable pain of a lack that had been denied up until then. Hence the urgency, the suddenness, the acute character, the orgastic colouring of the motor hallucination. It was the first phase of annulling the absence, an immediate and sexual possession of the object, a thought that had the value of an act. The second phase, the reaction formation, as well as words of magic value, sweeping aside both the content and the form of the orgastic hallucinatory experience, was the equivalent of saying, 'No, I haven't touched her, my analyst is taboo', re-establishing the usual image she had of her. Olga was at last able to smile.

Motor hallucination and words were combined to shrink magically, in the space of a breath, the time between the previous session and the first one after the break. When Olga rang the bell, the interruption of her sessions no longer existed, her affects were obliterated; even better, all that had never happened.

Once Olga was lying down, her sexual investment was so efficiently annulled that it would not produce any offshoots. So she could proceed as usual – namely, in a somewhat stifled tone of voice, the only sign of her permanent underlying anxiety, she recounted, associated, recounted, associated. Everything referred to the past. Memories, like model state employees, appeared, worked, and disappeared again. The centralising power of preconscious memory occupied the whole stage. Maurice Bouvet has described masterfully the use of memory by obsessionals, the purpose of which is to temper the immediateness of the object, to ensure a certain distance from it. This measure is indispensable owing to the vividness of their animistic thinking which threatens them with subject–object continuity, representation and perception. This threat is even greater in the case of the object's absence, which animistic thinking translates immediately into a hallucinatory presence.

During this first session after the break, owing to the magic annulment of the absence and to the over-investment of the past, nothing appeared in Olga's discourse concerning the interruption; there was no trace of the three sessions missed. The exclusion of any sort of representation of the absent analyst, with its concomitant affects, was so total that the analyst thought this signalled an amnesia with no point of return. Faced with this measure aimed at the non-existence of the perception of the lack, faced with Olga's lack of any representation of her, the analyst had a fleeting sense of derealisation that cannot be understood simply as a counter-transference thought in the order of castration or as belonging to the narcissistic register: 'My analysand is treating me as if I were a dead loss.' Her feeling of derealisation was immediately included in a retrogressive movement of her thinking reaching her consciousness with the flash of a ready-made expression, particularly loaded with intensity: 'No one'll be any the wiser.' Instead of a feeling of derealisation, the analyst now possessed a sense of assurance, the conviction that she had gained access to the essential aspect of the psychic economy of the moment and that her work of figurability would serve her, when needed, as a platform, a lever.

The analyst certainly could have avoided her feeling of derealisation, her formal regression, by remaining, for instance, at the level of her preconscious thoughts concerning the analysand's defence and eventually by giving the usual interpretation, namely, that Olga was acting as if the absence had not occurred. While justifiable in other cases, such an interpretation would have been ineffective here. The analyst had learnt with Olga that, had she done this, she would simply have been sustaining her analysand's preconscious which grasped rationally, without fail, all information concerning her functioning, immediately blocking any emergence of repressed ideas. Such an intervention would only have reinforced the demarcation line of a preconscious already cut off from its unconscious sources. Isolated from the unconscious, the preconscious becomes, for the obsessional, its own source of excitation. It shapes objects into objects–words–taboos and memories into memories–words–totems, into mortuary memorials. Its own functioning assumes the value of an auto-erotic object substituting itself for love objects.

(Under these conditions, any intervention by the analyst is in danger of being treated in this way, being disembodied, amalgamated with this auto-erotic preconscious. The only chance is to wait for the salutary flaw in the workings of such a pitiless mechanism, to wait for a failure signalling that the relationship with the object has been re-established.)

Towards the end of the session, Olga could not situate a date. Was it such and such a year? Her questioning ended with an outburst: 'And anyway, I couldn't give a damn about the calendar!' This blank in her memory, this act of forgetting, accompanied by lively affects, represented for the analyst the other much expected pillar of the bridge corresponding to his expression, 'No one'll be any the wiser.' She said: 'Ah!' Then, Olga's silence, a privileged moment in a hitherto continuous discourse, made the analyst continue. Spontaneously, in resonance with Olga's act of forgetting, her words came out in three phases, a sort of incantation: 'Is it one session, two sessions or three sessions? One death, two deaths or three deaths?' It was a way of approaching Olga's flaw, the 'gap in her memory', in an attempt to bring the perception of the lack that was not represented back to it. It might be said that the analyst was making dead people emerge so as to bring to life, or even create, the representation of her own absence.

Olga's reaction was instantaneous: 'Well, you're a surprise!', she exclaimed. A brief moment of pause followed when her drama seemed to be sinking in, but it was quickly followed up by the words: 'Oh shit, I hadn't thought of that!' Olga meant that, concerning the analyst's absence, she had not thought about her father who had died a few years before.

At this juncture, certain questions need raising. What did the gap between the analyst's intervention and Olga's association with her father represent? Did the expression 'no one'll be any the wiser' not correspond, above all, to the analyst's irrepresentable silent suffering, connected with the disappearance, the death of two of Olga's siblings, one of whom had died when Olga was just 1 year old? Did the nature of the analyst's psychic work not reflect or even reveal the otherwise ungraspable animistic character of the analysand's functioning?

The association concerning the dead father, which might have been considered as dynamic in another context was, for Olga, but an appeal to her preconscious memory, to the 'historical' deaths, in order to fight against the effect of the analyst's intervention, the uncanniness of the unexpected appearance of the missing sessions, the sudden appearance of the absent analyst. After a brief instant during which Olga seemed to grasp the import of such a universe, she emerged from the sense of uncanniness by suffocating it in the *déjà vu* of the recaptured memory. Her associations concerning her father's death were frequent and habitual, as if 'installed' in the sessions; they brought the associative links back to a status quo, to a dead point in their dynamics. The fullness of the representation of her father's death enabled Olga to evade the emptiness of the *non-representation* of the absence and to drown her affects in it.

It was totally impossible for her to elaborate the week of interruption; there was no trace of Oedipal issues; neither were there any representations of the primal scene with their corresponding defensive adjustments. Faced with the object's absence and unable to carry out a work of mourning, Olga's radical procedure was closely akin to the schizophrenic mechanism of withdrawing investment from the thing-presentation of the object. As an excessive impregnation by animistic thinking prevents the obsessional from establishing the double conviction '*Only inside—also outside*', from exercising the subtlety of 'No—Yes', he replaces it by the massiveness of a double negation of his investment of the object 'neither inside—nor outside', neither seen in perception nor known in representation. This procedure that will be reinforced by an auto-erotic investment of preconscious functioning. *The obsessional 'clings' to his own thinking, just as the paranoiac 'clings' to perception, each of them suffering from a weakness in secondary auto-erotism.*

The absence of representation of the lack is the point that Olga has in common with the Wolf Man for whom, at the level of the 'third current, the oldest and the deepest', there could be no question of a representation of the absence of the penis (Freud, 1914–18: *S.E.* XVII, 85). With Olga the absent representation of the object could only come back from the outside, just as castration reappears in the Wolf Man in the form of a hallucinatory perception of the severed finger. In Olga's case, in contrast with the Wolf Man, this could not occur in the waking state.

And if to this we add that the closest representation, the most representative of a negation of the investment of the object, is that of her death, one might as well say that recovering the investment of the object-analyst has every chance of taking the shape, as with animistic primitive man, of the return of a dead person, of a 'spirit'. Olga's exclamation, 'Well, you're a surprise', expressed her emotion on perceiving the 'unexpected thing'. 'So, you are there! You exist!' But, faced at once with the impossibility of dealing with such a test of the reality of the return of her investment of the analyst, Olga immediately imposed a work of memory, the recollection of a real death rendered familiar by its narration, by words.

The hallucinatory movement, immediately covered over by the memory, nonetheless left traces, as is shown by the dream that occurred during the night following the session. It can be seen that the analyst's intervention formed a smarting waking residue and erupted in the regression of sleep: 'I could see my face in a mirror. The inside of my mouth was disintegrating into shreds. People around me were lamenting: "We can't do anything, we can't do anything, we can't do anything." I woke up feeling oppressed, with the sense that the world was gloomy.' Olga eagerly brought associations related to the history of her infantile sexuality. She thought she was 'mortally' guilty for her sexual games and thought she was suffering from the 'illness of remorse'. With these thoughts about sexuality, then, she quickly exorcised the gloomy character of the dream. And the analyst remained alone with the affect awakened during the recital of the dream. With the memory from the day before of the expression, 'No one'll be any the wiser', in the background, the analyst once again felt a gap between herself and the analysand, between her associations and the atmosphere suggested by the dream. She tried to make a connection by taking up the formula, 'We can't do anything', which in its repetitive, rhythmic form, referred back to the session the day before and seemed to be the most representative element of what was at stake – namely, Olga's psychic death. A change occurred. Olga's voice began to tremble with emotion. 'I wonder if I was able to speak in the dream.' But she immediately overcame her emotion. 'Ah, yes, I know. I'm always constipated with words . . . words which kill.' Then she recovered her composure, as if in search of a 'truth': 'No, that's not what I want to say . . . It's words that failed me, which hurt me.' Troubled, Olga remained silent. 'Words which failed you?' Suddenly, Olga understood the absence by affectively investing the thought that now came to her: 'How is it possible that I didn't think for a moment about my sessions of last week!?'

At last, there was a convergence between the analysand and the analyst; except for the fact that Olga was only referring to words, to the absent sessions, but not the person of the analyst. It was words that answered, just as in her dream the phrase 'we can't do anything', repeated three times, corresponded both to the three 'deaths' and to the three sessions. This procedure was an indication of Olga's difficulty in regressing sufficiently to recover the thing-investments of the object. The words 'We can't do anything' show Olga was obliged to maintain the negation of the thing-investment of the object so as to avoid the danger of an animistic regression of her thought. Which is why, as she came near to perceiving the lack, she tried to verify her own image in the mirror of words. A nightmarish form of reassurance, it is true, but the depiction of the shreds of her mouth enabled her to begin to face her terrifying anxiety of losing the words that were the guarantee of her psychic life.

97

(If we consider the image at its manifest level, the mouth in shreds could be interpreted, beyond its specific interpretation relating to a genital, sexual content, as the manifestation of a sense of guilt originating in the destructive oral greed of the breast and of another child, the disappearance of the latter provoking, in animistic continuity, the depiction of the destruction of the mouth. But with such a genetic conception of Olga's drama, are we not in danger of rationalising the irrepresentable, of supplying the fullness of fantastic images created by the preconscious ego, precisely in order to blot out the emptiness of a *non-representation*, the gaping hole opened up by the withdrawal of investment from the thing-presentation of the object?)

Be that as it may, with Olga, we know that this type of approach simply nourishes the preconscious with words without their infantile flesh. It seems to us that the main theme of the dream can be understood, on the one hand, in terms of Olga's difficulty in refinding the object and, on the other, by virtue of the analyst's work of figurability, the sole witness of the analysand's psychic impasse.

Affect, devitalised and coloured by gloominess, would have remained the only possible representative of the negation of the investment of the thing-presentation of the object, a negation experienced as a destruction. Gaining access to such an affect was only possible for Olga with the support of the analyst's intervention. The affect foreshadowed the return of the object-analyst, under the prevailing animistic conditions – similar to those that led the Wolf Man to the dream of a threatening black demon with a raised finger, to an elaboration of the frightening hallucination he had once had of the severed finger. Thus, to avoid the terror of the hallucination of the lack and the pain of mourning, the obsessional denies the investment of the thing-presentation of the object for his thinking, like primitive man, is haunted by 'spirits'. With Olga it was the gloomy character of her word-presentations that indicated the return of the disavowed/killed object. Which is why the analyst heard herself saying in the session during which the dream was recounted: 'Like that, I come back during the night?' Olga responded with a dazzling flash of humour: 'Ah, there's the ghost!' But no sooner had she said this than she sank back into a state of distraught confusion: 'Then, I don't understand. There weren't any holidays? You were waiting for me?'

A breach had finally occurred in the isolation of the auto-erotic preconscious, allowing Olga's distress to appear. Humour, Freud wrote, is a means of recourse to the protective superego, an identification with the parental object in order to avoid pain. With Olga, the flash of humour: 'There's the ghost', allowing her to become aware of how it was impossible for her to invest the object, and opening the way to heaven knows what gaping hole, caused her reality testing to vacillate: 'Then there weren't any holidays?' But in contrast with session following the interruption, with the dizzy masturbatory phantasy of the motor hallucination, when the hallucination occurred in place of an object-investment, disavowing it, here, Olga's thinking implied the existence, the recognition of a full object-investment, of a mad desire for its presence and the magic realisation of this desire: 'So, you were waiting for me.' Here the negation of the absence was only there to impede becoming aware of the pain of the lack of the object that was at last perceived.

Olga made us understand that, in order to emerge from animism, there has to be a transformation of painful affects into the 'sensory power' of the hallucinatory fulfilment of the wish for presence. She made us understand that investing the memory is a way of fighting against the perception of a lack; it is at once a negation and a work of mourning. *It is the breaking up of pain into memories/ negations of absence that makes it possible to get beyond animistic thinking and to recognise the lack – a requisite of psychic evolution that is never really accomplished.*

A COMMUNITY IN THE
REGRESSION OF THOUGHT[1]

Jasmine

Jasmine comes from Vietnam. We do not know her age for certain. Her parents were killed by soldiers who attacked their village during the Vietnam War. Jasmine was about 2 years old when she was found beside her mother's corpse, although it was not known how long she had been there. As no members of her family were found, Jasmine was adopted by a French couple a short while after. She was good, obedient and did not pose her parents any particular problems – until they found out that she was having learning difficulties at school. When one of us took this little girl into therapy, she was at the age of latency.

This therapy was characterised by the fact that Jasmine was condemned to live in the immediate present: 'That's what I said'; ' It's like that'; 'What I say is what I say'; she would pronounce and repeat to the analyst in a rough, untiring fashion, preventing him from making any reference to the slightest conflict, to the slightest notion of the past. It was probably a case of a massive counter-investment protecting her against a serious deficiency. Indeed, although she had some notions of her past, her race, her colour, Jasmine could not believe in it.

The issues at stake at the start of this treatment were very particular: under the effects of the transference, the forced awakening of the past and buried perceptual residues risked compromising Jasmine's identifications with her adoptive parents who were white. In this connection, it is worth noting that Jasmine experienced her own reflection in the mirror as the resurgence of a ghost, which was a real torture for her. Contrariwise, in her drawings, she was eagerly searching for impressions through the effects of the colours she chose with passionate interest.

It was against a vast background of interpretative silence and on the basis of these beginnings of pictorial images that a rich work of figurability, shared with

100

the analyst, culminated progressively in the emergence of the image of the natal village nestled in a mountainous landscape under the radiant sun. The finesse of the drawing, its extremely delicate colourings, their shades and their harmony, were in astonishing contrast with Jasmine's rough manner of relating, with her tortured feelings concerning the difference of colour between herself and her adoptive parents. Her drawing, executed in a near hallucinatory state, was exceptionally vivid, suggesting the presence of an experience comparable to that of a night dream in which all the stimuli, internal and external, are transformed into dream perceptions, into sensory strength. In this way Jasmine's affects found their way into a dazzling image arising from its perceptual traces: the mirage of a landscape where, it might be said, the analyst and analysand encountered each other in the community of their thought unfolding in a quasi-hallucinatory retrogressive state.

With Jasmine, the habitual regressive course of the analytic session could not be brought to a halt at the level of the representable mnemic traces; the memories were unreachable or rather non-existent. At the same time, the force of the sensory traces liberated in the topographical regression of the session had such an impact that the session became a sort of machine for going back in time, for rendering credible, almost real, a past that was nonetheless without memories, an ahistorical past. Without a story or any memories, the drawing – a magic mirror capable of revealing, of giving presence, without horror, to the absent figures – was also an ardent mirror that excited the flames of a passionate transference: now that regression and perceptual identity had combined in Jasmine, she was convinced that the analyst, too, was born in Vietnam.

But Jasmine was not Alice; neither was the country of her amnesia called Wonderland. Once the drawing mirror had been put into words, it resonated between them, representing a third element uniting and separating them – Jasmine was not Narcissus either. Now that they were both complementary and distinct, like the two pieces of a *sumbolon*, the analyst and analysand were at last able to speak of a little Vietnamese girl named Jasmine. They made their way together along a traced path, created/found by virtue of the community of the regression of their thought processes. Instead of the habitual transference going from traces of the past towards the present, in this therapy it was the transference of actual affects, the passionate presence of the session that went towards the past, towards a memory destroyed by the trauma, investing it with images belonging to the child's sensory traces, in order to reconstitute a history that would gradually become a story. As in a fairytale, words emerged without violence. Jasmine's reality could at last be cathected by her libido; Jasmine was finally able to love herself, to believe in her history and to express her identity without suffering.

With traumatic cases such as Jasmine's, analytic theory undergoes an upheaval. We are far removed from the usual organisation of neurosis; without, however, being able to speak of psychosis; we are far from a problem of memory linked

101

to repression. We are faced with an alteration concerning, not the contents presented, but the function of memory itself. In this therapy, the mnemic images could only emerge from the past in the form of memory. Instead of the usual regression of thought in which the backward course stops at the level of memory, at the level of the images of a recollection accessible to consciousness, Jasmine's memory, without recollections, was awakened due to a mutual regression with the therapist and followed a common path culminating in a content accessible to consciousness. Thus Jasmine's recollection was revealed through the actual experience of the session; it emerged from a direct relationship between the non-presented 'sensory remains' of the past, and the present stimuli, absorbed in a work of figurability under the pressure of a principle of convergence–coherence including both psyches (we outlined this in Chapter 5).

With conditions as regressive as those obtaining in Jasmine's sessions, the gap between representation and perception disappears and psychic reality, dominated by an animistic mode of thinking, opens itself directly to the perception of the sense organs, which, as a result, are more under the sway of the pleasure principle than the reality principle. Accordingly, in the session, the identities of Jasmine and the analyst could no longer be the reflection of the internal mirror of each of them, of their memories, of their personal histories; their identities became the reflection of the regressive state of the present moment, in close connection with the immediate impact of their experiences as specular doubles. Jasmine's belief that the analyst was born in Vietnam, and the maintenance of the quasi-hallucinatory investment of the image of her natal village, had the function, in the early stages of the therapy, of protecting her against the return of pain, against the disorganisation that menaced this little girl faced with the irrepresentable terror of her trauma, the sight and sounds of her parents being killed, the disappearance of her whole infantile environment.

Characterised neither by psychosis nor psychoneurosis, Jasmine's psychic survival was organised essentially around a prevalence of the perceptual system and action. Even though her phantasy life, which had essentially been destroyed by the traumatic event, had left its stamp, it had left the child's psychic reality adhering instead to material reality, to action itself. In this respect, Jasmine's structure is akin to that of the behaviour neurosis described by Pierre Marty (1976).

Animistic thinking and the pre-animistic state

The particularity of Jasmine's mode of thinking, when the analyst began to see her, was linked, as we said earlier, to a powerful counter-investment, a disavowal of the perception of her own racial difference from her adoptive parents, a desperate attempt to be their daughter. Though Jasmine's functioning does not correspond to it in all details, one cannot help thinking here of the description of projective reduplication given by Marty, de M'Uzan and David (1963): 'The subject disavows his own originality, as well as that of others, . . . recognises himself wholly in the other, a complete image of himself cast in an identical form.' It is on this point, namely, the invasion of Jasmine's psychic life, at the beginning of her therapy, by this movement that might correspond in the infantile psyche to reduplication in the adult, that we are now going to reflect.

As we said earlier, Freud, drawing on Frazer's (1911) descriptions, defines animism in *Totem and Taboo* as man's first conception of the world, a conception based on the dualistic outlook of primitive man; that is, in his simultaneous recognition and denial of the existence of death, which entailed both a work of mourning of the dead person and the fear of his menacing return. The animistic world of primitive man was thus inhabited with the dead and with magic and its procedures were developed on the basis of this conception. In the child, the most unquestionable form of animism is omnipotent thinking, a magical mode of thinking that clearly persists in obsessional structures.

Thus understood, under the influence of primary processes and fortified by its mechanisms, animism represents a form of thinking akin to the model of dreams. We were interested in it at the very beginning of our writings as a formal regression of the analyst's thinking during the session capable of taking the form of a mode of *working as doubles*. But today, Jasmine's treatment confronts us with another mode of working in the session.

When the analyst's thinking pursues the regressive direction, there exists an experience of a certain quality, where speaking of animistic thinking is inappropriate; by the same token, it could be defined as a *pre-animistic state*, so as to differentiate it from animistic thinking in which the subject creates, through projection, a world that is identical with his own psychic processes. There is a passage in Freud that appears to endorse this. He suggests the existence of a state of 'pre-animistic animatism', drawing on the ideas of R. R. Marett (1909), who has described a pre-animistic religion. In essence, what we have understood is that, at the level of a *pre-animistic state*, in contradistinction to its evolution in the form of animistic thinking, there are neither thoughts nor contents, properly speaking. Prior to a sensory distinction outside–inside, without any possibility of projection, the conception of the world cannot be the image, the reflection of what the psyche itself is, as is the case in animistic thinking. The pre-animistic state may be said to consist in a state of quality dominated by a sensory continuity between the psyche and the world, between outside and inside. But although this is theoretically conceivable, can such a moment of evolution really exist in ontogenesis? For Freud it was indisputable, as we pointed out in the last chapter. Let us recall again the relevant passages: 'An infant at the breast does not as yet distinguish his ego from the external world' (Freud, 1929: *S.E.* XXI, 66–7); or again, 'To begin with, the child does not distinguish between the breast and its own body' (Freud, 1938b: *S.E.* XXIII, 188). The same idea is found in Freud's note of July 1938 describing the following sequence: 'The breast is a part of me. I am the breast.' Only later: 'I have it' – that is, 'I am not it' (*S.E.* XXIII, 299).

At certain moments in his practice, when the analyst's thinking is functioning regressively, it can approach a state where there is no distinction between hallucinatory endoperception and external perception through the sense organs. Such a state of non-differentiation is characteristic of the ego at night. One could thus defend the existence not so much of progressive or counter-progressive psychic moments in which the characteristics of a pre-animistic state dominate, but rather the permanence of such a capacity in the background of psychic life that is ready to actualise itself providing the conditions are favourable – for instance, while dreaming at night. It is a pre-animistic state of quality, which, comparable to that of the dreamer's ego, permits 'primitive modes of thought' to manifest themselves; it is neither thought itself nor – even less so – ideational contents, but a framing structure (in the sense given by Green to negative hallucination) which reveals them (see, in particular, Green, 1999a, 2002).

(In the evolution of the child's waking life, these animistic modes gradually recede as the object-representation is constituted, as the Oedipus complex imposes its order, before fading considerably with the onset of the period of latency, without however disappearing completely. The child's thinking, which is turned more towards external perception and oriented, particularly in western education, towards the concrete problems of life and towards finding solutions in accordance with the materiality of external reality, will develop secondary aptitudes. The price to be paid for this is the loss of a certain mental flexibility in being able to vary the levels of thinking.)

In this sense, at the beginning of the therapy, Jasmine's mode of thinking was characterised, like other children in latency, by an exaggerated concreteness, except that, in her case, there was something particular: Jasmine could speak well, with notions of her past, her origins, but she did not believe in it. Dominating the foreground was a sort of concreteness of her word-presentations and, in the background, the hallucinatory 'halo' that accompanies the actualisation of a representation was missing – the animation of the representation being entirely equivalent in her to sensory-motor activity.

Community in the regression of thought

As latency – Jasmine's memory in waiting – and the necessity of respecting her identifications with her adoptive parents, had rendered any form of analytic work based on manifest-latent dynamics impossible, Jasmine's treatment required the analyst to adopt a way of working centred not on the difference between dreaming and reality, but on considerations of the duality dreaming/not dreaming, a double expression of her reality. For Jasmine, transference was just a sort of dream; which is why, within the treatment, her primary identifications were animated and enriched by her reactualised perceptual residues. What was decisive for the evolution of this treatment was not so much being able, on the basis of everything she said, to form a picture, to understand empathetically what had happened to Jasmine, but to be able to render present her perceptual residues, containing the essential aspects of herself, to find means of representing them, so that this actualisation of her perceptual residues, implying a re-perception, could enable her to form a picture of herself, to own her identity. And it is perhaps only by means of this type of animistic regression, and by the breaking up of the quantitative into successive states of near hallucinatory quality, that a traumatic past without memory can be elaborated and, more precisely, acquire the psychic status of memory.

Jasmine was thus able to give up the counter-investment of her psychic reality to the extent of disavowing the perception of herself, thanks to a regression of her thought of a *pre-animistic*, then *animistic* order during the session. It was this regression to relations of identity between internal and external perception that allowed her to carry out an 'inspired' reversal. Instead of thinking, as she had before the therapy, 'I am not Vietnamese', thereby disavowing her own reality in a desperate attempt to be like everyone else, she reversed this relation: it was the world, the object of her over-investment at that particular moment, namely, the analyst, who became an image of her, her double. Jasmine had the unshakeable conviction that the analyst, too, was Vietnamese. The transformation of her pre-animistic wish 'neither my mother nor I are Vietnamese' into its animistic opposite in the transference, 'my analyst and I are both Vietnamese' was a true revolution in Jasmine's thinking, an indispensable movement through which her development had to pass. Nevertheless, without the participation of a certain degree of regression during the session of the analyst's thinking, converging with the analysand's own regression, in their *work as doubles*, it is probable that Jasmine would not have been able to achieve such a change.

In Jasmine's treatment, starting with an emotional experience, a *common psychic state* occurred in both the child and the analyst, a *community in the regression of thought*, extending as far as the pre-animistic state. When such a simultaneous mode of regression occurs, the convergence can be such that the analysand and the analyst have the same dream on the same night as is shown by the publication, already cited, by Rascovsky (1976). Claude Janin has elaborated the idea of a *mutual animism*, a regression, says the author, at the stage of omnipotent thinking exerting a '*detransitionalisation of thinking*' (Janin, 1996).

We cannot undertake a study here of the mechanisms at the origin of this common regression; nevertheless, we can point out that beyond the necessity for the analyst to tolerate the retrogressive movement of his thought, not to fear it, the mechanism in play in this mutual regression, does not seem to belong to the register of hysterical identification or to that of projective identification, but to a much more inclusive movement like a double primary identification operating simultaneously in both partners in the session.

Jasmine emerged from this *pre-animistic state*, from her fascination with the image of the drawing of her village, as well as from her belief in her perceptual identities, just as one emerges from a night dream and then gives an account of it. She passed from the regression of her thinking to telling her story, that of a little Vietnamese girl who had lost her parents and come to Europe. This was a change that may be considered as the transition from perceptual activity – the drawing, the view of her analyst as 'Vietnamese', having the value of immediate thing-presentations – to a transposition into word-presentations closely linked to their perceptual residues. Jasmine emerged from her pre-animistic regression by transforming her perceptual residues into memory traces. The investment of the representations linked together within a narrative, within a network of representations, re-established paths of circulation for the primary processes, even though they could not necessarily be deployed in a pre-animistic or animistic hallucinatory immediateness, for they conform to the symbolic values of the network. It was an indispensable transformation for Jasmine enabling her to have access to a non-traumatic discontinuity, to a past lost forever ('the past is what is screwed up' said one child on recovering from his psychosis and discovering temporal succession), to the reality of the 'existence' of her dead parents.

Like Denise Braunschweig, we wish to stress that in fact no representations are possible, or repressible, as long as the thing-presentations have not been linked up with word-presentations. In this sense, it is worth noting that during the period of the therapy, so to speak in a 'dream state', Jasmine never spoke to her parents about these sessions. This was quite simply for the reason that, as is often the case with 'fulfilled' dreams, because they do not seek a witness, any secondary gain, no registration occurs. It was only when she emerged from the *pre-animistic state* that she gave an account of it (in the sense of recounting a dream) with obvious pleasure. A topographical change had occurred in her.

PART THREE

The hallucinatory

10

THE NEGATIVE OF THE TRAUMA

We know that the psychoanalyst questions the past. A conference entitled *Psychoanalysis: questions for tomorrow*[1] sought to inverse his first vocation of predicting the past and to encourage him to listen to the future, to pose questions for tomorrow. In fact, such a purpose is profoundly analytic; for, from the very first encounter, there arises an acutely important question, or wager, for this tomorrow that is already present – namely, the issue of the end of the treatment.

Temporality, in the form of the pressure of the past, the present of the setting and the project of the end, is at the heart of analytic treatment. Yet, along with Freud, 'we have learnt that unconscious mental processes are in themselves "timeless". This means in the first place that they are not ordered temporally, that time does not change them in any way and that the idea of time cannot be applied to them' (*S.E.* XVIII, 28).

From the philosopher to the scientist to the mystic, yesterday as well as today, the notion of time has haunted man's thought in search of a better knowledge of the world and of himself. The research is crucial but the answers disappointing: 'For there is nothing more feeble than the discourse of those who wish to define these primitive words . . . time is of this sort. Who can define it?', asks Pascal. Indeed, is it not absurd to want to define something that is at once the 'movement of a thing' and the 'measure of the movement'? Time can only be intelligible, says Pascal by means of the geometric spirit, 'because nature herself has already given us, without words, a clearer knowledge' (Pascal, 1658). Only the analyst is not a geometrician and, what is more, he cannot do without words. Analytic ideas of the importance of Bion's or Lacan's have nonetheless culminated in formulations belonging to the mathematical order; and, as we pointed out to René Thom, 'doing geometry' is a requisite of retrogressive thinking.

Atemporality of the unconscious and temporo-spatiality of the preconscious

The difficulty of psychoanalysis thus stems from the very nature of the object it sets out to study – namely, the timeless unconscious whose quality, by definition, is to remain unknowable. We can only apprehend phenomena relating to it, such as the primary processes discernible in analytic observation or more or less remote consequences that lead us to infer its existence, without enabling us to grasp its nature. The latter can only be approached in reference, in opposition to the findings of our preconscious thinking, that is, in a negativity in relation to the sensory qualities of the system *Pcs.–Ucs.* The *Ucs.*, Freud insists, is nonetheless the principal component of psychical functioning; whence the refutation of 'the Kantian theorem that time and space are "necessary forms of thought"' (Freud, 1920: 28) – Freud was wary of limiting thought to the domain of the preconscious.

The best artifice at Freud's disposal for attempting the impossible task of approaching the *Ucs.* was the notion of its timelessness or, to be more explicit, its atemporality – but, let us not delude ourselves, this does not define it in any way. Among other things, it is this postulate of atemporality that led analytic theory to look for the roots of mental organisation in extra-temporal domains, namely, original phantasies, thereby linking up again with the notion of structure. This was a striking new theoretical prospect; but, like every fresh elucidation, it accentuates the opacity of what is left out of the field of light, paradoxically thickening the shadowy zones.

In fact, Freud's aim was less to situate the *Ucs.* in relation to temporo-spatialty itself than to make us sense a radical difference through the idea of its absence. Ultimately, the major difficulty standing in the way of our attempts to gain access to the *Ucs.*, to understand the complexity of the analytic session and to understand the resistance to change, does not reside so much in the tension repressing–repressed, in the resistances of the id or, indeed, in the mechanisms of psychopathological structures, as in the very fact that the human mind is organised by the plural nature of its constituents. The frontier between unconscious and preconscious is not only formed by the existence of the censorship created by repression; it is also a transitional zone between two contradictory natures rendering every attempt at passing between them necessarily incomplete and distorted, but equally transforming. There exists a radical incompatibility between the said atemporal quality of the *Ucs.* and any perspective of entering a formation organised on the basis of temporo-spatiality, like the systems *Pcpt.–Cs.* and *Pcs.–Cs.* How, on the basis of word-presentations or visual representation, even if originating in dreams, can we conceive of, think about, the unconscious? We can only infer it from its 'offshoots', the 'mixed race' of products that have certainly been created by the primary processes, by unconscious mechanisms, but not by the *Ucs.* itself. It is thus only by means of 'distorting filters' that we can have a certain vision of the *Ucs*. Which raises the problem that the essential elements of our analytic knowledge are based on mediate findings, although it does not prevent us from judging the theory derived from them as being 'sound'. However, the question arises as to whether we should be satisfied with gaining a certain degree of knowledge of the *Ucs*. solely via the intermediary of 'compromise solutions'. Should we not look for other means; see if other approaches are possible?

This is what we want to try and explore in the rest of this book, tackling, first of all, the simplest questions. What, in fact, is an 'offshoot' or 'mixed race'? Can an element from one system be transported to another? Or is it simply a question of delegation? Or, on the contrary, are we dealing with a real transformation? What is certain is that our preconscious thinking, formed by means of temporo-spatial markers, proves absolutely incapable of providing an answer. It can have the intuition of its own limits, but all understanding, owing to its passage via the chains of the preconscious, however enlightening it may be, is nonetheless a screen that hides and distorts everthing in the psyche that is not temporo-spatiality.

We have naturally not lost sight of the processes that develop in the conditions of the analytic setting: transference and transference neurosis, resistance, interpretation, the process of becoming conscious, without forgetting that today we can no longer maintain that these topical, economic and dynamic ensembles are the foundation of all psychic functioning. It has become an urgent issue to know if these constituents of the analytic process can, in themselves, account for the entire scope of the analytic encounter. For though they emerge from an active and indestructible past, they clearly do not correspond to any criterion concerning the notion of the absence of temporality, the only characteristic of the nature of unconscious processes. Apart from facilitating the setting up of the analytic process on the basis of products closely associated with the history of infantile wishes and the model of dreams as wish-fulfilment, the analytic setting also has the capacity of giving rise to other, quite different phenomena with the characteristics of immediateness, of actuality, that cannot be traced back to the contents of wishes in infantile history and follow the model of the dynamics of traumatic neurosis. The problem of articulating, of linking up this direct and immediate path with the mediate, progressive path of representation, of memory and recollections, represents, in our view, one of the major axes for understanding treatment and psychic functioning.

The position we take is to consider that the mechanisms of interpretation and the process of becoming conscious of an unconscious impulse require a change of quality at the same time as a change of level. The unconscious impulse only becomes fully accessible to the system *Pcs.–Cs.* if there is a possibility of transforming the traumatic neurosis, its atemporality, into the temporality of preconscious representation. Bion, as we know, made the notion of transformation the centre of his thinking; but we can already find in Freud passages tending in this direction. For instance, the difference he points out in 'The unconscious' (1915b) between the 'idea communicated' by the analyst an the 'repressed idea':

> To have heard something and to have experienced something are in their psychological nature two quite different things, even though the content of both is the same.
>
> *S.E.* XIV, 176

It is in the nature of the *Ucs.* to constantly elude our attempts at approaching it, to be ungraspable for processes of thought enclosed within the parameters of temporo-spatiality. There can thus be no question of claiming to study the nature of the *Ucs.*, but only the conditions permitting transformations in the nature of the analytic material. We need to understand how the analyst's thinking can have access, if not to the knowledge, at least to the intuition of such changes of quality; and how, in order to achieve this, it could facilitate, at certain moments, the particular conditions that favour the approach of this atemporal quality of the *Ucs.*

The unconscious and representation

The flexibility and mobility of displacements along a chain of representations is a necessary property of the analyst's thinking while working in a mode of floating attention. But we know that however indispensable it is, this dynamic no longer suffices today for understanding either the complexity of analytic work – especially the complex nature of the changes of quality in the analytic material during sessions – or for tackling treatments which get bogged down due to negative therapeutic reactions.

The works of Piera Aulagnier (1975) and Nicos Nicolaïdis (1993) are oriented towards the description of a realm 'beyond' representation; and the study of the sacred has led Catherine Parat (1988) towards hypotheses of the same order. Let us recall Freud's observation in 1900, in *The Interpretation of Dreams* (p. 525), when he establishes the existence of a 'dream navel', ' a tangle of dream thoughts which cannot be unravelled . . . the point at which it reaches down into the Unknown'; that is, 'to our very being which, though not representable, is yet the condition of all representation', as Francis Pasche (1999) puts it in the article to which we referred earlier.

The notions of the 'non-representable' and of 'non-meaning', which stand out increasingly in Francis Pasche's later work characterised by an original approach in which he studies the relations between metapsychology and philosophical systems as well as with theology, led him to the notion of apophatism which he defines in the last lines of his work *Le sens de la psychanalyse* (Pasche, 1988): 'Thus the notion of apophatism which defines a point, a nothing, an absence of content to focus on . . . a notion, we think, which our theory is in need of.' It is indeed true that, as soon as one takes interest in the backward course towards perception, one understands to what extent analytic theory today can no longer do without the study of a realm 'beyond' representation, just as it cannot economise on the notion of the 'work of the negative' developed by André Green (1993) throughout his work and particularly in the book of the same title.

In the preceding chapters, we have developed the hypothesis that the retrogressive state of thinking in the session is indissociable from the existence of a 'zone' of *non-representation* at the very heart of the psyche, constituting it and participating in unconscious functioning. *Non-representation* may be said to correspond to a psychic state that, owing to its absence of the quality 'representation' as well as of any sensory quality, and owing to its incapacity of exciting along the progressive path the pole *Cs.*, can only be described with a negative terminology. But it needs to be understood that this 'negative' does not define it in any way whatsoever, any more than the notion of atemporality defines the system *Ucs. Non-representation* is experienced by the ego as an excess of excitation; and if the mind does not arrive, by virtue of a transformation, at an experience of intelligibility accessible to the system of representations, the ego will experience it as traumatic.

The negative foundations of trauma

The theoretical upheaval introduced by the turning point of 1920 was not only due to the duality of the life and death drive; it came from two fronts: first, of course, the role of the death drive and its coexistence in every instinctual impulse; then, Freud's assertion in 1932 – which was announced more discretely, but was perhaps just as much of an upheaval for analytic theory – that a dream is not strictly speaking a fulfilment of a wish but 'an *attempt* at the fulfilment of a wish' (*S.E.* XX, 29). To this may be added, especially after 1920, the fact that the dynamic of traumatic neurosis was increasingly taken into account as a mode of functioning existing powerfully in every psyche, as well as its corollary – as was to be expected after *The Interpretation of Dreams* – that is, the reaffirmation of the definition of wishful impulses as pressure transforming the traumatic need into its contrary, the pleasure of allaying tension. On the basis of this evolution of Freud's concepts, we have framed the hypothesis of the existence, at the very centre of the organisation of repressed infantile wishes, of a traumatic element that defines it just as much as the pleasure principle. For his part, Michel Fain (1982) affirms 'the existence, at the very centre of the dream, the symptom, and the character trait, of a division which entails the coexistence of two contradictory systems, one of which functions on the model of the first topography . . .; the other functions as a traumatic short-circuit situated topographically outside the ego, "blocked out" and perceived simultaneously, unable to furnish substitutes for unconscious thing-presentations) What defines traumatic neurosis, according to Michel Fain, is its incapacity to 'furnish substitutes for unconscious thing-presentations'. The question is one of knowing whether this incapacity originates, as Freud thought, and as everything seems initially to suggest, in a perception qualified as traumatic, or if the investment of this perception and its hallucinatory repetition are defensive reactions of the psyche faced with a trauma. We tried to show in 1988, in an article entitled 'Trauma et topique' (Botella, C. and S., 1988), that the traumatic character cannot, under any circumstances, come from the content of an event which, in itself, is representable. Traumatic neurosis should be understood as a negativity – that is to say, a violent and abrupt absence of topographies and psychical dynamics, the rupture of psychic coherence and the collapse of primary and secondary processes as the ego loses its means. This brutal disorganisation has its origin, not in a perception, but in the absence of meaning in the violent excess of excitation and in the ego's state of distress; in the ego's incapacity to form a representation of them, to present them to consciousness. It is only secondarily that the ego will be able to find intelligibility, meaning and cause for its disarray, all of which are clearly linked to the immediate and simultaneous perception of a danger. The investment of a perception, followed by the cathexis of its hallucinatory repetition already form the first anti-traumatic acts of binding, the beginnings of an elaboration. Following up on this idea, traumatic neurosis seems to develop in situations where the binding capacities of the primary processes fail. Without a work of figurability, of coherence, instead of a series of displacements, of symbolic markers, culminating in a representation, a hyper-investment of a perception occurs; and, instead of a condensation forming an over-determined representation, an abrupt, massive investment of the hallucinatory–sensory pole is set in motion)

Such a way of envisaging traumatic neurosis complicates the notions of repetition–compulsion and the death drive; and consequently the comprehension of the turning point of 1920. This theme deserves to be developed, but we shall have to confine ourselves here to a few considerations concerning the repercussions of our conception at the level of the notions of infantile trauma and infantile neurosis.

At the end of his work, in *Moses and Monotheism* (1937b), almost 50 years after his description of traumas retroactively (*nachträglich*), Freud entirely revised the notion of trauma. He conceived, for the first time, of a trauma with negative effects:

> The experiences in question [i.e. traumatic] are as a rule totally forgotten, they are not accessible to memory . . . They relate to impressions of a sexual and aggressive nature, and no doubt also to early injuries to the ego (narcissistic mortifications) . . . The effects of traumas are of two kinds, positive and negative. The formers are attempts to bring the trauma into operation

114

once again – that is, to remember the forgotten experience . . . to revive it. The negative reactions follow an opposite aim: that nothing of the forgotten traumas shall be remembered and nothing repeated . . . These negative reactions too make the most powerful contributions to the stamping of character. The symptoms of neurosis in the narrower sense are compromises in which both the trends proceeding from traumas come together.

S.E. XXIII, 74–6

Freud was probably inspired by Ferenczi who, in 'Some thoughts on trauma', a chapter in *Final Contributions to the Methods and Problems of Psycho-Analysis* (published posthumously in 1955), asserts that 'no memory traces remain, even in the unconscious, and thus the causes of the trauma cannot be recalled from memory traces.'

It is worth noting that Freud does not say that two different types of trauma are involved; on the contrary, he discusses two forms of reaction to the event. One can understand, then, that for him the new formations comprise both positive and negative forms, as much where psychoneurotic symptoms are concerned as affections of the ego organising 'character'. Freud concludes that ultimately the content of the event is not the essential aspect of the trauma; and he introduces the positive value of the preforms:

When we study the reactions to early traumas [i.e. before the fifth year], we are quite often surprised to find that they are not strictly limited to what the subject himself has really experienced but diverge from it in a way which fits in much better with the model of a phylogenetic event and, in general, can only be explained by such an influence. The behaviour of neurotic children towards their parents in the Oedipus and castration complex abounds in such reactions.

S.E. XXIII, 99

Every trauma, then, can be said to have two sides to it. There are the 'positive reactions', closely linked to primal phantasies, constituting themselves generally on the model of *Nachträglichkeit*, and giving form to psychoneurotic symptoms, infantile neurosis and to the organisation of the transference neurosis. And then, there is its hidden, reverse side, the 'negative reactions', that is to say, a negative 'residue', an unrepresentable 'residue' that cannot be repeated any more than it can constitute a neurotic symptom. Consequently, the expressions of trauma with 'negative effects' are limited to 'character', to symptoms 'without content', in the order of inhibitions, to ego 'restrictions' or to affects that pass for so-called normal attitudes to life and here one will speak, for instance, of sensibility towards the facts brought by perception. This coincides, at least in its formal aspect, with the outcome of war neuroses, once they have been cured. The analyst is nonetheless left with a troubling question, since this negative side, often presented

115

as being a normal aspect of affect, character or inhibition, is totally absent both from the associations and from the transference/counter-transference interplay and can easily elude the action of analytic treatment. We have come to consider this negative residue, which is destined to give way to the precedence of primal phantasies, as the basis of infantile trauma.

Today we are convinced that the traumatic character of infantile trauma corresponds neither to the model of traumatic neurosis nor to that of *Nachträglichkeit*. It stems neither from the intensity of a perception nor from the content of a representation, but from the incapacity to transform, to give psychic quality to a state that, owing to this very incapacity, becomes an excess of energy, an unbound perception, without, for all that, setting in motion a traumatic neurosis. Situated outside the dynamics of repression and the system *Ucs.*, and unable to give preconscious offshoots, to be taken over by primary processes, or to supply energy to the mechanisms of displacement and condensation, infantile trauma is of the order of a *non-binding: there is a total absence of intelligibility and, a fortiori, of content*, and not of a perception with traumatic content. There is a gaping hole in the perceptual realm doubled by a gaping hole in the representational realm: neither inside nor outside. There is a fracture, a gap in the tissue of representations, in the tissue of the investments of the infantile neurosis. Its existence can only be suspected through certain disturbances, 'accidents' of thought, bearing witness to the presence of a perturbation due to a *non-representation* and not to the content of the event. It is a question of what the infantile neurosis cannot include in its system of investments and anti-investments, representations and conflicts; of a zone of psychic suffering exceeding the possibilities of representation, and thus referring to object losses that cannot be represented and elaborated in a work of mourning – a zone where the violence of liberated affects disorganises the mind. This state of psychic quality can only be defined as a non-cathexis, a non-object. In order to differentiate it clearly from the memory trace, bearing contents, it could be qualified as a *perceptual trace* – on the condition, however, that this is understood as an absence of intelligibility, doubled by an absence of quality – even if only in a sensory form. *It may be described as the potentiality of an excess of energy tending to deploy itself in an unbound hallucinatory-perceptual movement, a potential effect without content.*

Ultimately, *the negative of the trauma has its origin not in a quantifiable positive, but in the absence of what, for the child's ego, for his narcissism, should have occurred as a matter of course. Something fundamentally evident for the subject that should have happened did not happen, even though he is not aware of it and, a fortiori, cannot form an idea of what this negative is.* The difference here with Winnicott's intuition – probably also inspired by Ferenczi – when he speaks of 'a past event that has not yet been experienced' (Winnicott, 1974) resides in the fact that what 'has already been' is, in our view, a negativity.

This is why the theoretical status of the negative of the trauma is not easy to delineate. In certain respects, it can be likened to the *Verwerfung* of psychotic hallucination, as Freud (1911b) understood it in the passage of the text on Schreber:

> It was incorrect to say that the perception which was suppressed internally is projected outwards; the truth is rather, as we now see, that what was abolished internally returns from without.
>
> *S.E.* XII, 71

Let us add, though, that in contradistinction, the negative of the infantile trauma is not the product of the abolition, the 'negativisation' of a representation, but the consequence of a lack at the outset, of a missing inscription, at any rate in the form of a representation. And even if a certain connection can be envisaged between the mechanism of Freud's *Verwerfung* and the negative of the trauma in that, in both cases, access to consciousness can only come from the outside, a fundamental difference remains, for the path of return cannot be the same. Psychotic hallucination proceeds, after an 'internal catastrophe', by a subversive distortion of reality testing capable of transforming a representation into a perception, into what is 'only outside', whereas the return of the negative of the infantile trauma corresponds to a very curious situation in which, strictly speaking, there is no distortion of reality testing. Its strange status, 'neither inside–nor outside' does not allow it either to return from the outside, like the *Verwerfung*, for it is not an abolition, nor to return from the inside, as is the case of the repressed, for it is not a memory trace. In fact, the negative of the trauma is only discernible in the regression of the analytic situation, in the retrogressive encounter of two psyches, in this complex process of psychical work that we call the analyst's figurability. Otherwise, one has to be content to consider the manifestations of the 'negative effects' of the trauma in the same way as Freud does; that is to say, as 'defensive reactions', as 'restrictions of the ego', or again as 'permanent modifications of character', even going as far as the idea of the existence of 'elements of the ego dissociated by the trauma', without however qualifying this state as a splitting of the ego. They may be described as pre-psychic/psychic modifications that are non-representable, not to say inaccessible to classical analytical technique.

At a congress on the subject of trauma, we heard about the following case. After a serious attempt at taking his own life, a man was brought into a psychiatric emergency unit specialising in trauma. He was in a suicidal, mute state of stupor, cut off from society and alcoholic, after having been acquitted for the following set of circumstances. His 1-year-old baby had died from a fall while he was playing with him and throwing him up in the air. He was a happy young man who had been transformed by the birth of his son and who, to his son's delight, constantly wanted to play with him. So much so that his wife, whom he did not listen to, fearing a fall, had become so worried that she had gone to the police for help, but they could do nothing for her. The young man had lost contact with his own father, who had left home when his son was still a baby. Throughout his childhood, his mother had told him endlessly how his father had been violent towards him; how, on many occasions, he had nearly killed him. But the young man had no recollection of this violence. Our hypothesis is the following: the massive investment of the baby was charged with a violent return of his own infantile impulses that had been blown apart under the traumatic conditions of his childhood, i.e. those of violence and his father's disappearance. But the accident should not be understood so much as the fulfilment of an infantile wish linked to the object-father and the image he had of him as to a violent experience, even though the latter could not be perceived, depicted and represented so that a trace might remain of it. Solicited by his son's investment, his own infantile impulses towards his father brought out the negative, the negative effect of his trauma. The latter, deployed freely in broad daylight, provoked a continuity between hallucinatory activity and 'acting out' (*agieren*), a radical transformation of the relation between the perceiving subject and the object of perception: the object dissociated itself, breaking off its links with the representation. The violence of his infantile impulse, under the impact of the negative of the trauma, transformed the young man's game with his baby into the equivalent of a direct realisation – he himself becoming the baby being thrown into the air – a movement that is perhaps comparable to the typical dream mentioned by Freud in chapter VI of *The Interpretation of Dreams*, where jumping, flying through the air, are said to originate in an actual sensation experienced by the dreamer during sleep, relating to the perceptual traces of the baby's state of elation as he is thrown into the air by the adult. But, by letting go of his child, in the middle of these hallucinatory acts, the young man woke up to a reality as terrifying as that of a nightmare, to the reality of the beginning of his life. He had re-established the continuity of his history. His act filled the white of the irrepresentable nature of his trauma with the black of melancholy, the representation of his own life and death at the hands of his father. His act violently positivised the negative of his trauma. It was a case of a blinding disorganisation of the psychical apparatus, in which one can clearly distinguish the dual valency of the trauma, the positive intensity of the sensory implosion and the explosion of negative intensity in the extreme act. Whether we are talking about the baby or about the young man himself may be said, in the last analysis, to be one and the same thing (see Balier, 1988).

The question arises, then, of knowing what the conditions for the reversibility of such a process might be. How can the negative intensity of the trauma be positivised except through action?

One of the major problems for the analyst, then, is of knowing what technical approach to adopt towards these irrepresentable 'negative effects' of traumas for which there seems to be no real psychic solution. Furthermore, the infantile traumas are so well covered over by all the complexity of the representable and repressable traumas, linked to primal phantasies, with their systems of logic, of causalities, constitutive of the infantile neurosis that occupies the foreground entirely, that most of the time, they go totally unnoticed.

Ferenczi, who, as we know, was preoccupied by the treatment of trauma, denounces 'the insufficiency of analysis in the waking state' and recommends an 'elasticity of analytic technique', an active technique, analysis 'in a state of trance'. In effect, as the infantile trauma is deprived of the possibility of taking the form of a representation, it is not accessible to habitual interpretations based on the model of the interpretation of dreams and of the first topography. Are we obliged, then, as Ferenczi thinks, to create, during the analytic treatment, the conditions necessary for the actual repetition of the trauma, 'for bringing it, for the first time, to perception and motor discharge'? In reality, Ferenczi's 'state of trance' only succeeds in re-enacting the state of distress, the motor agitation and creates a new trauma without elaborating the original one. Ferenczi came to understand this and, in a note dated 8 August 1932, declared that 'the reproduction of the trauma is, in itself, inefficient from the therapeutic point of view' (Ferenczi, 1932).

We will not enter into the debate between Freud and Ferenczi concerning the 'active technique', except to point out that, Freud's severe criticisms of it notwithstanding, the questions Ferenczi raised in regard of remembering influenced Freud. Pursuing, then, a path of research that did not lead to a change in technique, to an act, but to a broadening of metapsychology, Freud left us precious indications in 'Constructions in analysis' (1937a) concerning the possibility of gaining psychic access to these negative effects of infantile trauma, which otherwise remain inaccessible to consciousness. Two new notions concerning analytic practice, which we have already discussed, are of inestimable value in this respect: first, that 'conviction' has the same economic value as actual recollections; and second, the complementary notion of the quasi-hallucinatory returns of forgotten events.

From this point of view, and taking into account that the retrogressive state of thinking, characteristic of dreams in traumatic neurosis, facilitates the understanding of the trauma, we think that in analytic practice in general, traumas are only accessible on the condition that the retrogressive movement of thinking accedes to the hallucinatory level. Only a retrogressive duality subject–object, at the basis of the analyst's mode of *working as a double*, the essential aspects of which we have outlined earlier, has the capacity to gain access to the contents, to render presentable that which had hitherto never been intelligible.

There is an image in quantum physics that is very enlightening in this connection. Faced with the negative of infantile trauma, the analyst finds himself in the situation of a fisherman teasing a 'quantum fish', which only materialises once it has been caught. It is as though, before rising to the bait of the analyst's work of figurability, this negative of the analysand were only a potentiality of 'fish trauma' occupying the whole pond of the id, at certain places more concentrated and at others more diluted, like André Breton's surrealistic image of the 'soluble fish'.

Is, then, the negative of trauma concrete or abstract? In this connection, we wish to quote Paul Langevin: 'The concrete is the abstract rendered familiar.'

11

THE HALLUCINATORY[1]

Although Freud revealed the unconscious thanks to his associative capacities and brilliant intuitions, one should not underestimate the fact that he owed his discovery to the study of dreams and especially to the study of his own dreams. Analytic research, psychical work and the atemporality of the unconscious can only be approached or grasped by means of a particular state of thinking that proceeds along the backward, retrogressive path.

In Freud's work, topical, temporal and formal regression 'are one at bottom and occur together as a rule; for what is older in time is also more primitive in form and in psychical topography lies nearer to the perceptual end' (Freud, 1900: *S.E.* V, 548). We have opted for the preferential use of the term formal regression in order to stress the fact that regression concerns a change of quality, a change in the form of psychic elements – the model being the transformation of the ideas into a hallucinatory dream image. Freud writes:

> This regression, then, is undoubtedly one of the psychological characteristics of the process of dreaming; but we must remember that it does not occur only in dreams. Intentional recollection and other constituent processes of our normal thinking involve a retrogressive movement . . . In the waking state, however, this backward movement never extends beyond the mnemic images; it does not succeed in producing a hallucinatory revival of the *perceptual* images.
>
> *S.E.* V, 542–3

During waking life, 'it is necessary to bring regression to a halt before it becomes complete, so that it does not proceed beyond the mnemic image' (*S.E.* V, 566). Freud means that without the break of the 'perceptual images', without the intervention of memory, the mind could very well regress, in daytime, to a 'primitive state' of its functioning, which would result in hallucinations.

Free-floating attention and the renunciation of preconscious 'purposive ideas' represent a minimum of necessary modification in the analyst's thinking; they facilitate free association, access to a psychic work of binding, ranging from the search for simple connections charged with meaning to the articulation of vast sets of meaningful links. This work forms the analyst's habitual means of thinking about events, of understanding the psychic changes in the session, referring to the terms of unconscious desire and representation, transference neurosis, history and temporo-spatiality. It retained its exclusivity for Freud up to a certain theoretical evolution corresponding to the turning point of 1920. Thereafter, although it was still valid, this conception of the analyst's work no longer sufficed to explain the whole economy of the session. The way forward opened up by 'Constructions in analysis', in 1937, is evidence of this; Freud transcended his own pessimism by indicating to us implicitly eventual theoretical and technical solutions to the impasses of the analyst, which, barely a few months earlier in 'Analysis terminable and interminable' had been seen as insurmountable. This practice of construction, giving rise to the 'quasi-hallucinatory' character of 'conviction', which Freud recommends, is a relatively convenient path of access to what is irrepresentable, for it only requires a minimum of formal regression of the analyst's thinking. When pushed further, this formal regression does not fail to awake a feeling of uncanniness, which, as a consequence, the ego tends to avoid. But the analyst's constructions do not always give the result expected and the irrepresentable, which causes the treatment to get bogged down, is then only accessible on the condition that the analyst can tolerate a more important regression of his thinking.

As we have already indicated, our approach – to the extent that we favour the study of unforeseen, unexpected relaxations, drops in the tension of thinking, taking the ego by surprise, in spite of itself – is contrary to the practice recommended by Bion, implying an active, strong attitude of the analyst's ego. In fact, we are interested in the ruptures in the analyst's habitual psychic work, facilitated by the regression of his thinking; in the 'accidents' occurring in the course of his thinking marking temporary pauses in the connections of free association. These are 'flaws' in the thick tissue of the bindings and investment of ideas that open the analysis up to a work of transformation, of figurability.

What Freud evokes in terms such as the 'sudden fall in intellectual tension' of parapraxes, the 'sudden shortcoming' of forgetting, the discharge obtained from laughing at a joke when 'one senses something . . . indefinable which resembles an absence', the 'disturbance of memory', the *déjà vu*, the *déjà raconté* – all psychic phenomena that could be grouped together under the denomination of *accidents of thought*, and that he initially considered solely as products of repression – prove, in the light of fresh findings at the end of his work, to be more complex processes for which explanations that only take into account the psychopathological models of the neuroses and psychoses remain insufficient. In 'A disturbance of memory on the Acropolis' (1936), these 'accidents' of daily life, in particular the *déjà vu*, the *déjà raconté*, accompanied by feelings of derealisation and playing the role of 'occasional hallucinations in the healthy' are treated by Freud as memory of an immediate past, as 'positive counterparts' of the negative of the derealisation. A connection is thus established between the failure of alterity and hallucinatory memory. Their indissociability helps us to understand better the reticence and the mistrust, even the incapacity of the ego, when faced with such regressive qualities. Accounts of sessions endorsing this have been reported in the previous chapters (Florian, Olga, Thomas, Jasmine).

Aline: an 'accident' in the course of the analyst's thinking

Aline, a little 5-year-old girl who has been in analysis with one of us three times a week, for one year, recounted the following dream: *She did not have her mummy and daddy any more; she was alone, lost in the forest. Some large nasty animals appeared which made big eyes at her and cried out 'you little . . . you little . . .'.* At that point, she could not move. She woke up in a state of anxiety and called for her parents.

Aline told us that the day before she had had a bad day. Her parents had stopped her from doing several of her activities. Due to the rain, she did not have permission to go and play with a friend; then, at table, feeling a little disappointed and limp, she was told off for the way she was dressed; finally, she could not listen to her 'consoling' records owing to a technical problem that her father had not had time to repair. That evening Aline could not go to sleep and so she went to her cupboard to look for a handkerchief that she had not used for a long time and, by sucking it, was able to fall asleep.

The role of the waking residue, the feeling of frustration, of unhappiness, can be understood in the following way: during the night, in her sleep, 'with an aching heart', Aline imagined a fairytale: 'Once upon a time . . . there was a little girl, with no parents, who had got lost in the forest.' But with Aline, on this particular night, the fairytale's function as a protective shield and censor could not resist the force of the hostile impulses towards her parents and her analyst. The dream image of big animals, which were reprimanding her by making big eyes at her and insulting her with the words 'you little . . . you little . . .' is already the effect of a double instinctual reversal; namely, of Aline's preconscious wish to aggress her parents and her analyst; and, of the unconscious dream wish, introducing the disapproving look of the big animals, a violent exhibitionist phantasy, doing something very silly aimed at attracting their attention.

With the help of Aline's games and associations, the complete analysis of the dream unfolded over several sessions, the details of which we will not go into. In the dynamics of the transference–counter-transference, several paths of interpretation emerged involving sequences such as unhappiness–anger–vengeance, the wish for exhibition–self-punishment, or again primal scene–abandonment–

seduction. The analysis also pursued paths referring to the figures of the oral and anal sexual theories as well as to the castration complex–penis envy concerning the 'little pipe' of her little brother. In short, it was a classic analysis of a dream corresponding to an 'ordinary' organisation, so to speak, of a little 5-year-old girl. And yet the analyst had a barely perceptible feeling that something was not right in the apparently good work that the analyst and analysand were accomplishing. It was in this climate that, during an intervention, an 'accident', a disturbance of memory, occurred in the analyst's thinking: he suddenly forgot the child's first name. This act of forgetting was no doubt complex, but what we want to underline here is the fact that this 'accident', a 'shortcoming' in his thinking, would enable the analyst to grasp the traumatic nature of the child's waking residue, which, up to that moment, had seemed to him to be related to a mere frustration.

When the act of forgetting occurred, the analyst felt uneasy for a while, experiencing a sense of derealisation that disappeared as suddenly as it came. In its place, he thought of one of Andersen's fairytales; to be more exact a particularly clear auditory image forced itself on him: 'But Her Majesty is completely naked!' And he immediately understood that the situation of the emperor, the beauty of whose finery is much praised by his subjects – while in reality he is walking completely naked – and that of the analytic relation of the moment, both had the same meaning. Thanks to his act of forgetting and the imagery of the fairytale that emerged out of it, imposing itself through perceptual identity, accompanied by feelings of conviction and aptness, the analyst understood that the dream and its interpretation, beyond their context linked to customary psychoneurotic conflictuality, had the function of shining finery. The analyst and the child, blinded by the vividness of the dream and the brilliance of its interpretation, could not perceive the naked truth, namely, the distress of Her Majesty, the Baby Aline. A 'shortcoming', an 'accident' was necessary for another meaning to emerge – namely, that the exhibitionist wish that governed the dream was already, beyond the conflictual pleasure, aggressive and erotic, relating to the infantile neurosis as a whole, an anti-traumatic measure, an attempt to give meaning to an irrepresentable waking residue. Furthermore, it is important to note that the analyst's complete analysis of his forgetting of the child's first name was related to traumatic aspects of his own infantile neurosis.

Aline had no awareness of her analyst's fugitive thought disturbance – which does not, of course, mean that she had not perceived it unconsciously. In any case, the analyst said to her: 'I forgot you for a moment, Aline', without suspecting, at that moment, the significance of this intervention. He considered it simply as a product of his counter-transference. In fact, the intervention proved to be much more complex, for it was owing to this remark by the analyst, arising from his formal regression, from his work of figurability, denouncing and naming the momentary loss of the investment of the child, that the latter would be able to approach what had been unrepresentable the day before.

In the course of the sessions that followed this particular intervention of the analyst, a traumatic trace made itself felt in the shape of successive 'quasi-hallucinatory' movements that were at odds with her games and associations. Sudden ideas came to her, for instance, such as that 'the analyst could not see her', 'was not looking at her', to which she responded by laughing and saying, 'What funny ideas!' These sudden accesses to consciousness of a traumatic trace were then tempered by being integrated into chains of representations, sometimes by means of a displacement onto a friend whom the parents 'did not care about', at other times, within the transference: 'If I don't have a dream, you don't care about me, do you?', which announced an Oedipal causality, the logic 'because castrated', giving the irrepresentable the meaning of a lack.

Thus, by virtue of a traumatic trace of his own infantile neurosis and the wavering of his own identity, the analyst was able to understand that the apparently commonplace disappointment of the day before the dream had affected Aline so deeply that her otherwise excellent capacities for forming images, for representing had collapsed. The rage, the insults towards the analyst-parents who had been unable to find a remedy for her misfortunes the day before were not really the essential factors, at that moment, of her psychic economy. The essential issue was the impossibility for Aline to be able to imagine herself uncathected by the object, to imagine the irrepresentable character of her own absence in the object's eyes, that is, a disorganising state at the limits of the psychic and inaccessible to elaboration, which may be described as *non-representation*; an ensemble relating to the positive and negative effects of the infantile trauma.

For Aline, therefore, the origin of the problem stemmed from the day before. In the absence of any representation of the adults' inattention to the child's troubles and unable really to become aware of her state of distress, she wore her psychic suffering on her sleeve, so to speak, without there being any possibility of a work of binding. During the day, Aline behaved as if she were involved in a typical dream of nudity, in which the spectators are indifferent to the nudity of the subject. The traumatic *non-representation* had borrowed a direct path of discharge that invaded the psychic stage in daytime, taking the form of a mode of behaviour modelled on typical dream imagery. The day before, Aline was living more at the motor (behaviour) and hallucinatory pole than at that of representations and memory traces.

The following day, the mere fact of bringing a dream to her analyst was already a satisfaction for Aline. Moreover, the fact that the dream was that of a small child meant it was an object of admiration. Aline and the analyst shared, in this way, within the homosexual transference–counter-transference, the 'exhibition-admiration', which, in the formal regression inherent to the traumatic situation, took on the value of an immediate and direct realisation in the form of a sort of reciprocal primary admiration between mother and infant. Thus, for Aline, the session became a true wish-fulfilment acting as a substitute for what had not occurred in her dream, recuperating the trauma of the previous day; while for the analyst it was pleasant work up to the point when there was a rupture of the investment of the word-presentations in the forgetting of the name, opening the way to the traumatic traces of his own infantile neurosis. It was due to the actualisation of these traces in the act of forgetting, rendered intelligible by a work of figurability, that the real meaning, the anti-traumatic value of the homosexual transference–counter-transference of the moment, was revealed. Only the sequence: accident of thought image of the fairytale, followed by the 'I forgot you for a moment', had the capacity to reveal to Aline the unrepresentable nature of the negative of her trauma.

The problematic of the hallucinatory

Basically, we are perhaps only speaking about the same problem as Freud in 'Constructions in analysis' that is to say, how certain events of the very distant past, 'at a time when the child could still hardly speak' (1937a: *S.E.* XXIII, 267) can only force themselves into consciousness, as he writes, in a 'quasi-hallucinatory' mode. As we have just seen with the case of Aline, this comparison is of interest on two accounts: first, because these events are 'distant'; not so much in time, in fact, as in their impossibility of operating a return via the habitual path of memories and ideas; and, second, because their obligatory mode of access is 'quasi-hallucinatory'.

Although Freud had been fascinated by hallucination as early as *The Interpretation of Dreams*, he did not make any real study of it, apart from certain passages of the 'Wolf Man' and 'President Schreber' – for complex reasons that we cannot enter into here – until 1915 in 'Metapsychological supplement to the theory of dreams' (1917a). There, Freud sensed to what extent, beyond psychotic phenomena, the study of hallucination would necessarily become a study of the hallucinatory in general and how, given its implications, it would be unavoidable in analytic theory. At the end of his work, he reconsidered the problem in 'A disturbance of memory on the Acropolis' and then in 'Constructions in analysis', both fundamental texts, let us repeat, for the evolution of psychoanalytic ideas, in which Freud – refusing yet again to restrict and limit his thinking to the theoretical schemas he had already elaborated, and asserting that hallucination was not confined solely to the terrain of pathology – allowed himself to be confronted once more by a 'beyond', this time to a 'beyond' of memory and representation.

The question of hallucination is much vaster and cannot be reduced to the domain of pathology. Certain contemporary authors are investigating it and seeking, like Freud in his last writings, to detach the notion of hallucination from that of psychosis. Bion's increasing interest in hallucination, in our opinion, fits into this line of research, notably when he investigates the links between hallucination and analytic intuition. The same is true of the concept of negative hallucination described by André Green (1993) as a fundamental element of the mind and of Jeanneau's notion of the 'hallucinatory position' (1985).

For our part, we are wondering if it is possible to make a differentiation between the psychotic hallucinatory mechanism – i.e. the Lacanian foreclosure, the 'abolition on the inside', the 'negativisation' of a representation and its transformation back into an external perception – and the hallucination of nocturnal dreaming. How can one fail to establish a difference, on the one hand, between the hallucinatory regression of dreaming in which the dreamer, owing to the withdrawal of investment from his sense organs and motility, doubled by the astonishing 'partial cathexis of the system *Pcs.–Cs.*', hallucinates a psychic reality in which he can see himself taking part, just as he forms an integral part of the psychical scene in daytime, and, on the other hand, psychotic hallucination in which the subject, unlike the dreamer, is not present, for he is the victim of a 'negativisation' of his psychic reality. The psychotic lives his delusional conviction through sensory elements that are hyper-cathected in an auto-erotic mode, with all the characteristics of an external perception – 'endopsychic perception' or 'self-perception' being beyond his reach. If the psychotic loses his capacity to dream during hallucinatory periods, it is precisely because these two forms of hallucination are mutually exclusive.

Bion was particularly interested in the role of psychotic hallucination during the session, and in the analyst's difficulty in unearthing it, since it is frequently, as he says, 'invisible'. He thus looked for a procedure by means of which the analyst could gain access to it.

Our study is essentially concerned with non-psychotic, occasional hallucination, that is, with the possibility of expressions, outside the psychic state of sleeping, of a hallucinatory regression as in night dreams. Certainly, the hallucinatory 'primitive state' has to be 'surmounted'; the pleasure principle, under the influence of reality, evolves and is transformed into the reality principle. But, at the same time, Freud consistently maintained that 'primitive states can always be re-established; the primitive psyche is, in the full sense of the word, "imperishable"'. Just as we know that the pleasure principle is part of normal functioning and that, by adapting itself, it remains constantly at work, are there not grounds for thinking that the dynamic tendency towards hallucinatory expression is not confined to dreams at night and remains a potentiality of the mind, even a permanent psychical activity, albeit obscured or transformed by psychic requirements, such as those of reality testing and the system preconscious?

Our hypothesis is as follows: there exists a normal aptitude of the psyche for hallucinatory expression, that of dreaming at night, that is permanently restrained during the day by the necessity of maintaining the reality principle. This hallucinatory quality is not the consequence of a rejection or of 'an abolition on the inside', but a regressive capacity for thinking akin to the form of a 'primitive state of the psychical apparatus in which wishing ended in hallucinating' (Freud, 1900: 566) of which the night dream is a relic. This regressive capacity is more or less active depending on the individual and is facilitated by certain circumstances, notably those of the session.

This linking of regression and hallucination is by no means simple. To get an idea of this, it is sufficient to follow Freud who, in 1900, initially believed that hallucinations and 'normal visions' could be explained in the same way: 'they are in fact regressions – that is, thoughts transformed into images' (p. 544); then, in 'Metapsychological supplement to the theory of dreams' (1917a) he considered their relation in a more complex way:

> If the secret of hallucination is nothing else than that of regression, every regression of sufficient intensity would produce hallucination with belief in its reality. But we are quite familiar with situations in which a process of regressive reflection brings to consciousness very clear visual mnemic images, though we do not on that account for a single moment take them for real perceptions.
>
> *S.E.* XIV, 231

Later, Freud was to describe as 'quasi-hallucinatory' images impregnated with a sense of conviction, with a sense of the truth of construction in analysis.

Hallucinatory modalities: hysterical, 'normal people', psychotic

Hysterical hallucination

The principal example remains the repetitive hallucination of Frau Cäcilie. This patient in the *Studies on Hysteria* (Freud and Breuer, 1895) had a hallucination on being seized by sudden and violent feelings of anger against her two doctors, Freud and Breuer: she repeatedly saw both her doctors hanging from two adjacent trees in her garden.

Symbolism, as we know, is at the heart of hysterical symptoms. Another case in the *Studies on Hysteria* shows how much this is so. Elizabeth had a conversion hysteria when, standing in front of her dead sister, she had the following thought, which was immediately condemned and repressed: her brother-in-law was now free to marry her. The conversion consisted in having great difficulty in remaining standing. Freud discovered the repressed thought at the origin of the symptom: 'I do not want to remain single.' The astasia-abasia took its origin in a displacement of symbolism: 'remaining single' can be expressed in German by *alleinstehen*, 'remaining single' = to be standing; and in Hungarian – Elizabeth had spent her childhood in Hungary – by *egyedulallo*, which means both 'single' and 'standing alone'. Symbolism, along with other primary processes, displacement and condensation, is the lynchpin of hysterical conversion that follows the model of wishful dream-fulfilment.

128

It is precisely at this level that hysterical hallucination poses a problem. Although the analysis of Frau Cäcilie shows that her repetitive hallucination took its origin, as in Elizabeth's case, in the transformation of a repressed thought: 'There's nothing to choose between the two of them; one's the pendant [match] of the other' (*Die zwei sind einander wert, der eine ist das Pendant zum Anderen*), it is probable that, in Frau Cäcilie's case, under the impact of an intense emotion, the transformation of the hateful thought into a truly nightmarish hallucination did not come about with the help of primary processes, in a movement equivalent to the dream-work. Under the effects of a brutal shrinking of the symbolic field, opening the way to the perception–hallucination, *pendant* (hanging) becomes *pendu* (hung), probably as an image in conformity with the thing-presentations, and not as a product of a work of figurability intimately attached to the repressed, to the historical and personal unconscious roots of Frau Cäcilie's (Silberer, 1909) infantile sexuality, whereas in Elizabeth's case, 'standing' was related to infantile complexes towards the father.

As Freud says, sometimes hysteria does not take linguistic symbolism as a model, but it may be that they 'draw their material from the same source' (Freud and Breuer, 1895: *S.E.* II, 181). In the case of Frau Cäcilie, the regression immediately pursued a retrogressive path such as one finds in traumatic neurosis, a short path that does not accede to infantile mnemic traces (we will come back to this in the next chapter). The traumatic element – the violent investment of her two doctors with feelings of hate rather than the usual libidinal feelings – functioned as a sudden, external traumatic perception, extraneous to the ego. Without bindings, the latter took over this minimal link of the equation 'hanging–hung', the image of which was a vehicle for the investment loaded with hate.

Thus, notwithstanding the fact that this repetitive hallucination represented the fulfilment of the wish to take revenge on her two doctors, the existence of the repetition of the hallucination shows that the issue at stake here is more one of an economic order than of a realisation of a content of a repressed wish. Which is why there is justification for thinking that the repetitive hallucinatory discharge of hysterics is to be considered, up to a certain point, as being similar to that of traumatic neurosis; that is to say, akin to the violence of a reflex motor discharge in response to physical pain.

However, a further question needs to be raised: if hysterical hallucination follows the model of traumatic neurosis; if there is a failure of the primary processes, a failure of the habitual mechanisms of hysteria, why describe this type of hallucinatory expression as hysterical hallucination? Ultimately, we think that when the ego's possibilities of binding are sufficient, which is usually the case, the hysterical symptom will take a more complex form as, for instance, in the case of Elisabeth where it made the detour of the roundabout path via infantile mnemic traces. Frau Cäcilie, for whom the mechanism of hysterical conversion failed, nonetheless realised a psychopathological modality of a fundamentally hysterical nature, that of crisis.[2]

Taking account of the development of Freud's thought, the dream, we have already recalled, is not a wish-fulfilment but, more precisely, an 'attempt at wish-fulfilment', which the psychical capacities of binding must deploy in the face of traumatic elements, in particular irrepresentable infantile traumas. The failure of this work of binding, of this effort to restore meaning, leads to the hallucinatory repetition of the trauma. The same may be said at the level of the formal regression of waking thought. Like the dream, formal regression of waking thought extends its field between, at one extreme, the disguised fulfilment of an unconscious wish, the product of a complex work of figurability characteristic of night dreams, namely, phantasy; and, at the other extreme, the failure of this work and the resolution of regression on the model of dream hallucination in traumatic neurosis. In the case of Frau Cäcilie, where the work of binding, of the primary processes, and, in particular, of displacement, had failed, the traumatic element (the violent investment of her two objects, Freud and Breuer, with feelings of hate instead of libidinal feelings) that overwhelmed the representative possibilities, as it had no representable meaning, deployed itself freely, took control of her sensory-motor functioning and made it possible to render the equation 'hanging–hung' intelligible in the guise of a hallucinatory projection.

Hallucinations in 'normal people' ('the smell of fir')

Should what Freud calls 'occasional hallucinations in the healthy' (Freud, 1936: *S.E.* XXII, 244), that is to say, a non-psychotic hallucination, be called psycho-neurotic or normal? It may be characterised, globally speaking, by the conservation of the investments of object-representations and of reality testing, for the ego will experience the hallucinatory image as a false perception. What is involved is an 'accident', a momentary regression, in the course of neurotic or normal psychical processes. In the conditions of the analytic setting, facilitating regression, as much of the libido as of the ego, the retrogressive path used is most frequently that which leads to a disguised realisation of a repressed wish. These regressions can sometimes have the characteristics of night dreams: Olga's motor hallucination, related in an earlier chapter, is such an example.

Here is another. It took place, as in Olga's case, after a week of interruption due to the analyst being on vacation. An acute re-actualisation of the suffering caused by the absence occurred, putting the capacities of the psyche for elaboration to a severe test on the analyst's return. Scarcely had the analysand (psychoneurotic, with a fundamentally Oedipal structure) laid down on the couch, without waiting for the analyst to settle in his armchair, when he exclaimed: 'There's a smell of fir in here!'[3]

On the basis of the initial associations that came to him, one can understand that this reference to the 'smell of fir' allowed him to discharge his hate aroused by the analyst's absence and to realise, in a hallucinatory manner, an unconscious wish: 'It smells of the fir of your coffin', the aggressive anal connotation of which collaborated with the olfactory form of the hallucination, disavowing his feelings of abandonment in connection with a primitive scene reduced to a 'smell'. However, 'smelling the fir' was also a way of experiencing the joy of starting his sessions again: this was based on childhood memories, happy gatherings around the Christmas tree, the image of his mother taking him 'in her arms'. The hallucinatory act had the value of realising contradictory wishes, a remarkable condensation of feelings of hate and love. It was related to causalities that the analyst is accustomed to in his daily practice and that can be described as representational causalities linked to temporo-spatiality and the relation to the object. Only these causalities were not able to explain why these wishes – it was not the first time he had been faced with them – assumed on that particular day a hallucinated perceptual mode of expression. Under normal circumstances, the analysand would, in the course of the session, have expressed these same wishes in the form of representations. Something else entered the equation on that day; something that must have been the cause of the hallucinated perceptual form. The analysand, who had arrived full of transferential joy rooted in childhood, found, once the analyst had opened the door and was standing in front of him, close to him, that he was suddenly seized by violent feelings that took over his ego. It was an acute, traumatic moment, outside time. No more thoughts, no more representations; just a non-represented elan of childhood, pure affect comprised solely of motility and action: rushing forward into the analyst's arms, as a child does with his mother. In order to get beyond this state deprived of any representational solution, the analyst had to effect a radical change of psychical register: the acted affect had to be replaced with a hallucinatory expression. Only the hallucinatory solution was capable of handling both the unthinkable elan and its inseparable contrary, just as unthinkable, violent, and true: a negative. Something in the transferential regression that should have happened as a matter of course did not take place: 'the analyst-mother not taking him in her arms', something unthinkable, irrepresentable, constituted the negative foundation of the trauma.

Faced with this massive appearance of the negative, there followed a deep narcissistic regression comparable to that of the sleeping state in that it is also accompanied by a tendency to withdraw cathexes from objects, perception and motility – traumatised patients often give descriptions of a state of motor and psychical paralysis. For Ferenczi (1955), '"shock" is equivalent to the annihilation of self-regard' (p. 253); and for Freud, to the destruction of the feeling of self-love, to the 'early injuries to the ego (narcissistic injuries)'. 'Loss of love and failure leave behind them a permanent injury to self-regard in the form of a narcissistic scar' (Freud, 1920: 20). As we said in our account of Aline's analysis: *the negative foundation of every infantile trauma resides, in short, in the impossibility for the child to imagine himself non-invested by the object of desire; to imagine the irrepresentable character of his own absence in the object's eyes.*

To put it in another way, when, in an entirely unexpected manner, the child's perception is brutally confronted with the absence of any investment of himself on the part of the invested object – this is the very meaning of any trauma in a child's life – the link between the endopsychic perception of representations and the perception of the sense organs is smashed to pieces; the internal mirror is shattered. The *symmetry representation–perception* is ruptured (this notion is developed later). Without content, instinctual life deploys itself freely and the conditions are then propitious for the occurrence of a traumatic neurosis and the phenomenon of the hallucinatory repetition of a perception. In the contrary case, if an endopsychic perception, a representation, imposes its force against the perception of the absence of investment of the subject by the invested object, a distortion of reality, ranging from denial to its delusional reconstruction becomes possible.

The best solution remaining is clearly that of perceiving the absence of investment and urgently 'finding-creating' (Winnicott) a causality capable of supplying an explanation for the negative. Thirdness – the logic of, 'because daddy', giving a glimpse of the possibility of one day winning one's place with the object conserved by virtue of this found/created causality – is preferable to the unthinkable withdrawal of love by the loved object. Likewise, traumatic as it may be, the idea of castration, of the missing penis, is better than the narcissistic nothingness of the absence of investment of the subject by the object. Consequently, while being at the origin of traumatic after-effects, primal phantasies, inasmuch as they protect against desubjectivisation and give rise to a relational richness between subject and object, have unquestionably an anti-traumatic value. The specific feature of what are considered as the traumas inherent to the Oedipus complex (castration, seduction and primal scene), however much anguish they cause, is paradoxically their structuring role, their organising force, which is indispensable for the constitution of the subject. In this sense, describing these complexes as traumatic is not altogether justified for, strictly speaking, only that which cannot be elaborated psychically deserves to be described as traumatic.

Psychotic hallucination

We know that the famous passage of the text on the 'Wolf Man' concerning the hallucination of the child Sergei, 'a third current, the oldest and deepest, which did not as yet even raise the question of the reality of castration' (Freud, 1914–18 *S.E.* XVII, 85) is one of the major points on which Lacan developed his conception of foreclosure as a specific mechanism constituting psychotic phenomena. We also know that Lacanian foreclosure is equally defined by another passage of the text on President Schreber mentioned earlier: 'It was incorrect to say that the perception which was suppressed internally is projected outwards; the truth is rather, as we see now, that what was abolished internally returns from without' (p. 71), whence Lacan's formula, 'what has been foreclosed from the symbolic reappears in reality'. Foreclosure and hallucination, thus entangled, determine psychosis.

Psychotic projection is, then, to be considered – not in the way it occurs in neurotic projection, that is, as a form of defence in which the repressed representation both remains in the unconscious system and is projected on to an external object, the investment of the representation being retained – but as the annihilation, the total destruction (in the sense of atomic physics, where mass is entirely transformed into energy) of a representation that disappears from the system of unconscious representations and is thus impossible to interpret. *The essence of the mechanism of psychotic hallucination may be said to be the 'negativisation' of a representation.* Such a negativisation is the opposite of a retrogressive process; it is its contrary, a mode of inhibiting hallucinatory expression consisting in clinging to the sense organs, to the concrete nature of what they can generate in terms of meaning, even if it is delusional. It is this sensory positivisation through a perception, instead of a representation, that characterises psychotic hallucination. Paradoxically, one could say that psychotic hallucination does not belong to the hallucinatory domain, in the sense we attribute to the retrogressive path, but rather to a fundamentally perceptual-sensory order, to the domain of the sense organs. Our hypothesis is that, owing to its being concretised in an perceptual-sensory over-investment, it represents a barrier against the anxiety felt by the ego when faced with the fear of a brutal rupture of all representation, of all investment; with the fear of a Screberian 'end of the world', the projection of an 'internal catastrophe'. The error of psychiatry and Freud's too – one that we continue to make – is to employ the same term 'hallucination' for both the psychotic and the dream phenomena, when, in fact, different and even opposing mechanisms are involved.

(But what is the interest of approaching the psychotic phenomenon with the formulation 'negativisation of the representation'? What does it offer with regard to Freud's idea of 'abolition on the inside' and Lacan's idea of foreclosure? It allows us to draw special attention to the rupture of the fragile equilibrium of reality testing as a duality representation–perception, instead of reducing the distortion of reality to the consequence of a defensive procedure of the ego alone.)

Let us return to the case of one of Tausk's patients, Emma A. (Tausk, 1919a) studied by Freud in his 'Papers on metapsychology' (Freud, 1915c: *S.E.* XIV, 197–8). After a quarrel with her lover, she was complaining that *her eyes were not right; they were twisted.* This she herself explained by bringing forward a series of reproaches against her lover: 'She could not understand him at all, he looked different every time; he was a hypocrite, an eye twister (*Augenverdreher*), he had twisted her eyes; now she had twisted eyes; they were not her eyes any more; now she saw the world with different eyes.' In face of the object-loss, the

133

intolerable reality had to be denied and to that end the unconscious object-representation was disinvested; in its place there was an over-investment of word-presentations, 'eye twister'; the lost object had become a word through the double aspect of '*verdrehen*': literally, twisting, turning something round; and figuratively, to turn somebody's head. And, as she was unable to effect a formal regression like Frau Cäcilie, or a displacement like Elizabeth, this patient over-invested the sensory value of the word, the latter becoming inseparable from her body. And, what is more, at the end of the process, the representational value of the word could be entirely effaced and with it the remains of the object-investment, in favour of auto-erotic investment. Psychic suffering disappeared by being transformed into a hypochondriachal malaise, a delusional bodily change.

Object-loss, the loss of the investment of the thing-presentation of the object provokes psychic chaos. Such a disobjectalisation, in André Green's sense, and the consequent disorganisation, a 'negativisation', were in this case, compensated by the sensory over-investment of the word, by the word-body (S. Botella, 1983) in place of the lost object. Instead of hallucinatory activity occurring in the retrogressive direction, the delusion unfolded along the progressive and perceptual path culminating in the formation of a sensory-motor object which, in the place of the 'negativised' object-representation, became the unifying pole of an ego stuck to perception.

A metapsychological definition of 'the hallucinatory'

From the metapsychological standpoint, 'the hallucinatory', in different forms, is a constituent part of psychic paths.[4] But if we adopt a descriptive point of view, the hallucinatory must be envisaged as a regressive capacity of psychic functioning akin to the primitive form of the apparatus. From this perspective, the natural, spontaneous response to which the psyche tends is always of a hallucinatory order. And it is an inhibition of the hallucinatory deployment by the waking ego, regulating it and relativising its power by means of reality testing, that gives birth to representational modes of thinking.

Usually, the hallucinatory participates during the day in certain daily psychic processes; it underlies the daytime work of figurability in the same way as it underlies night-time dreaming; it participates in the vividness of memories, just as it contributes to arousing the sense of evidence, of conviction, sometimes culminating in 'very vivid sensory elements', almost hallucinatory, says Freud. By way of example, one can take the vividness of the yellow of the flowers in Freud's screen memory, or again Proust's beautiful descriptions. We concur with Michel Neyraut in *Les logiques de l'inconscient* (Neyraut, 1979), in particular when he considers that 'hallucination (we would say "the hallucinatory") is at the basis of logic'. It is the failure, the flaw or the absence of regulating agencies of the hallucinatory that may give the latter a pathological colouring. Given that the aim of the usual work of analytic treatment is to become conscious of the repressed, the process of rebinding at the preconscious level of the thing-presentation, repressed along with the preconscious word-presentation, occurs in the forward direction; the latter is not, in itself, a spontaneous path for unconscious wishing which, in its atemporality, tends towards the hallucinatory. Just as, according to Freud (1900), thinking is a 'detour', the process of becoming conscious of repressed material involves a 'detour' via word-presentations – it 'thinks' the repressed wish instead of fulfilling it.

As a complement to the problem of the hallucinatory, we can inscribe Freud's conception, above all in *Totem and Taboo*, and in 'The "uncanny"', of an unconscious 'derived from primitive animism' and defined by atemporality and the absence of spatialisation. The essence of the preconscious system, the reason for its existence, its vital function for psychic growth, is to overcome these primitive states and to introduce into psychic processes temporo-spatial discontinuities. At the theoretical level, one could thus hope to associate closely, or even render identical, the hallucinatory and the functioning of the system *Ucs.* What seems reasonably certain to us is that the hallucinatory, like the *Ucs.*, represents in the psyche a real pole of attraction; and in this context we would see the primary processes as having the role of tempering this attraction – we have seen their failure in the case of Frau Cäcilie.

With a view to formulating a definition of the hallucinatory, we are going to make use of two ideas: the first, which is relatively integrated within theoretical elaborations, is that, in 'primitive hallucination', the thing-presentation constitutive of the unconscious is the equivalent of the object of perception; the second maintains that unconscious wishes, even in the adult psyche, are formed on the model of primitive hallucination and therefore that it does not tend in any way towards preconscious representation but towards its hallucinatory fulfilment. If we accept these two ideas, in themselves truly Freudian, we can go further and consider that *it is not enough to say that the wish tends towards its hallucinatory fulfilment; it would be more exact to say that the hallucinatory is a constituent part of the unconscious wish, as is non-representation too.* We should then ask ourselves if the hallucinatory quality of the unconscious wish concerns exclusively the definition of wishing or if it also concerns the very notion of the unconscious. The problematic of the hallucinatory thus brings us back to the impossible question of the nature of the unconscious. Which is why we will have to be content with the following formula: *the state of psychic quality, which we call 'the hallucinatory', only concerns the unconscious in as much as it is its 'natural' means of expression. It is a 'natural' tendency prompted by the pressure of the non-representable traumatic zone of the unconscious wish,* which comes to light when the preconscious system does not oppose it, when the forces of binding and the investments of representations weaken or when the 'detour' via thinking does not take place. These conditions obtain during the production of a night

135

dream and, partially, during a formal regression of thinking resulting in a work of figurability in daytime.

If, in fact, as we think, the primordial quality of the hallucinatory is its atemporality, we should conclude that such a quality, regarded by Freud as a characteristic of the *Ucs.* belongs in reality to the hallucinatory tendency of unconscious wishes and not to the *Ucs.* itself. Apart from its derivatives, of which the hallucinatory is a part, the *Ucs.* remains unknown.

Reality testing and psychic temporalities

The question raised at the beginning of the third part as to how the transition from the atemporality of the unconscious to the temporo-spatiality of the preconscious occurs can thus now be thought about in a different way. How is the atemporal hallucinatory tendency of unconscious wishes transformed into a temporo-spatial and bound preconscious representation? The problem of the change from atemporality into temporo-spatiality should, then, within our theoretical hypothesis, be envisaged as a transformation of a state governed by the hallucinatory into a state in which the representation, in particular, word-presentations and language, marked by the organising and regulating value of object cathexis, holds back the violent aspiration of the unconscious wish to obtain its satisfaction by the shortest route. In fact, this change obliges us to assume the existence of a permanent psychic work which, at each instant, finds itself excluding or using the hallucinatory tendency by adapting it, in order to differentiate representation from perception; we mean, of course, the work of reality testing, without whose study nothing pertaining to retrogressive processes and the links between the preconscious and unconscious systems can really be understood.

Although at moments the notion of reality testing seems simple in Freud – for instance, a motor action capable of distinguishing what is outside from what is inside – it emerges from Freud's texts as a whole that this simplicity is just a particular aspect of a vast process. Reality testing is a complex psychic work constituted by multiple and varied relations between the ego and the object and its representation and of the circulation of their cathexes between systems unconscious, preconscious and perception consciousness. The encounter between the ego and material reality is a consequence of this work.

The two famous phrases of 'Negation': 'The first and immediate aim, therefore, of reality-testing is, not to *find* an object in real perception which corresponds to the one presented, but to *refind* such an object, to convince oneself that it is still there'; then, 'what is unreal, merely a presentation and subjective, is *only internal* [our italics]; what is real is also there *outside*' (Freud, 1925b: *S.E.* XIX, 237–8) have led us to develop a personal conception of the work of reality testing (see Chapter 8). The essential point boils down to the fact that the 'primitive' psyche finds it is subject to a double constraint: first, in order to avoid the distress of the object's absence, the experience of *Hilflosigkeit*, he is obliged only to perceive the object in its hallucinatory form; and second, faced with the insufficiency of this hallucinatory solution, he is obliged, in order to survive, 'to form a conception of the real circumstance in the external world' (Freud, 1911a: *S.E.* XII, 219). The whole problem is to know how one can form a conception of the external world as an apparatus would do it, by recording 'the real state' of this world. Comparable to this improbability, the 'original reality-ego' of which Freud speaks in *Instincts and their Vicissitudes* (1915b), is a hypothesis, in our view, that cannot be defended; moreover, he never speaks of it again in his later elaborations, even when he is dealing with the beginnings of psychic organisation in 'Negation' in 1925 where, on the contrary, he asserts that, 'the antithesis between subjective and objective does not exist from the first' (*S.E.* XIX, 237). The same is true in *Civilization and its Discontents* (1929) when he discusses the 'oceanic feeling' dear to Romain Roland.

On the basis of these Freudian approaches to reality, we formulate reality testing as a psychic process of great complexity involving, at one and the same time, a denial of perception in order to be able to invest the object in a hallucinatory manner and a perception of the object in its hallucinatory form so as to be able to refind it in the denied perception. These investments form a double movement that, in reality, is only one, the formulation of which, as we were saying earlier, could be that of a double contradictory conviction: the object is 'Only inside–Also outside'. It is a contradiction, in our view, that structures the essential, constitutive dynamic of the work of reality testing, establishing simultaneously a union and a separation between outside and inside. It is thus by means of a contradictory contraction in the order of 'only–also' that the 'representation of the external world' and, more broadly, the psychical capacity to represent, can be constituted. Paradoxically, the work of reality is thus based at the same time on a continuity that, elsewhere, we have called animistic thinking and a pre-animistic state and on a structure that has certain similarities with that of splitting (represented by the dash between the 'only' and the 'also'), in particular with its classical model to which we have already made allusion in this book: 'I know father's dead, but what I can't understand is why he doesn't come home to supper' (Freud, 1900: 254). This vast work on a set of contradictions – the simultaneity of an object cathexis coinciding with a cathexis of narcissistic omnipotence; the coexistence of splitting and animistic continuity; the recognition of reality and its denial – is the only means of constituting in a permanent way the foundations of reality testing, psychic movements constantly going back and forth between representation and perception.

The problem of the origins of memory thus comes into play here. We have just spoken of the necessity, for the mind, of denying the perception of the object in order to be able to cathect it by hallucinating. Such a *negativisation of perception* is the consequence of repeated traumas due to the object's absences and failure in its function of binding.

Psychic discontinuity has the immediate effect of a truly instinctual appeal; the instinctual impulse, solicited by absence, provokes a qualitative change, the accession of a meaning, a logic, a primordial binding, which every mind has to create in order to overcome distress when faced with the object's absence and, more precisely, with the terror of the state of non-perception: 'disappeared/eaten' (like food). The organisation of this experienced/thought 'oral theory' is inseparable from the conviction 'only inside'; its complete formulation would be '*disappeared–eaten–only inside*'. By the same token, the return of the object will also be experienced/thought in the oral mode enriched by a new relation: '*disappeared–eaten–spat out–also outside*'.

In fact, the return of the 'spat out' object, the 'also outside', already requires a function of memory; it assumes the capacity for 'remembering' the existence, both simultaneous and, at one time, hallucinatory, of the object. *If, as Freud says, consciousness appears in the perceptual system in the place of mnemic traces, we can suppose that, in its turn, memory appears in the place of the hallucinatory.*

In the session, one notices how the appeal to memory puts a brake on formal regression limits the hallucinatory tendency to reactualising the sensory traces of memory images.

MYSTICISM, KNOWLEDGE AND TRAUMA[1]

Stressing the importance played by Bion's development of the notion of mysticism in the evolution of Freudian theory represents, it seems to us − although we are not particularly Kleinian or Bionian, but rather attached to Freud's thought and the potential developments it contains − the best homage that we can offer Bion.

In Bion's theory, the notion of mysticism is situated at the crossroads of the psychical processes of analytic interpretation and scientific discovery. What we are concerned with is an ensemble, knowledge, the approach of which, in Bion's view, cannot be separated from mystical practice. We will focus on two central ideas of Bion. The first is that 'psycho-analytical observation certainly cannot afford to be confined to perception of what is verbalised only' (Bion, 1970: 82). The second − inspired by, among others, Freud who asserts in *An Outline of Psychoanalysis* (1938b) that, 'Reality will always remain unknowable' (p. 196) − is that the human being cannot have access to knowledge of the object itself; he can only know emanations from it, emergent qualities, evolving characteristics, which have repercussions on it as phenomena; but these sensible and perceptible qualities, verbalisable or representable, differ from the object's 'ultimate reality'. There exists in every object of study an essence, noumen, or thing-in-itself, in Kant's sense, that remains inaccessible to the observer owing to the very nature of his psychic system, of his incapacity to apprehend non-sensory phenomena, such as the analysand's 'ultimate reality', or 'ultimate truth' in the case of the analyst, or the object of investigation in the case of the scientist. This reality or ultimate truth, Bion calls 'point O'; and, all we can know of it is its transformations or emanations. However, Bion thinks that we should try to reach this realm beyond or short of what is sensory, representable and thinkable; and that the only means to do this is through mystical practices.

Bion says that the analyst, just like the mystic, should, 'through an effort of the ego', follow a 'rigorous', 'positive discipline' consisting of renunciations −

Bion's famous three Nos. By renouncing all memory, desire and understanding, the analyst gains access to what Bion qualifies as an 'act of faith'. By that, he means that the essence of the analytic encounter is the analyst's effort to attain the analysand's point O, to be one with O, 'to be O', a 'state of union'. The same holds true for every process of scientific discovery.

By rehabilitating the notion of mysticism, Bion placed himself within a current of thought scorned by positivist science. In the 19th century, any interest taken in mystics was much more aimed at criticising them than trying to understand their sensibility; accordingly, the term mysticism was relegated to the domain of the irrational and became a synonym of obscurantism.

The importance of Bion's approach is thus considerable. In order to measure its significance, it is worth recalling the definition of the term mysticism in Lalande's *Dictionnaire Philosophique*: 'Belief in the possibility of intimate and direct union of the human mind with the fundamental principle of being, a union constituting at once a mode of existence and a mode of knowledge foreign and superior to normal existence and knowledge.'

We can see, then, that mysticism is a major and inescapable problem, not only for the religious – it would be very convenient to reduce the problem of mysticism to the world of religion (in this connection, see Hulin, 1993) – but also for the scientist and for the psychoanalyst who, for his part, claims to know the 'fundamental principle of being'. In fact, the problem of mysticism, as a 'mode of knowledge', has been a concern of psychoanalysis since its beginnings, to the point that we can only grasp its importance for Bion and, more generally in analytic theory, by starting with Freud's study of it.

Freud used the term mysticism in a critical manner until he formulated the new theory of the drives and the second topography in the 1920s. The fact that the scientific context was no longer the same as in the 19th century, and that science had just undergone the shock that attended Einstein's discoveries, must have had a considerable influence on the evolution of Freud's thought. The theory of relativity, calling into question the principles of Newtonian physics and mechanics, along with the conception of space and time, could not leave someone like Freud indifferent; for he wanted to explain the functioning of the mind according to the models of Newtonian mechanics – that is, in terms of different movements linked together primarily owing to the pressure of the past, with a linear development and reversible in time. Like Newtonian principles, this conception of Freud's was to prove inadequate as a container for the growth of analytic theory.

With the second topography introducing the notion of the id, Freud operated a certain decentring of the notion of a repressed unconscious system. From then on, while forming part of a greater whole, the *Ucs.* had a somewhat relativised role compared with that it had had previously. It necessarily followed that psychoneurosis, as an organising structural model of the mind, would also have a lesser role. To this may be added the fact that Freud discovered both the economic and dynamic impact of traumatic neurosis and also the determining action of its equivalent, actual neurosis, forming part of the very structure of psychoneurosis at the heart of normal psychic functioning. What Freud understood was that, when circumstances require it, the psyche has the potential to discharge itself repeatedly, without the participation of representations, effacing the topographies and psychoneurotic functioning, permitting perception to be transformed into hallucination. A conception of mysticism now became accessible to Freud: he was able to say, in 1932, in the *New Introductory Lectures*, that the mystical method also entails an erasure of the psychical topographies, carrying with it temporo-spatiality.

But Freud went still further. In the same text, he considered that 'the therapeutic efforts of psycho-analysis have chosen a similar line of approach' as mysticism, and that 'certain mystical practices may succeed in upsetting the normal relations between the different regions of the mind, so that, for instance, perception may be able to grasp happenings in the depths of the ego and in the id which were otherwise inaccessible to it' (Freud, 1932a: *S.E. XXII*, 79–80). On the behalf of the creator of psychoanalysis, this reference to the 'otherwise inaccessible', which could only be grasped by means of mystical practices, was a courageous observation of the limits of his discipline, as it was practised at that time. Francis Pasche was the first person in France to conceive of what he called 'psychoanalytic asceticism' (Pasche, 1962).

(Mystical thought functions, then, from the Freudian standpoint, with the habitual psychic equipment which, being subject to an erasure of the psychical topographies, coincides with a dynamic for which the model is traumatic neurosis. Only, instead of the repeated hallucinatory discharge of a so-called traumatic perception, mystical thinking has the peculiarity of conferring a new aptitude on perception.)Thus, it is by trying to understand the nature of this psychical efficiency reaching the 'otherwise inaccessible' that we will be able to grasp the mystical method better.

The astonishing quality of perception evoked by Freud is all the more difficult to delineate in that he never really took the trouble to define what he meant, metapsychologically, by the notion of perception; he was concerned principally with the notion of representation, of words and things. In all domains, the notion of perception comprises a certain ambiguity for it represents at once a function, the act through which this function is exercised and its result. For his part, Freud did not escape this ambiguity. Throughout his whole work, he associates perception with consciousness in the form of a system *Pcs.–Cs.*, which he situates on the periphery of the psychical apparatus. A system endowed with free, at the very least, mobile energy and opposed to the systems of mnemic traces and representations, that is, the preconscious and unconscious. In other words, when in metapsychology one wants to approach the notion of perception separately from the system *Pcs.–Cs.*, it has to be conceived of as being situated topographically outside the realm of representations; or again, as that which escapes the dynamic of the investments of representations and, consequently, equally that of psychoneurosis. We are reduced to defining it, not in terms of its qualities, but in terms of what it is not, that is, by a negativity. From the analyst's point of view, perception, like reality 'will always remain unknowable'; or, put in another way, it can only be defined in function of a reality that is equally unknowable. We will come back to this in more detail in the following chapters.

In metapsychology, perception retains all its ambiguity of function, act and result. More precisely, it should be considered as a dynamic operating permanently between a traumatic pole and the result of a work of transformation carried out on the latter; it is to be looked on as one of the possible dynamics of a 'living organism' with complex laws whose spontaneous functioning, when faced with the same problem and without the intervention of the work of reality testing, leads to hallucinatory wish-fulfilment. This would be the investment of 'what remains' when the dynamic of hallucinatory satisfaction is prohibited, when energy can borrow neither the immediate path of hallucinatory and/or traumatic discharge nor the path that Freud calls in the *Interpretation of Dreams* the 'roundabout path', the mediate path of the investment of small bound quantities of representation and thought. Perception, which represents an indispensable discontinuity in the hallucinatory continuum, operates less in function of a so-called objective reality principle than a reality principle which Freud considers as a modification of the pleasure principle – thus still reliant, at least partially, on the unconscious wishes of the id and superego, impregnated with intrapsychic conflictual issues, notably those of infantile neurosis. It is a principle that obliges the psyche to create simultaneously two specific qualities, complementary and contrasting, those of perception and representation, thus provoking a double fissure in the original indiscernibility between perception and hallucination, a double distinction necessary for maintaining an element of differentiation with hallucination. It is via this dynamic of the tripartite perceptual field, between hallucination, perception and representation, that we will be better able to grasp the problem of mysticism.

Arthur Koestler has recounted in *The Invisible Writing* (1954) a series of experiences of a mystical character that he had when, in 1936, he was a prisoner in Seville, and, charged with spying, was in danger at any moment of being shot by Franco supporters. While he scratched symbols on the wall of his cell in an attempt to rediscover Euclid's method of the infinite numerical series, he had the following experience:

> I must have stood immobile for some minutes, entranced, with a wordless awareness that: this is perfect – perfect'; until I noticed some slight mental discomfort nagging at the back of my mind, some trivial circumstance that marred the perfection of the moment. Then, I remembered the nature of that irrelevant annoyance: I was, of course, in prison and might be shot. But this was immediately answered by a feeling whose verbal translation would

be: 'So what? Is that all? Have you got nothing more serious to worry about?' – an answer so spontaneous, fresh and amused as if the intruding annoyance had been the loss of a collar-stud. Then I was floating in a river of peace on my back under bridges of silence. It came from nowhere and flowed nowhere. There was no river and no I. The I had ceased to exist . . . When I say 'the I had ceased to exist', I refer to a concrete experience that is verbally as incommunicable as the feeling aroused by a piano concerto yet just as real – only much more real . . . the 'I' ceases to exist because it has, by a kind of mental osmosis, established communication with, and been dissolved in, the universal pool. It is this process of dissolution and limitless expansion which is sensed as the 'oceanic feeling', as the draining of all tension, the absolute catharsis, the peace that passeth all understanding.

With remarkable lucidity, Koestler concludes by remarking on the necessity of taking experience in its 'raw' state, and of not falling into the trap of making an interpretation (pp. 351–3):

Religious conversion on the deathbed or in the death-cell is an almost irresistible temptation . . . That temptation has two sides. But because the experience is inarticulate, has no sensory shape, colour or words, it lends itself to transcription in many forms, including visions of the Cross or of the goddess Kali; they are like dreams of a person born blind and may assume the intensity of a revelation. Thus a genuine mystic experience may mediate a *bone fide* conversion to practically any creed: Christianity, Buddhism or Fire-Worship.

It cannot be said better. The mystical state may be said, then, to be a particular psychic state giving rise to an original solution: the mystic, whether Far Eastern, Sufi or a St John of the Cross prescribing an attitude of detachment from sensations, thoughts, desires, memories and any investment of representation, transforms the world of loss and the affect of terror attached to it, into a feeling of plenitude, a state of union. The trauma of non-investment and *non-representation* is avoided in favour of a hallucinatory state of happiness.[2] In the same spirit, the painter Zoran Music (1995), relating his imprisonment at Dachau in 1944, at the age of 35, has given a marvellous description of this transformation that plunged him into a state of exaltation while drawing, on bits of paper that he had managed to spirit away, the horror of corpses being piled up.

I drew as if in a trance, clutching morbidly at my bits of paper. It was as if I was blinded by the hallucinatory magnitude of these fields of corpses. While drawing, I grasped at a thousand details: what tragic elegance there was in these fragile bodies! Such precise details: their hands, their thin fingers, their feet, their mouths slightly open in a last attempt to get some air. And the bones covered by white skin, turned slightly blue. And my obsessive concern not to betray in any way these diminished forms, to succeed in reproducing them, precious as they were to me, reduced to their essentials. (My translation)

As Simone Korff-Sausse (2000) points out in a remarkable article, far from being a nightmare, far from wanting to get rid of it, the horror of the experience takes on the value, for Zoran Music, of a precious treasure that he does not want to lose at any cost. A strange dream he had many years after his release from captivity bears witness to this: in it, he finds himself in a stadium surrounded by an immense crowd in the terraces, all corpses.

It was something magnificent for me, because it was like an inexhaustible vision. And then, suddenly, the terraces began to slide to the left, out of sight. And I woke up, desperate, certain that I had lost for good something extremely precious to me.

Mystical experience, on the model of hallucinatory wish-fulfilment, masters the hallucinatory solution of traumatic neurosis – we will see later how – while seeking, behind the scenes, to bring about a genuine reversal of the psychic order, that of conflict, sexuality and infantile trauma – that is clearly incompatible with analytic practice.

What is the situation, then, as far as Bion's practice is concerned? One must not confuse the mystical state, as we have just described it, and Bion's concern with attaining 'ultimate truth'. Perhaps by associating his practice and the mystic model too readily, Bion runs the risk of leading us astray with regard to the thinking he wants to transmit. In fact, as soon as one ceases to let oneself be fascinated by the great pregnancy of the idea of ecstasy, of union – whether with God, the universe, oneself or the analysand – one can understand that mystical practice is nothing but a consequence of a particular form of mental functioning, i.e. the retrogressive tendency of all its constituents. In this sense, one can find a few rare passages in Bion in which he expresses himself more in terms of regression than in terms of mysticism but, curiously enough, without comparing them: 'First it is to be noted that the submergence of memory, desire, and understanding appears not only to run flat contrary to accepted procedure but also to be close to what occurs spontaneously in the severely regressed patient.' And he concludes: 'There are real dangers associated with the appearance; this is why the procedure here adumbrated is advocated only for the psycho-analyst whose own analysis has been carried at least far enough' (Bion, 1970: 47).

Rather than 'real dangers' for the analyst, what is involved here are anxieties of a particular order, for which the analyst's own analysis, however thorough it has been, has not really prepared him. For the organisation of the work of the session, the transference/counter-transference dynamic, the economy related to it, protect the analysand from the retrogressive character of these uncanny phenomena of which we were speaking, which are triggered when psychic functioning begins to take the backward direction. The analysand is relatively well protected against the threat of losing the sense of alterity generated by the approach of this form of regression (which we discussed particularly in Part Two) by his libidinal regression inherent to the transference nourishing relational links and the work of memory. For the analyst, it is not the same, provided that he abandons these dynamics or, as Bion says, is without memory, desire and understanding. In effect, if in the usual economic and dynamic conditions of the session, with sensory perception partly excluded – facilitating the waking formal regression of thinking, as in sleep – regression continues in the analyst to the point of inducing a withdrawal of his cathexes of object relations and memory, it sometimes happens that the limits of his ego are erased. It is only at moments like this, and at this price, that the mind can attain a state of the formal regression of thought and, via this, 'otherwise inaccessible' perceptual qualities.

The retrogressive capacity of thinking, as we know, is more or less developed in different psychic structures; it can be absent in certain psychotic and, above all, operative ways of functioning. As far as the mystical procedures are concerned, we have already said that, when he is following the retrogressive path and faced with the traumatic approach of the *non-representable*, the mystic 'opts' for the radical solution of a hallucinatory reversal – as he once opted for of the terror of distress – into an experience of union that he will describe as sublime, which he will call God or the universe.

From our point of view as psychoanalysts, this experience of union can be nothing other than a transformation of the effect of the disappearance of the sense of alterity, a disappearance that is ineluctably concomitant with the pain of loss. But the drive, freed from its ties of object cathexis, cannot transform pain, as in the work of mourning, into the repetition of hallucinatory states limited to the evocation of memories. It is thus in this free deployment of the drive, with the attendant threat of an irreversible traumatic solution entailing a total upheaval of the psychic order, that the hallucinatory irruption will be experienced in its immediate aftermath as a happy state of union with an immaterial object that is idealised in place of investing the object and oneself. It is a mechanism for disavowing mourning with a hallucinatory outcome, as one can observe in certain pathological states of mourning, in particular in children.

But then, when Bion uses, with insistence, the formulation 'feeling of union', how are we to understand it within his own theoretical context? For him, the 'state of union' refers at once to the notions of mysticism and genius, two entities he considers as similar, notably in their relations to the group. Although, unquestionably, one can only agree with Bion's assertion that mysticism and genius have a common basis, the point of departure being, in our view, the formal regression of thinking, fundamental divergences exist concerning the respective outcomes of their methods, which even seem antithetical.

In order to enter the question more thoroughly, a detour via Freud's work will once again be necessary. Between 1932 and the end of his life, Freud's thinking

145

followed a subtle evolution, the richness of which we are still far from having exhausted. This evolution allowed Freud, in 1938, to reconsider the notion of perception awakened by the practice of mysticism and capable of grasping the 'relations in the depth of the ego and in the id' as 'the obscure self-perception of the realm outside the ego of the id' (*S.E.* XXII, 79, *S.E.* XXIII, 300). These famous formulations, so often cited, imply that, instead of a union – for the believer, with God, or, for other mystics, with the universe – Freud preferred to envisage the mystical phenomenon in the solely intrapsychic terms of 'self-perception'. Should we, then, take this orientation literally and conceive of the outcome of the regression of thinking as a self-perception of the id? By using the term 'id', Freud probably wanted not only to reduce the problem to a purely intrapsychic phenomenon, but also to connect it with what, in the psychical apparatus, is neither part of the system preconscious and the secondary processes nor part of the dynamic unconscious and primary processes. In short, to under-stand it independently of everything in the mind that is structured and organised. For him, mystical practices are related to zones of mental disorganisation, to an 'obscure' zone, self-perceived, for there can be no question here either of the habitual sense organs or of their intrapsychic equivalents. Thus, at this same date of July 1938, he wrote in the *Outline of Psychoanalysis:* 'The id cut off from the external world has a world of perception of its own' (1938b: *S.E.* XXIII, 198). From then on psychoanalytic theory opened itself to the study of a different kind of perception from that of the system *Pcs.–Cs.*, of a state at the limits of the psychic, apt at grasping what we condense in the term *non-representation*.

By denying loss, the mystic transforms the pain of loss into a state of hallucinatory union, terror into ecstasy. Whereas the genius, recognising trauma and loss, faces up to the sense of uncanniness aroused by the approach of the complete loss of investment and tries to 'perceive obscurely', to understand everything in his state which could give it shape and meaning. If Freud speaks of 'self-perception', it is perhaps also because it is possible, beginning with this state, to 'opt', like the genius, for the position of an observer, in continuity with the 'observed', without however losing oneself in the feeling of mystical union. To be more exact, when alterity disappears, the act of perceiving and its result become indissociable, perceiver and perceived indistinct, without, for all that, producing a 'state of union'. 'Self-perception' represents an intelligibility in the absence of object and narcissistic cathexes, an intense hallucinatory act without 'union' with perception through the sense organs. Bion would speak of the 'ultimate truth' of the object. Thus it seems clear that while analytic practice can in no case be directly compared with that of mysticism, at least as we understand it, it can, at certain moments, and in certain respects, be compared with the practice of the genius.

It has seemed indispensable to us to recall the problem of Freud's relation to mysticism and its evolution in order to refute the somewhat simplistic idea, in Bion's theory, which reduces the importance of mysticism to a sort of private

146

hobby, to a consequence of the influences of his early childhood in India, to his interest for the mystics, Sufis in particular, or again to the impact on him in London, after the war, of a personality like Krishnamurti. Even if one thinks that the weight of mysticism in Bion's theory stems from the fact that Bion himself had a mind that was rather attracted by it, this in no way diminishes the importance of the problem raised in his work by the relations of psychoanalytic practice and mystical practices – any more than the idea that Freud was undoubtedly a neurotic discredits his discoveries on neurosis.

Whereas, in Freud's conception, the analysand's psyche is governed by the pressure of his repressed memory, by his unconscious wishes, and the cure is defined by the transference neurosis and its counterpart of counter-transferential memories and unconscious wishes, Bion, on the contrary, thinks that: 'memories and desires are "illuminations" which destroy the value of the analyst's capacity for observing'; or again that 'the importance of the *Ucs.* must not blind us'; statements that bear witness to his intention not to hide his difference from Freud. He spoke of his analytic practice as being a 'different' and 'complementary' analysis (Bion, 1970: 67) laying claim to such a theoretico-clinical gap with Freud that each analyst is obliged to reflect on this gap. Are Freud's and Bion's forms of practice really 'complementary', as Bion thinks? Is it just a question of depth or of 'vertex'? Some evade the question by condemning Bion's thought en bloc.

In reality, the problem with which Bion's thought faces us goes far beyond his analytic practice. The theoretical issues at stake are more important than with other theoreticians, owing to the importance of the relativisation of the repressed unconscious in Bion's work. And even if we consider that this relativisation is simply the inevitable consequence of the decentring of the *Ucs.* operated by Freud himself in the second topography (1923a), it is still true that Bion's theory represents numerous aspects of a crisis in analytic theory, if only at the level of the notion of interpretation that he defined as being 'an actual event in an evolution of O that is common to the analyst and the analysand' (Bion, 1970: 27), refuting its accepted sense of being the principal means of access to repressed wishes rooted in the past. Thus Bion confronts us with the necessity of no longer thinking about psychoanalysis solely in terms of what can be considered as its sole paradigm.[3]

Whether one is Bionian or not, the truth is that it has become increasingly difficult to uphold a conception of psychic functioning limited to the Freudian topographies alone and to the dynamic of the repression of representations that stems from it. Other dynamics can be taken into consideration without there being any risk of the Freudian edifice crumbling. It is in the nature of Freud's thought that it can be enlarged on permanently. We would readily speak of a system of thought in expansion, which would be impoverished if one reduced it to established formulations, if one neglected its spirit in order to restrict ourselves to a textual interpretation. Bion saw this sharply. We will conclude now by rendering homage to him with a final citation:

The mental domain cannot be contained within the framework of psycho-analytic theory. Is this a sign of defective theory, or a sign that psychoanalysts do not understand that psycho-analysis cannot be contained permanently within the definitions they use.

Bion, 1970: 72–3

PART FOUR

Outline for a metapsychology of perception

A PSYCHOANALYTIC APPROACH
TO PERCEPTION

*The primary memory of a perception
is always a hallucination.*
Freud, 1895: 339

*Perception plays the part which
in the id falls to instinct.*
Freud, 1923a: 25

The unknowable

Whatever the means used to gain knowledge of the world, whether it be the sense organs or thinking, the problem is that knowledge has to fulfil certain conditions in order to lead to what Freud calls consciousness – that is to say, it has to acquire the characteristics of a form that is perceptible to consciousness. However psychical it may be, consciousness is nonetheless looked on by Freud as a 'sense organ for the apprehension of psychical qualities' (Freud, 1900: 574). The subject is far from being simple, for excitatory material 'flows', he continues, 'into the *Cs.* sense organ from the *Pcpt.* system, whose excitation . . . is probably submitted to a fresh revision before it becomes a conscious sensation, and from the interior of the apparatus itself, whose quantitative processes are felt qualitatively in the pleasure-unpleasure series when, subject to certain modifications, they make their way to consciousness' (p. 616). In both cases there is a transformation of the initial product; the unknowable is generated at all levels:

> In its innermost nature it is as much unknown to us as the reality of the external world, and it is as incompletely presented by the data of consciousness as is the external world by the communication of our senses organs.
>
> *S.E.* V, 613

The human being can only know the object, whether internal or external, from the emanations, the qualities emerging from the sense organs, characteristics in a state of evolution that have repercussions on his consciousness; but these sensible and perceptible qualities, which can be verbalised or represented visually, differ from the object itself.

The unknowable is inevitably an integral part of the psyche. It originates as much in the problem of perceptions closely dependent on the sense organs and their limits as in that of the limits of thought. At the outset, deprived of the quality of consciousness, thought has to transform itself into preconscious thought in order to acquire such a quality, which requires its passage via word-presentations and their perceptual residues, especially auditory. The drama of thought is that, in order to accede to the quality consciousness, it is submitted to the double diktat of the sense organs and the obligatory detour via perceptual qualities capable of arousing consciousness. Between lure and transformation, the unknowable is perpetuated. The 'dream navel' bears witness to this. The domain of what can be represented is a crude reduction of the vast domain of the unknowable. The problem is thus no longer one of the knowledge of an absolute and unattainable exterior. Rather what is at stake is knowledge at the level of the capacity of the psychical apparatus and its degree of reliability for reflecting, via the intermediary of representation and the quality consciousness, something of this unknowable domain. The study of thinking, notably in its association with perception, has become a fundamental issue for both psychoanalysis and science.

Fifteen years after *The Interpretation of Dreams*, Freud (1915c) suggested that psychoanalysts were, from the outset, in possession of means that give them a certain advantage over scientists:

> We shall be glad to learn that the correction of internal perception will turn out not to offer such great difficulties as the correction of external perception – that internal objects are less unknowable than the external world.
>
> *S.E.* XIV, 171

Owing to certain characteristics of their daily practice – the fact, for instance, that their object of study is the *Ucs.* of the 'similar other' (Green), an external object that is, however, similar to the observer; and that their objectivity involves the observation of their own subjectivity and functioning during the observation – psychoanalysts find themselves at the centre of the contemporary scientific debates on knowledge. Due to their increasingly thorough understanding of how the psyche functions, they can – and perhaps should – rise to the challenge, in the near future, of making a considerable contribution to scientists. This they could do by providing better knowledge of the instrument and its limits so that the gap between what is perceived through observation and the object itself might be better identified. In other words, our approach to reality itself, to its 'unknowable' nature could be refined.

Bion was the first to take this path. In order to have access, however small, to the unknowable, in order to reach what lies beyond or short of sensory reality, of the representable, Kant's noumen or thing-in-itself, which Bion calls the 'point O', the psyche, he suggests, has to operate not by means of the senses but through an 'act of faith' on the part of the analyst, which he considers similar to that of mystical practice. We discussed in Part Three the great interest but also the dangers entailed in this comparison between mysticism and psychoanalysis. But whatever one may think of it, it cannot be denied that Bion managed to centre the problem of the knowledge of reality on the study of thinking; and to impose, as its corollary, the necessity of not circumscribing the latter to the dynamic of representations.

In parallel with the expansion of contemporary scientific thinking, which is obliged to try and transcend its own limits so that it can approach both the domain of the infinitely small as well as that of the infinitely great, psychoanalysts have understood during recent years that the limits of their means of thinking and those of their knowledge converge and are inseparable. Hence their effort to take interest in how their own psyche functions in the analytic situation, in the hope of finding a means of gaining access to the comprehension of a psychical dimension and sufferings other than those of neurosis – a domain where intelligibility refers neither to certain expected causalities nor to the notion of representation alone.

The irrepresentable

It may seem paradoxical that psychoanalysts write about the irrepresentable, so much is analytic theory determined by the notion of representation and, in particular, by the sense it has of unconscious representation. A certain number of questions arise imediately: what is the relation between the metapsychological concept of unconscious representation and this notion of irrepresentability that has appeared so often in the analytic writings of recent years? In an analytic theory that claims to be rigorous, should one not envisage that the irrepresentable is nothing other than one of the characteristics of unconscious representation; and, in this case, is not all this interest in the irrepresentable exaggerated or unjustified? Or alternatively, this appreciation is summary and, beyond the fascination that such a suggestive term, with its romantic aura, can exert, the pre-occupation of analytic authors for the irrepresentable is the consequence of an increasingly fine analysis of the metapsychology of the session and a fresh awareness of the role in the treatment of the limits of the psychical apparatus and its capacities for representation. However that may be, what can be said here and now is that the irrepresentable can seemingly only be defined in terms of a singular negativity of representation that includes the latter; and, consequently, the study of irrepresentability rightly falls to psychoanalysts and

153

refers them to the indispensable prior condition of establishing a definition of representation from a specifically analytic point of view.

The real problem begins here, for throughout Freud's entire work, the notion of representation remained rather imprecise and was impregnated with diverse meanings. He used the term as it is habitually used. The notion of representation sometimes has the sense, in his writings, of the psychical repetition of an external perception and sometimes the more sophisticated sense of delegation (the psychical representative of the drive). It is this last sense, only, which would be given a definition of a strictly metapsychological order: the concept of *Vorstellungsrepräsentant* was to be indissociable from primal repression and would determine what constitutes the system *Ucs.* itself. It is thus in this respect that analytic theory, for better or for worse, one might say, is closely and inextricably bound up with the notion of representation. Without going any further, we could then conclude that, in analytic writings, the use of the term irrepresentable should be reserved for that which does not fall within the scope of this *Vorstellungsrepräsentant*, for that which has no possibility of gaining access to a chain of representations governed by unconscious wishes, by the drive and its fixation to its psychical representative.

Defining itself by the foundational concept of 'unconscious representation', analytic theory is organised around a paradox: it seeks to maintain, within the same concept, both the idea of a representation located in the unconscious and, by definition, cut off from consciousness, and the opposite idea, contained in the term representation, of 'presenting before the eyes or before the mind'. It is this semantic irreconcilability that radically differentiates analytic theory from any other discipline. Dialogue with other sciences will thus pose apparently insurmountable problems, not so much, as it has often been thought, due to resistance in scientists towards psychoanalysis, originating in their own repressions, but due to this conception that is deeply incompatible with the rationality necessary for all positivist scientific thought, at least in the form it has taken up to a short time ago. Perhaps now, with the revolution introduced by relativity, quantum theory and their repercussions, profoundly modifying scientific thinking, dialogue has become possible between analysts and scientists. We like to imagine that analytic theory, with its major concept of unconscious representation, can be the first model, at the heart of the evolution of scientific thought, of a new conception of science that is capable of breaking with the limits imposed by preconscious logic, temporo-spatiality and the ego's need for tangible evidence.

Caught then as it is, between one definition, that of the delegation of an *Ucs.*, by definition unknown and inaccessible in itself, and another, that of the reproduction of an external world, the study of representation and, consequently, of the irrepresentable, poses psychoanalytic theory with considerable problems – namely, those of knowledge, consciousness, and perception, all notions which been given little treatment in psychoanalytic literature.

In 1938, in line with the spirit of science that was already modern, asserted that:

> In the meantime we try to increase the efficiency of our sense organs to the furthest possible extent by artificial aids; but it may be expected that all such efforts will fail to effect the ultimate outcome. Reality will always remain 'unknowable'.
>
> Freud, 1938b: S.E. XXIII, 196

This observation is still valid today, in spite of the spectacular progress of science, as Bernard d'Espagnat (1990, 1994) concludes. The same can also be said of all those in other domains who endeavour to approach reality. The description made by the Nobel Prize novelist, Camilo José Cela (1990), is exemplary:

> But things are never described as they are, but only as they are perceived. The essence of a bit of grass, for instance, remains a mystery for man, an inaccessible arcanum. And yet we define it and reduce it to its green colour, its form, its flexibility or its bitter taste.

And so we are faced, not without a certain sense of perplexity, with the problem of a reality that is 'unknowable', while at the same time being the source of our perceptions. What is more, this source of perceptions is charged with a sense of self-evidence, of certitude as to the existence of the lost object, of unshakeable truth. In other words, however 'unknowable' reality is for man, it nonetheless brings him a certain type of knowledge from which he can no longer free himself. It could be said that, just as the falcon lured by the bait returns to the hand, the psyche is trained by the lure of the sense organs.

The scientist has recourse to particular languages, like mathematics, in order to be able to conceptualise certain external elements that are independent of the sense organs, whether they are the universe or the infinitely small. Indeed, every man uses word-presentations, whether absolute or infinite, that have a meaning for him, although he is incapable of imagining their content. In parallel to this, insofar as his internal world is concerned, he is faced with experiences that he cannot easily represent, and poetry or music will be the means of approaching them. It is a matter, in all cases, of the limits of our systems of representation. But this is only of relative interest to psychoanalysts, for the specificity of analytic research resides, above all, in the study of the *Ucs.* and, in a more general way, in the study of psychical inscriptions more than in the study of their means of expression.

We know that studying the mechanisms of neurosis leads us to the comprehension of our psychic functioning in relation to the instances and causalities between the representative contents that are part of the neurotic structure. In this context, the term irrepresentable defines a content with a meaning that can eventually be named but not represented – words like absolute or infinite would be the model for this. But analytic practice teaches us that when listening to the whole range of the experience of the session, without limiting this to the comprehension of the underlying relations of the neurosis, the irrepresentable becomes something different, that is, neither content nor meaning. The very term irrepresentable turns out to be improper from this perspective. In fact, in this wider context of the session, what we understand by irrepresentable can only be signified in terms of a negativity.

In *Inhibitions, Symptoms and Anxiety* (1925a: *S.E.* XX, 170) Freud writes: 'Thus, the first determinant of anxiety, which the ego itself introduces, is loss of the perception of the object (which is equated with loss of the object itself).' Following this model, and extending Freud's conception, we wrote at the beginning of this book that the loss of the perception of the object cannot be traumatic as long as its representation is maintained; that it is not the loss of the perception of the object but the loss of its representation, the danger of *non-representation*, which is the mark of infantile distress.

We can see, then, how the problem of knowledge, that is, of knowing what the relations are between the observer and the observed, between the inside and the outside, boils down to an investigation of the laws that organise the relations between perception and representation. The problem of knowledge necessarily entails the study of perception, which is inseparable from the study of consciousness.

This being the case, the original question concerning psychoanalysts and their way of envisaging irrepresentability, now returns in another form: is the notion irrepresentable simply the sign of a sense of impotence in relation to our current knowledge and, in this case, can the irrepresentable be surpassed each time that our knowledge progresses? Or, on the contrary, is it irrevocably the ultimate representation possible of our psychical reality, marking the limits of what can be represented, and of thinking at its most abstract?)

A brief reminder on perception (act /content)

Throughout Freud's work, perception as well as its definition suffer, as we know, from a certain lack of rigour. In this, his work merely reflects a problem of a general nature – namely, that none of the different definitions of perception is entirely satisfying. Accordingly, it is sometimes envisaged as the very act of the sense organs and sometimes as content. The latter can thus be considered in psychoanalysis as a signifying content referring to an infantile sexual theory and to a basic complex of infantile psychoneurosis. Is it because of this diversification, this indetermination, that, after Freud, psychoanalysts were not tempted to study perception? At any rate, the real difficulty is probably due to the specific nature of our psychoanalytic discipline which is essentially constructed as a theory of representation and, further, of unconscious representation; that is to say, of repressed phantasy charged with prohibited instinctual impulses. It is a theoretical corpus whose formulations are particularly far removed from any psychological notion, such as perception.

However, at certain moments in the development of his theory, Freud was himself obliged to introduce the problem of perception. Apart from the 'Project for a scientific psychology' (1895), a pre-analytic text, and *The Interpretation of Dreams* (1900), which inaugurated psychoanalytic theory, it was above all during the 1914–18 war, when he was confronted with the study of traumatic neurosis and with the hallucinatory repetition in dreams of a traumatic perception. Then during the 1920s, Freud set about the difficult task of establishing a meta-psychology of the distinction inside–outside, through the study of psychosis initially, followed shortly after by the study of fetishism and the disavowal of perception involved. This shows *a posteriori* that psychosis and perversion were of less interest to Freud in themselves than as means of broaching the relations of the psyche with the real world. (For more details on the relation of Freudian theory to perception, see Green, 1999c: 202, 211.)

Today, psychoanalysts are at last concerning themselves with the problem of perception, led not, as one might suppose, by the expansion of cognitivism, but by a movement specific to their own preoccupations which has its roots in Freud's reflections on traumatic neurosis and the disavowal of perception. In fact, far from being the initiator, the expansion of cognitivism may be said, rather, to have had an inhibiting role for psychoanalysts. For perception involves a risk of deviating towards a new model of the treatment where observation of the concrete, of products arising solely from a relation based on the concreteness of the sense organs – like the psychoanalyst who, in good faith, observes attentively the facial expression of his analysand in order to discover an affect, a hidden meaning – would take precedence over the free-floating attention allowing the analyst to listen to the analysand's unconscious phantasy and, in a more general way, to the changes of levels in the different modes of representation (*représentance*) of the psychoanalyst's thinking. In short, such a research model would sweep aside the determining and organising components of the analytic process that are inaccessible to any form of direct observation, however fine it may be. In this respect Winnicott's practice is exemplary. Even though he was always very fond of baby observation and extremely attentive to the play activities of children, he always maintained that it was the transference, exclusively, that held the key to the understanding of the psyche. It is not by observing the sleeper, even by means of the most sophisticated recording techniques, that the dream becomes visible, even less its meaning.

There is a risk of going adrift each time one neglects the fact that psycho-analysis is the fruit of a very particular evolution in the practice of Freud who was distancing himself increasingly from medicine and phenomenology. A series of renunciations concerning perception gave rise to psychoanalysis – the medical exam, hypnosis, suggestion, pressures applied to the forehead were all abandoned – and then, Freud's stroke of genius in withdrawing out of the patient's view, the analytic setting comes into being and is maintained on the condition that it is determined by not being able to see the analyst, by the fact that the perceptions of the sense organs are reduced to a minimum, so as to facilitate the emergence of internal psychic life, the dimension of representation and phantasy. This places psychoanalysis in a specific and thoroughly original position for studying perception.

In reality, there is surprisingly much less distance today between psycho-analysis and certain trends of cognitivism and neurobiology than there used to be. Especially when one thinks of the 1970s, and the temptation at that time, particularly in the USA, with Hubert Dreyfus, of translating psychoanalysis into cognitivist terms. By establishing an oversimplified connection, to say the least, between psychoanalysis and cognitivism, the Freudian notion of representation was reduced and confused with that of Brentano, on the pretext that Freud had attended his courses in Vienna. And Dreyfus went so far as to associate the tendency towards fulfilment, specific to the representations located in the system *Ucs.*, with the idea of intentionality, an idea which, as we know, also came from Brentano and constituted thereafter the basis of the thinking of another pupil of the same epoch, Husserl. To come to the conclusion, on the basis of these facts, that, in its very conception, psychoanalysis is cognitivist, proves the readiness of some to ignore the Freudian theory of the unconscious, whether it is the *Ucs.* as a system of the first topography, or, as from 1923 (*The Ego and the Id*), the *Ucs.* integrated within a much larger whole, the id, a new psychical agency in which drive activity is then described without being linked to representational systems. And even if one takes into account the fact that 'an instinct can never become an object of consciousness – only the idea that represents the instinct can' (1915b: *S.E.* XIV, 177) – one cannot forget the role of affect, which can also be a representative of the drive. Things become more complex if, following Green (1986b), one accepts that: 'the object reveals the drive'. Far from being a mere reproduction of a perception, and notwithstanding certain passages in Freud that tend in this direction, Freudian representation is considered today by the majority of authors as a vast network of meaning constituted, under the influence of infantile sexuality, through transformation of the arepresented instinctual activity of the id. The recent reduction operated by Erdelyi (1985), cited by Varela (1988), applying cognitivist terminology to the Freudian concept of repression, is yet another outrageous simplification. As for the ideas of Davidson and Dennett and the notion of a 'mind without a subject', we refer the reader to the excellent critique offered by André Green in his article 'Philosophie de l'esprit et psychanalyse' (Green, 1996b).

Fortunately, an important current of theoreticians from the cognitive sciences has become increasingly aware that, however neurobiological and rooted in so-called objective information perception may be, its theorisation cannot for all that escape the conditions of the very particular relations established between what is perceived and the perceiver and between what is perceived and knowledge. In this sense, the majority of scientists today accept that, while perception certainly depends on sensory receptors, it cannot be confined to them. Local physiological responses are far from being capable alone of defining the complexity of the perceptual process that, including the psychical, has to be understood at a global level. Psychoanalysts are not the only ones to assert this; recent works of neurobiologists, those of Ecclés and Edelman, as well as those of Francis Crick, come to similar conclusions. Indeed, at the present time, most authors agree in considering that perception cannot be conceived as a simple entry of information in the central nervous system: 'it is the brain and not the environment which decides what we see' (Barlow, 1990, cited by Bourguignon, 1994). Jeannerod (1993) was more precise: 'It is not the environment which solicits the nervous system, shapes it or reveals it. On the contrary, it is the subject and his brain which question the environment, inhabit it gradually, and finally master it.' The same is true of the cognitive sciences: J. P. Dupuy (1994) points out that, in 1948, McCulloch had already discovered that the eye only transmits to the brain a fraction of the information that it receives; that the organism has to 'pay in information' for gaining access to the certainty that there is a world that exists outside us. According to McCulloch, this loss is in fact programmed; and, according to Pitts, what we are dealing with here is a law of nature the existence of which translates its very great redundancy (McCulloch, 1948–53). What is more, a tendency that is currently making its weight felt within the cognitive sciences proposes a functional approach that even goes as far as formulating the hypothesis that perceptual processes are characterised by psychical 'constructions'. Thus Francisco Varela (1988) asserts that: 'Perceiving is the equivalent of constructing invariants by a sensory-motor coupling which permits the organism to survive in its environment.' And, in 1994, this same author concluded that the basis of cognition is an autonomous 'global activity': 'It is this autonomous activity of the system that needs to be put at the centre of our investigations, rather than our entries . . . The key point consists in considering as central, and not as a secondary problem, the question of the interpretation, the emergence of meaning . . . It is no longer a question of the information which is given, but of information as something which is literally in-formed (formed from within); and it is this creation of meaning as an autonomous activity which is capable of accounting for what is most interesting in knowledge.'

One cannot be more explicit and the psychoanalyst can only be delighted by this perspective, for it corresponds to a path that psychoanalysis has explored since its creation, namely, hallucination. An explanation is necessary here. Owing to the fact that dream hallucination excludes perception, there is a tendency to oppose perception and hallucination or to reduce hallucination to an error of judgement concerning perception. However, it is being understood increasingly that the relations between them are far from simple. Thus very recently, Jeannerod, who directs the Inserm (Institut national de la santé et de la recherche médicale) research unit 'Vision et Motility', declared in an interview for the journal *La Recherche* (Jeannerod, 1996b) that, by using techniques of cerebral imagery applied to patients who were hallucinating, he had been able to discover that 'hallucinations activate the primary zones of perception, the very ones which process external sensory information . . . whereas one might have imagined that hallucinations activate neither the receptive zones, nor the executive zones, but rather the central regions managing "second hand" information . . . This means that perceiving an object and imagining it is in the end the same thing.'

This astonishing relation between perception and hallucination has not escaped René Angelergues (1992), who asserts that: 'Perception is hallucination.' René Diatkine taught us a long time ago, in the form of jest, that perception is a perversion of hallucination. In the same vein, we have been interested in the idea defended by John Steward (1994) that, 'the capacities of cognition are ultimately hallucinatory'. The same idea may be found in one of the conclusions established by Isabelle Billiard (1994), concerning the meetings of a multi-disciplinary workgroup in which she urges psychoanalysts to 'reconsider from a different point of view the question of the primal mode of being of psychical activity, that is, its hallucinatory capacity'. This is of special interest to us because, through purely psychoanalytic means of reflection and through the experience of treatments of neurotics and borderline cases, this idea was one we also defended during a UNESCO Conference, in 1989. We insisted then on the need for analytic theory to introduce the notion of the hallucinatory as a process beyond or short of the representational and the perceptual of which it is both a source and a result. Nothing in the psyche would take place without the participation of the hallucinatory, including perceptual processes.

The relation perception–consciousness

Although there is undeniably a general tendency in psychoanalysis, even in Freud, to reduce perception to an elementary function, to a non-complex unity, the notion is at the same time used in other senses: self-perception, endopsychic perception, internal perception, or again perception specific to the id.

As for the notion of consciousness, it is defined in *The Interpretation of Dreams*, as we have already recalled, as 'a sense-organ for the perception of psychical qualities' (*S.E.* V, 615). As an organ, it remains, throughout almost the whole of Freud's work, united with perception constituting one and the same system, the *Pcs.–Cs*, situated at the periphery of the psychical apparatus of which 'consciousness is the subjective side of one part of the physical processes in the nervous system, namely of the perceptual processes' (Project, *S.E.* I, 311). Then, once he was involved in the study of the unconscious, Freud no longer really interested himself in either of them and they were practically left on one side until 1915. Then in the space of ten days – according to the *Standard Edition*, between 23 April and 4 May exactly – Freud simultaneously wrote *Mourning and Melancholia* (1917b) and 'A metapsychological supplement to the theory of dreams' (1917a) (and they were published in the same edition of the *Internationale Zeitschrift Psychoanalysus*). These were two fundamental texts and their confrontation opened the way towards a new theoretical conception. In the latter, the union of perception and consciousness is asserted, but an inversion occurs in what Freud now calls the system consciousness–perception (*Bewusstsein– Wahrnehmung*), giving priority to *Cs.* over psychical processes. This was probably the consequence of a new objective that Freud had given himself by writing the 'Metapsychological supplement'. Instead of focusing his interest on the dream content and its interpretation, as he had done until then, and being concerned to acquaint himself increasingly with the functioning of repression and that of the system *Ucs.*, he now gave priority to the processual, to the study of the hallucinatory quality of dreams, by linking the latter up with the theory of narcissism elaborated one year earlier. Dream hallucination was thus no longer understood solely as a product of formal or topographical regression; it acquired the status of a narcissistic process.[1]

We get a measure of the complexity of the Freudian approach – which never falls into the temptation of simplification and often treats the subject at a certain level of explicit elaboration while, at the same time, remaining open implicitly to other solutions – if we take into account the fact that, during these same ten days, in 'Mourning and melancholia', which truly complements the 'Metapsychological supplement', Freud tried to situate the notion of the object at the centre of analytic theory; that is, he opened the latter to the link with the external world. Thus, with these two articles which close his papers on metapsychology, initiating a notion of perception closely bound up with narcissism, hallucinatory in nature, and open to the world, a psychoanalytic approach to traumatic neurosis became possible and the premises of the second topography were laid.

After an extension in *Beyond the Pleasure Principle* (1920), where one again comes across the priority of the system *Cs.*, it was in *The Ego and the Id* (1923a) that perception took precedence definitively. There it is either a question solely of the system *Pcs.* or of an inversion of the formula used in the 'Metapsychological supplement' of the system *Pcpt.–Cs.* (*Wahrnehmung–Bewusstsein*). The articles that follow, i.e. those devoted to the loss of reality in neuroses and psychoses or the article on the 'mystic writing-pad', or again 'Negation' (1925b), bear witness to Freud's growing interest in perception. This evolution was confirmed and concluded in *New Introductory Lectures on Psychoanalysis* (1932b) in which Freud, studying this subject for the last time, openly grants perception its autonomy, the right to be a system in itself, the system *Pcpt.* (*Wahrnehmung*) and maintains, as he does in the Project, that 'during its functioning the phenomenon of consciousness arises in it' (*S.E.* XXII, 75); that is to say, consciousness becomes a quality of the system *Pcs*. The schema at the end of the chapter is evidence of this; it reproduces the schema in *The Ego and the Id* (1923a), although consciousness does not appear in it.

But it was his investigations into the perversion of fetishism (1927a) which would offer him the possibility of really approaching the connection between the ego and reality and of coming to terms with the complexity of the role of perception. By constituting a fetishistic object, the fetishist acknowledges in his own way the missing penis in a woman and thus accords sense perception its full importance; but, at the same time, he retains, in his endopsychic perception, something irrepresentable and terrifying from his infantile sexuality, the anti-traumatic outcome of which is the belief that women do have a penis. Gilbert Diatkine (1994) has already pointed out that Freud's conception of perception then undergoes a change. In fact, due to this possible division between sense perception and endopsychic perception, the study of perception can no longer be reduced to one of a sensory content inasmuch as the endopsychic perception can simultaneously have a different content.

The ambiguity of the notion of consciousness considered both as a system and as a quality was thus removed; henceforth consciousness could be conceived of as that which, during the functioning of the system *Pcs*., detaches itself from it and, momentarily, becomes quality.

An important question persists nonetheless: how are we to define perception as a system, to describe its dynamics and, in particular, its relations with consciousness, when perception and consciousness do not lend themselves at all easily to temporo-spatial metaphors, to being part of a schema, their main characteristic being immediateness, atemporality, the absence of permanent investment? Just as, for the spectator, 'the dancer and the dance are one', perception and consciousness cannot establish a distinction between what is perceived and the process under way. The problem is one of knowing whether the metapsychological apparatus, as Freud handed it down to us, is really able to take this into account

Freud was certainly not taken in by this problem or by the manner in which he was obliged – courageously, considering the scientific thinking of his time and the rigorous character he wanted to give to the metapsychology – to leave certain concepts somewhat vague, with a possibility of contradiction, if he wanted to pass on to us the most exact approach to the functioning of the psyche. Indeed, the true coherence of the metapsychology and, more broadly, of Freud's thought, resides as much in its rigorous character as in its capacity to integrate a tolerance for openness to new possibilities and developments. This is undeniably the case for the evolution concerning the character of perception and consciousness.

As we know, consciousness, like the sense organs, is only excitable under certain conditions; without their presence, it is incapable of perceiving psychical activity; it does not even have the slightest suspicion as to its existence. These conditions which are capable of awakening the quality consciousness depend on a phenomenon whose essential aspect is the investment of attention, the link with presentations, those of words principally; and more exactly to 'memories of words', says Freud, thereby linking the problem of the quality consciousness with the system of memory, in short, with the inevitable temporo-spatiality without which the phenomenon of consciousness cannot occur. Thus the exacerbation of the investment of attention maintains a strong link with the quality consciousness. But that is not all: what is important, says Freud in the *Outline* is that:

> [S]ince memory-traces can become conscious just as perceptions do, especially through their association with residues of speech, the possibility arises of a confusion which would lead to a mistaking of reality. The ego guards itself against this possibility by the institution of *reality-testing* . . .
>
> S.E. XXIII, 199

The distinction representation–perception is a permanent and arduous task of the ego and all the more essential in that it is erased periodically during regressive states in sleep when, as is made clear in 'Metapsychological supplement to the theory of dreams', as the system *Cs.* is uncathected and reality testing is abandoned, 'the excitations which, independently of the state of sleep, have entered on the path of regression, will find that path clear as far as the system *Cs.* Where they will count as undisputed reality' (*S.E.* XIV, 234).

And Freud himself immediately acknowledges in a footnote the theoretical impasse implied by this observation:

> Here the principle of the insusceptibility to excitation of uncathected systems appears to be invalidated in the case of the system *Cs.* (*Pcpt.*). But it may be a question of only the *partial* removal of cathexis; and for the perceptual system in especial we must assume many conditions of excitation which are widely divergent from those of other systems.
>
> S.E. XIV, 234

(There exist, then, two ways of achieving endoperception: either in the waking state, via residues, the sensory residues of words and things, or in the retrogressive state when excitations are subjected to another treatment.)

The retrogressive psychic state, momentarily cut off from these cathexes, represents a certain perceptual quality that can also manifest itself in daytime, notably in the regressive conditions of the session. With a 'partial withdrawal of cathexis from the system *Cs.*', accompanied by a 'partial' abandonment of reality testing, a quite original quality can occur during the day – namely, a capacity for intelligibility, which, without the participation of primary and secondary processes, beyond sensory experience, without having right of access, along the forward, progressive path, to the quality of representation and to the system *Pcs.-Cs.*, offers a direct path of access to endopsychic perception, to the accessibility of certain mental 'zones' that are otherwise unreachable.

In the 1980s, with the study of border concepts (*concepts-limites*) such as negative hallucination (Green, 1983), the perception of the lack (Denise Braunschweig and Michel Fain (Braunschweig and Fain, 1975; Fain, 1982)), the zero imago and apophatism (Francis Pasche, 1983), or again, our own concept of *non-representation* (Botella, C. and S., 1983b), there appeared in French analytic literature what might be described as a relativisation of the stability of the topographies and of their dependence both on the direction and the scale of time and on the hegemony of the content; for all these concepts have emerged from research into the erasure or collapse of the systems of representations.[2]

The usefulness of privileging the study of these border concepts becomes all the clearer now that we know, since our study of *non-representation*, that the absence of representable content does not mean an absence of an event. What was suggested by the evolution of Freud's thought now becomes clear. In order to study perception and consciousness, as well as the deep connections between perception and representation, we can no longer continue to limit our thinking to the classic conception of the psychical apparatus and to the specific points of view of the metapsychology.

From perception to the perceptual process

We were saying earlier just how imprecise the notion of perception remained in Freud's work. It inevitably stands in a difficult relationship with analytic theory owing to the fact that the latter is centred on representation, leaving it only a marginal place. Located at the limits of our theory, disliked by psychoanalysts, entirely ignored by the index of the *Abstracts of the Standard Edition*, only figuring in *The Language of Psychoanalysis* by Laplanche and Pontalis under the heading of 'consciousness' (psychological), and considered by many as a notion that should be left to psychologists, neurophysiologists or cognitivists, it has never been the object of a truly psychoanalytic study.

In terms of content, its status is relatively clear: namely, a traumatic content or a primal content necessary to the organisation of the psyche. Freud's insistence on the role of perception for the constitution of the principal phantasies, castration and the primal scene – for one, the sight of the difference between the sexes; for the other, certain evocative signs – bears witness to the importance that he accorded to it. The two phases of the complex of castration comprise, not only a gap in time and consequently a work of memory, and thus of elaboration, but also the participation of the simultaneous perception of the present and the past. In order for phantasy to organise itself at the heart of the infantile neurosis on which it is founded, it is indispensable to be able to recall seeing the difference between the sexes at the moment of hearing the threat that had hitherto been inoperative; or conversely, to recall hearing the threat of castration on seeing the difference between the sexes that until then had remained indifferent. And if the reality of perception does not appear in ontogenesis, phylogenesis will take charge of it.

Let us return, however, to one of the major problems, already raised, that Freud handed down to us: How are we to conceive of perception as a system, that is, as an integral part of the psychical apparatus like the other systems, preconscious and unconscious, when the term system presupposes the idea of a 'set of elements which depend reciprocally on each other in such a way as to form an organised whole' (Lalande) that does not correspond to the nature of the relations of perception? Instead, Green (1993: 212–13) proposes that:

[T]he perceptual quality be considered from the angle of 'making present to oneself' which infers . . . implying a change of state and a plurality of modes of existence, each of which can take over from the other, without linking these to a 'conscious' phenomenon. We shall thus be freed from this aspect of immediateness which perceptual experience comes up against in contrast to the discursiveness of understanding. Perception is discursive, just as thought needs to become perceptible to be be thought about.

In order to cover this vast field of the perceptual quality, we will make use of a more general term, that of the perceptual, which we will employ in the sense of *The Interpretation of Dreams* (1900: 499) based on a citation already used, but whose importance obliges us to repeat it:

Our waking (preconscious) thinking behaves towards any perceptual material with which it meets in just the same way in which the function we are considering behaves towards the content of dreams [i.e secondary revision]. It is the nature of our waking thought to establish order in material of that kind, to set up relations in it and to make it conform to our expectations of an intelligible whole.

This, then, is how Freud freed himself right away from the limits of a psychological conception and opened up the metapsychology of perception to a conception akin to that of dreams, to be more exact of the dream-work; to what might be called the '*work of the perceptual*'. We subscribe to this, while nonetheless preferring to use, instead of work, the notion of *process*. By that we mean a set of phenomena presenting a certain unity, while taking account of the fact that perceptual processes depend on a psychic reality that includes as much the perception of the sense organs as endopsychic perception.[3]

The new understanding furnished by the study of fetishism, namely, the possibility of psychic functioning operating through the simultaneity of two perceptual processes, with different meaning and content, would at last enable Freud to analyse, in 1936, his disturbance of memory on the Acropolis that had occurred in 1904, more than 30 years earlier. It is one of the major texts of the Freudian corpus in which all the complexity of a multidimensional psychic universe could now be revealed in the brilliant analysis that Freud carried out so meticulously, highlighting the relationship, in simultaneity, between (a) memory, the endoperception of a recollection, 'So all this really *does* exist, just as we learnt at school!'; (b) the barely stifled disavowal of the perception of the sense organs, 'What I see here is not real'; and (c) 'feelings of derealization' which he calls 'complicated processes' and which are equivalent to phenomena of a hallucinatory order. At the end of this analysis of this disturbance of memory, protecting him from a split, an alteration of the self-presentation, Freud discovered just how intense the investment of an object-representation, the loved father, could be, and became aware of the sense of guilt involved in surpassing him. An immoderate infantile wish was at the origin of the onset of the disturbance, of the simultaneity of these different hallucinatory-perceptual processes, memory, disavowal, sensations of derealisation, and the cause of the rupture of the equilibrium of what we will call, in the next chapter, the *symmetry representation–perception* – a situation akin to the case of the analysand we reported earlier under the title 'the smell of fir'.

'THE LOST OBJECT OF HALLUCINATORY SATISFACTION'

The concrete is the abstract
rendered familiar through use.
                    P. Langevin

The strange encounter between the orchid and the wasp

In order to help the reader get a feeling of how difficult the metapsychological approach of perception seems to us to be, we will refer to Rémy Chauvin (1992) who, in *La biologie de l'esprit*, describes the encounter between a flower, the orchid and a species of wasp, the Gorytes.

In this species, the male is born before the female and searches desperately for a partner until the moment it notices on an orchid's corolla a rather precise form representing a wasp, in its own image. And when it settles on the corolla, a smell similar to that of the females in its species rises from the bottom of the orchid. Without hesitating, the Gorytes plunges in and starts wiggling. By stirring up the masses of pollen, it makes them stick to the pistil and the flower is pollinated. It is not until a month later that the female Gorytes are born, but the orchids have already faded.

Such, then, with their overtly sexual content, are the unexpected relations between the perceiving Gorytes and the perceived orchid! What sort of perception, what sort of memory, what sort of temporality are we dealing with here? Is the relation between the perceiver and the perceived one of a discovery? The orchid may have already discovered the Gorytes in the past; the Gorytes, for its part, does not discover the orchid, it only perceives its own image in it.

'You would not seek for me if you did not possess me', runs Pascal's astonishing formula in his *Pensées* (1966). Comparable to the story of the Gorytes, the drama of perception is that man is only able to perceive when he is goaded by the absence of his object of satisfaction, when he is searching for an object, lost forever, of which he will only be able to find again a mark, a misleading message, a lure.

The gap between what is perceived by the perceiver and the object cannot be bridged. *The perceiving subject will forever be affected by the failure of the hallucinatory solution, by the mark of his own existence in the object of satisfaction that has been lost forever.* When he first opens his eyes on to the world, he searches desperately for his object satisfaction, but will only find the mark of its loss, deluding himself in the joy he experiences in front of his own mirror image or in being persecuted by the double. If one thinks of the perceiving subject, Lacan is right: 'The substance of the subject is nothing other than the *jouissance* from which he is cut off.')

This marking by the 'lost-object-of-the-hallucinatory-satisfaction' constantly represents a truly instinctual appeal to which the perceiver is continuously subjected – except when he achieves the retrogressive performance of gaining access to the royal road of the hallucinatory satisfaction of dreams. The instinctual appeal, kept in a state of alert night and day, seems to be destined to find satisfaction by hallucinatory means. Even its fulfilment in action will only have a real value of realisation on the condition that it is accompanied, reduplicated, at a hallucinatory level; that is, on the condition that the perceiver can find the trace in it of his own existence that has been lost in the failure of the hallucinatory object satisfaction. *his own existence ≈ his desire*

(The relation between the perceiver and the 'lost-object-of-the-hallucinatory-satisfaction' is obviously not of the same order as that of the subject–object relation at the basis of every explanation of the dynamics of neurosis. Indifferent to temporality, localisation and conflicts, the relation between the perceiver and the 'lost-object-of-the-hallucinatory-satisfaction' does not produce any psychic work, neither is it the product of any such work, any more than it is at the origin of a development in space time. Its effects are more comparable to an expansion than progress; they represent the possibility of suspension and extension of the limits between inside and outside, between the ego and the world, between the *déjà vu* and the unknown, the familiar and the unfamiliar. The relation between the perceiver and the 'lost-object-of-the-hallucinatory-satisfaction' opens up the path to the perception of a lack, the basis of the quality consciousness, of all perception, whether the object is a representation, concrete object, phantasy or dream.

The perceiver is neither really the subject nor the 'I'; it is close to the body ego, to a cathexis of something bodily associated with the 'lost-object-of-the-hallucinatory-satisfaction'. It represents the auto-erotic potential of the retrogressive path where every idea 'is turned back into the sensory image from which it was originally derived' (Freud, 1900: 543).

It is this hallucinatory, sensory quality of the perceiver that makes the existence, the reality, of what is perceived evident. For its part, the 'lost-object-of-the-hallucinatory-

satisfaction' is, in itself, closer to the trace left in the very flesh of the perceiver, than to something separate, autonomous. Unknowable in itself, it is clearly not in the order of an object in the usual analytic sense; it may more readily be compared with a groove, a concave mark revealing the perceiver–perceived.)

After these first steps towards a metapsychological understanding of the psychical activity of perception that is as indivisible as it is complex – first steps guided by the astonishing story of the Gorytes, a story that has the function in our research of a sort of dream whose work of figurability has subjected our understanding to 'a necessity to combine all the sources which have acted as stimuli into a single unity' (Freud, 1900: 179) – we are going to tackle the problem of perception by means of the opposite procedure. In what follows, we will transform this global process of the indissociable triad perceiver–perceived–'lost-object-of-the-hallucinatory-satisfaction' into temporal sequences, while bearing in mind Freud's warning in connection with the subject of auto-erotism and narcissism, to take as 'a defect . . . in the interests of lucidity, the conceptual distinction between the two phases . . . as though it were also a separation in time' (Freud 1905b: 194). As early as *The Interpretation of Dreams*, Freud had postulated the existence of an original experience of satisfaction whose conception is based on the idea that the state of internal tension, of distress (*Hilflosigkeit*), outside help and satisfaction constitute a unity. The unitary vision of this conception is particularly clear in the famous footnote in 'Formulations on the two principles of mental functioning' where Freud defends the idea:

> of an organisation which was a slave to the pleasure principle and neglected the reality of the external world . . . The employment of a fiction like this is, however, justified when one considers that the infant – provided one includes with it the care it receives from its mother – does almost realize a psychical system of this kind.
>
> *S.E.* XII, 220

One therefore has to ask oneself if, in such an organisation, the real object can really be experienced as existing on the outside, as being separate. In the section of *The Interpretation of Dreams* devoted to the experience of satisfaction, Freud eludes this difficulty. Admittedly, he speaks of 'outside help' and of a 'perception of nourishment', but this does not answer our questions as to the nature of the object that comes into play here. Let us recall, rather, that an essential element of this experience is the appearance of a particular perception: 'The mnemic image of which remains associated thenceforward with the memory trace of the excitation produced by the need . . . Next time this need arises a psychical impulse will at once emerge which will seek to re-cathect the mnemic image of the perception and to re-evoke the perception itself.' 'This wishful activation', Freud notes elsewhere, 'produces the same thing as a perception – namely, a hallucination' (Freud, 1895: *S.E.* I, 319).

Given that, by definition, there is absolutely no distinction between the actual 'specific action' and its hallucinatory production, should we not conclude that, at the beginning, this 'outside help' cannot be experienced as coming from outside? Consequently, is there not a case for supposing, especially if we want to stick as closely as possible to Freud's conception, that initially, the irreducible nature of the distress is the consequence from the newborn baby's point of view, not of the absence of specific action, but of the loss of hallucinatory satisfaction? That, in reality, is it the loss of the object of the hallucinatory satisfaction that gives rise to distress and not the loss of the real object? And further, that it is through searching for 'the object of the hallucinatory satisfaction', for this first 'lost' object, that the real external object will be discovered with the experience of a rediscovery. Indeed Freud (1925a) tells us:

> At birth no object existed and so no object could be missed. Anxiety was the only reaction that occurred. Since then repeated situations of satisfaction have created an object out of the mother; and this object, whenever the infant feels a need, receives an intense cathexis which might be described as a 'longing' one.
>
> S.E. XV, 170

It is thus indeed the child who creates as much the perception as the representation of the mother, in place of the 'lost-object-of-the-hallucinatory satisfaction'.

The primal trace of the lack

We think that the transition from the state of tension to the hallucinatory state constitutes a model which marks the whole of psychic life definitively and permanently, erasing the difference between the order of the primal and the order of functioning. In this mythical moment of 'implosion' of the dawn of psychic life, reproducing itself, from our metapsychological standpoint, at each instant of all psychic life, there is from the outset a transformation of the state of tension into a hallucinatory state and, at the same time, a 'split', which together provoke the detachment of the quality perception–consciousness at the heart of sensory experience, at the heart of what should have been a satisfaction of the need by the 'lost-object-of-the-hallucinatory-satisfaction', in place of the latter. The quality consciousness thus unfolds against the background of a hallucinatory perception of the lack of the object satisfaction. This initial perception–consciousness is not the same as the perception of the external world via the sense organs.

The primal perception is in the order of a self-perception. Freud had intimated as much in 1915, in *Instincts and their Vicissitudes*, when he put forward the idea that 'for the beginning of its activity the scopophilic instinct is auto-erotic' (1915b: *S.E.* XIV, 130). The hallucinatory perception of the lack of the object satisfaction, the basis of self-perception–consciousness, may be said to constitute the matrix of all reflexivity, which we have already depicted by the ternary relation perceiver–perceived–lost object. This first form of reflexivity faces us with the problem of an initial entanglement of the instinctual and the perceptual and of their links with the erotogenic zones and the sense organs.

In order to be able to think about this initial entanglement, including the instinctual and the perceptual, *it seems necessary to postulate the existence of a primal trace, namely of the lack; an indiscernible trace between the loss of the object and the loss of the hallucinatory satisfaction. It is a negative inscription taking the form of an incessant hallucinatory deployment without the possibility of discharge, of a hallucinatory quest that is all the more desperate in that what determines it is indeed the lack itself. The original perception is, at the same time, a movement and an impression of this movement activated by the pulverisation of the model 'experience–object of the hallucinatory satisfaction'; it both exerts the value of an instinctual source and captures the impulse, merging with it.*

The primal mark of the lack will be decisive in the inscriptions of the recognition of the difference between the sexes and the sexual infantile theory of castration, reorganising all the cathexes and offering thenceforward a causality, an explanation, for every perception of the lack, every sense of the lack, re-inscribing them within a history of the object. As a result, in our analytic practice, this hallucinatory movement, constitutive of perception, cannot be distinguished from the infantile sexual cathexes occupying the foreground.

In this domain, where things are not clearly distinguishable, there also arises the fascinating problem of the link between such a negative inscription, arising from the ontogenetic evolution of the loss of 'the object-hallucinatory-satisfaction' marking the psyche definitively and the Freudian idea that man's psyche is constituted under the stamp of phylogenetic structures, of matrices that are already there, transcending it; namely, of primal phantasies.

Owing to its nature, we are necessarily unaware of the characteristics of the *primal trace*; nevertheless, by likening it to *non-representation*, we can say that it is not that of a memory that can be recollected and that such an inscription can only come back with the character of something present, either hallucinatory or real. Freud says as much in his letter to Fliess dated 4 December 1896, where he calls *Wz* [*Wahrnehmungszeichen* (indication of perception)] 'the first registration of the perceptions; it is quite incapable of consciousness and is arranged according to associations by simultaneity'; in contrast, he continues, 'with the registration arranged according to other, perhaps causal, relations' of *Ub* [*Unbewusstsein* (unconsciousness)] (Masson, 1985: 208).

From what we have just said, *it follows that hallucinatory experience, the primal trace and the ternary relation perceiver–perceived–lost object, are different forms or facets of one and the same psychic reality. Likewise, infantile trauma, non-representation with its negativity and its hallucinatory tendency, converge with the primal trace and its relations.*

171

Each night, there is a re-actualisation of this trace. In a primordial conflict, the dreamer's psyche has to survive between the wish for a limitless narcissistic regression and the danger of *non-representation*. When we abandon ourselves to the regression of sleep and withdraw cathexis progressively from external objects and their representations, we are in danger of triggering the anxiety of a total loss of representation. We are thus exposed in our sleep to the risk of traumatic *non-representation*, which tends to reawaken the absolute distress of the lack contained in the *primal trace*. From the loss of the real object to the *original trace*, the activated hallucinatory movement will be resolved either by a brutal awakening at the level of perception or by an attempt at hallucinatory dream-fulfilment. Dreaming is an immediate and momentary means of escaping the *original trace* owing to the hallucinatory re-cathexis of the object from which the dreams proceeds.

The representation of the world

All aspects of psychic reality are traversed by the sense of loss and by its halluci-natory tendency. One can imagine that the primal trace, with its deployment – which, left to its own devices would extradite us towards the irrepresentable nature of the self-perception of the lack, towards the infinite of an 'objectless perception' – must be 'mastered' by returning to oneself, by the property of a reflexive movement that now bears the stamp of the object (although not as yet cathected as such). We are referring to the auto-erotic activity of 'looking at oneself' which is marked by the fact of 'being looked at' by the object. This secondary auto-erotic dynamic provides the basis for the work of reality testing as well as the distinction representation–perception.

(At the same time, the tendency towards the hallucinatory deployment of the original trace also finds its limits in other forms – namely, in isolation, in the shackles of the sense organs, as well as in the libidinal cathexes of the erotogenic zones, constituting a sense of bodily limits, of outside–inside, of the object's external reality.)

All these processes, under the effects of the negative of the *primal trace*, represent an upheaval for the psyche which 'had to decide to form a conception of the real circumstances in the external world' (Freud, 1911a: *S.E.* XII, 219). It is only after this upheaval that it becomes possible to speak of perception in terms of a real object. Hallucinatory activity is relegated not only by the quality consciousness but, above all, by the capacity for remembering. In a psychic life that is proceeding in a forward direction, the backward movement never extends beyond mnemic images and the beginning of the so-called retrogressive path towards 'the hallucinatory-object-satisfaction' can only occur under the peculiar conditions of sleep.

The relegation of hallucinatory activity behind the qualities of consciousness and memory goes hand in hand with opening one's eyes onto the world: the perception of the world emerges out of unpleasure, just as the representation of the real object emerges from the pain of its absence. '*At the very beginning, it seems, the external world, objects, and what is hated are identical*' (Freud, 1915b: S.E. XIV, 136). That said, the perception of the world is nonetheless a libidinal cathexis of that which is capable of substituting itself for the quest for the hallucinatory object satisfaction. It is the cathexis of a psychical act in which the *original trace* and its negativity, are transformed with the participation of memory into *déjà vu*, into the discovery of a satisfaction refound, something that has already happened.)

Quite clearly, the representation of the world cannot be conceived of as the result of a simple mechanism of registration, the reproduction of what is outside; it is the end product of a complex work. It seems it is constituted by borrowing the two psychical paths conjointly: the forward path towards representation, certainly, but also the backward path towards hallucination, under the respective impulsions of the reality ego and the pleasure ego. The two paths are created, undone and recreated continuously, in a double instinctual movement seeking, along different paths, even if it involves a detour by thinking, the same aim: namely, wish-fulfilment. Originating in this entanglement, the representation of the world seems to us to be a process that is as ungraspable as it is complex, irrepresentable for our thinking, which, with the participation of our sense organs, terminates in an apparently simple perception accompanied by a sense of reality: what I see, hear, touch or feel. What is perceived and what is represented by consciousness is the reduction of a complex process organising itself against a hallucinatory background. Whether the final product is experienced as a representation, that is to say, as 'only inside' or as perception, i.e. 'also outside' will depend on the work of reality testing that we have already described.

The symmetry representation–perception

If there is to be a cathexis of the perception of the object, hallucinatory self-perception must necessarily be effaced by the cathexis of sensory perception; by the same token, the cathexis of the object in representation is inherent to the absence of the object in perception. Two negatives work on the psyche: for representation, there is the negative of the absence of the cathected object; for perception, there is the negative of the loss of the 'hallucinatory-object-satisfaction'. Together they constitute a *negative duality*.

As for the duality corpuscle–wave, the duality *representation–perception* refers to an object that can be defined in two contradictory ways. However, unlike quantic expression, the main quality of reality testing is the simultaneous coexistence of two modes of work, the effect of a double demand for work imposed on the psyche by the double negative. It constantly forms a *symmetry representation–perception*. This *symmetry* defined by their negativity enables us to understand perception and representation in a way other than in terms of their duality based on the exclusion of one of them; to understand better the conditions of their particular modes of intelligibility and not only to identify them through discrimination. As long as they are only designated by the quality that the ego assigns to them, namely, either inside or outside, their original relation remains hidden. As in the game of the cuckoo, in shutting and opening the eyes, the ego identifies the same content now as a representation, now as a perception. Yet, this result, depending on the work of the ego, does not prevent an invariability of their negative duality from being maintained permanently by the properties of this symmetry. The latter regulates the global functioning of psychic life constituting a dynamic that is comparable to that of the magnetic poles where one unfailingly obtains a north pole and a south pole, at whatever point one cuts the magnet. The fact that one can present itself without the other in the to and fro between two qualities in waking life should not be substituted for investigations into the correlations and principles constantly governing the psyche as a whole. The latter possesses qualities that are different from those of the parts that are identifiable in relation to each other. We are not arguing here in favour of the conception of a 'whole' as a stable ensemble that lacks nothing – as is the case, moreover, for the depiction of the topographies or of the psychical 'apparatus'. On the contrary, our conception of the psyche as a 'whole' corresponds to the image of the *initial psychic implosion split* we described earlier and equally to that of the emergence from trauma. That is to say, to the permanent power of a general mobilisation of the psyche in an intense activity with a hallucinatory tendency nourishing itself on the negative potential of the *original trace*; an unstable 'whole' making and unmaking itself continuously.

The symmetry representation–perception of the negative duality guarantees psychic coherence. In its double instinctual determinism, it is also constrained, guaranteeing the commensurability of our experiences as well as that of their openings. Without the limitation it imposes, without a constant correlation with the finite system of word- and thing-presentations, we would be faced ineluctably with the infinitely irrepresentable nature of the lack of the object satisfaction; our psychical life would be ephemeral; we could not last. At the same time, the effect of the opening up of the perceptual pole that it exerts on the systems of representations is a constraint towards change, ensuring new representations. Otherwise, the systems of representations in themselves, namely, memory, could not cathect the new ones. They would become more complex and would constantly form links, but always with the same elements, until the psyche was completely confined within the most perfect example of what is 'already known'. These are facts that are confirmed for us in our analytic practice by infantile trauma: the *non-representation*, provoking the actualisation of the instinctual implosion, splits the *symmetry representation–perception* of adult thinking, which is then condemned either to exhaust itself through a 'sterile' perceptual activity, since it is cut off from its infantile traces or to the poverty of 'devitalised' representations, since they are cut off from their animistic sources. In other words, it seems that there exists a deep entanglement between the organisation of infantile neurosis and the *symmetry representation–perception*.)

The formation of this duality out of the instinctual 'chaos' of the id can only be envisaged without the presence of the pre-existent forms, the primal matrices. Taking interest in the general characteristics of primal phantasies represents for us the possibility of a new perspective for the theory of the drives, i.e. of acceding to a point of view where the coherence of the organisation of the whole is given precedence over that of isolated contents and their relations. In the absence of the object, the 'primal' ternary link that emerges from negativity, 'mummy not there because daddy', opens the way for us all to the representations and all the explanations in the world. The third, the cause, the 'because daddy', positivises the terrifying 'neither mummy–nor baby'. *The primal scene is the positive side, the representable outcome of a cause emerging from the negative.* Now that the irrepresentable has been transformed into a concrete form, the ego can face the absence in another way than by auto-erotic withdrawal.

(To sum up, the *symmetry representation–perception*, understood both as continuity of a negative duality and discontinuity of a qualitative duality at the heart of a fundamental work of binding–unbinding, is thus neither an effect of mirror reflection nor a stable cathexis of two distinct qualities. Rather, it is an invariable psychic property, an organising principle of drive activity as a whole, governing, by virtue of its double 'demand for work', by its double determinism, the permanent traumatic potentiality of the psyche.)

The perceptual and psychic causality

It is the sexual that allows us to transcend what is unthinkable for us, i.e. lack, absence, difference, etc.; to reveal the figurative power of the psyche in the infantile sexual theories; to create different logics, dual or ternary; to establish complex causalities: Oedipus, castration. Oedipal causality and the causality of castration relativise absence, difference, protecting us from the tidal wave of the affects of terror, of distress.

It is the sexual in its universal form that imposes fragmentation on us, the recognition of difference on the basis of general facts. The 'universal penis', of which Cournut-Janin and Cornut (1993) speak, is a hypothetical entity requiring that every conception of difference refers to it. But 'universal' seems more important than 'penis'. The universality of complexes refers less to the truth of their content than to the value of the conjunction of the relations they organise.

(Our complexes inscribe us within a succession of models, cathexes, conflicts between wish and defence and within the determinism of a temporal series of events in which every effect has a cause. They ensure the stability of entities

175

whose cohesive relations define both the structure that is destined to evolve and the events of this evolution. They constitute our representational power and guarantee the permanence of the cathexis of the object–presentation, obscuring the negative aspect of infantile trauma. Representations of sexuality, infantile wishes towards the object, the causal, form the basis of the first topography, whereas the second opens out directly on to the sphere of the drives, of 'chaos'.

In the example of the 'smell of fir', among others, we have seen at work the negative basis that usually disappears in face of the precedence of primal phantasies and causal, representational organisation. The irrepresentable 'negative residue' was discharged directly through the hallucinated smell and the hallucin-atory act was so successful in overcoming the storm of affects that the latter disappeared completely. As with Olga, the session often began in the most ordinary way. Such hallucinatory acts, having direct recourse to the sense organs, are not rare and have, in fact, the value of a discharge, with the capacity of eliminating completely the entire instinctual quantity in play at that particular moment. It has to be said that most of the time we do not concern ourselves with this; we pass over these fleeting impressions that are outside the usual mode of transference.[1]

In the hallucinatory act, such as the 'smell of fir', there is no question as to the link that exists between the cause, that is, the negative, the non-represented, and the effect, namely, the hallucinatory movement discharging itself in the form of a content, the smell. But this link, which does not correspond to the nature of representational infantile causalities, poses a conceptual problem.

Today, the psyche can no longer be thought of as a mechanism that can be explained solely in terms of the causal relations between its different delimited entities such as the representations or agencies of the first topography. Analytic theory will only be able to respond to the new questions arising from the extension of practice to borderline cases with a conceptual outlook that is capable of taking into account not only the representational transference/counter-transference elements and the conflicts between the agencies, but also the processes, the psychic movements traversing both psyches at every level. A re-evaluation of psychic temporality has become inevitable.

(Let us take, for instance, the genetic point of view. Undoubtedly it opens the way to explanations, to multiple causal analyses, but these are limited to the linearity of phases conceived within a temporal succession: oral, anal, urethral, phallic; or of successive properties: adhesive, paranoid, depressive; or, alternatively, of organisational levels: primary/secondary, pre-genital/genital, etc.)These formulas work very well, are easily applicable and represent a great economy of thought. In his time, however, Freud – and we know how attracted he was by the genetic point of view – always remained reserved on this subject. As we have already recalled with regard to the transition between the auto-erotic phase and the object phase, he qualifies such an approach, culminating in a temporal succession, as a 'defect' of thinking 'in the interests of lucidity' (footnote of 1910 in *Three Essays on Theory of Sexuality* (Freud, 1905c: *S.E.* VIII, 194). For Freud, while auto-erotism can be localised as a component of an early phase, it is just as much an inherent and actual tendency, a process of adult psychosexuality that is for ever being renewed. Then there is the temporal revolution introduced by Freud marking the psychic functioning of an unavoidable particularity, namely, the notion of *Nachträglichkeit*, a causality that may be qualified as retroactive. We shall not, however, dwell on this here, as it has already been discussed sufficiently and we would like to come directly to the heart of our subject.

At certain moments of the session, every psychoanalyst experiences the fact that our topical or temporal constructions, which had seemed the most meticulous, the most exact, and the most solid of our causal theories attaching to them, prove insufficient or even unsuitable. It is such moments that call into question our habitual working models, originating, notably, in the interpretation of the dream narrative of the first topography. With the practice of analyses of so-called borderline cases, we are truly pushed towards the necessity of transcending or going beyond this model and its modes of explication of causal relations limited to relations between representations or systems of representations and we need to know how to deal with the relations between all the psychic processes in the session. What we have in mind is the simultaneous confrontation of processes, for example, between dreaming and waking thought processes; between hallucinatory deployment and memory; between the negative of the infantile trauma and the work of figurability; or again, between reflexivity, the double, and the splitting of thought processes. We should be able to adopt a point of view that endeavours to embrace the plurality of perspectives concerning the psychic reality of the session – a sort of 'aleph', as Borges (1949) writes: 'the place where, without admixture or confusion, all the places of the world, seen from every angle, coexist' (1949: 127). It is a vision that does not imply the idea of the permanence of a localisation or that of temporal succession; but rather tries to grasp the simultaneity of the processes of the session in relation to the plurality of their meanings. It takes into account the habitual representational causalities that are relatively simple to grasp, including the phenomenon of *Nachträglichkeit*, while being open, at the same time, to other causal relations that are also operative in the session, but in a manner that is less accessible for the analyst – namely, those that are related to the processes of the session.

At the time Freud was elaborating the first topography, he expressed, in his letter to Fliess dated 6 December 1896, an initial intuition aside from the topography, which is no less brilliant, on the general functioning of the psyche. Thanks to a new elucidation involving a change of perspective, he gives us a very fine example of the possibility of understanding the same thing in a different way. 'What is essentially new about my theory', Freud writes, 'is the thesis that memory is present not once but several times over, that it is laid down in various kinds of indications . . . I do not know how many of these registrations there are – at least three, probably more.' He calls them: *Wz* [*Wahrnehmungszeichen* (indication of perception)], *Ub* [*Unbewusstsein* (unconsciousness)] and *Vb* [*Vorbewusstsein* (preconsciousness)]. They are 'not necessarily topographically' separated, he notes. And he adds: 'The first registration of perceptions is quite incapable of consciousness and is arranged according to associations by simultaneity.' Without topographies and without temporal succession, by simultaneity, such a description of the psyche represents the first Freudian schema that includes perception in the order of psychic constituents.

One gets a glimpse, then, in this letter, of a conception to which Freud accorded great importance. 'If I could give a complete account of the psychological characteristics of perception and of the three registrations, I should have described a new psychology.' But from the moment, shortly after this letter, that Freud's interest became focused on conflict, the dialectic would be subject to rules and causality to the binary logic of conflicts: pleasure/unpleasure; primary/secondary; thing-presentation/word-presentation; self-preservative instinct/sexual instinct; life instinct/death instinct. In this theoretical context, the perspective opened up by this letter, of an order of indications simultaneously inscribed in different forms would be reduced to the relation representation–perception based on the optical model of the lens.

Over 100 years on, what can be said about this letter in the light of contemporary thought? The problem is vast. Let us simply say that, in our opinion, the conception abandoned by Freud corresponds to the most current scientific preoccupations and deserves to be reconsidered, in particular with regard to the value of the perceptual in relation to temporality. In the Freudian order of the levels of registration of memory, what is qualified as an indication of perception represents all the simultaneous associative power of indications: it is both a constituent element of memory and a guarantee of the unity and intelligibility of the latter by virtue of its deployment towards all the registrations. This is what we call the perceptual. The registrations of the causal relations of unconsciousness and those of the linguistic relations of preconsciousness are of themselves inaccessible to consciousness; they are unintelligible unless reactivated by hallucinatory means, that is to say, unless they acquire the perceptual quality. Through this necessary process of perceiving, the perceptual is present at all levels, in each indication.

(Following Freud's intuition, one may suppose, therefore, that the connections between the indications are of a quite particular nature; they depend on a perceptual-hallucinatory quality that cannot be restricted either to the limits of the sense organs or to those of the temporo-spatiality of the preconscious. A coherence exists that has no knowledge of determinism or of the notion of cause as the succession of cause and effect; it is the simultaneity of the indications of the dream-work, of the work of figurability, representing in itself a causal potential.)

In front of a psychic event in the session such as the the analyst's work of figurability with Aline, or the 'smell of fir', rather than speaking of causality, it would be more exact to speak of cause as a potentiality of causalities in evolution. We should employ the notion of causation insofar as it 'designates the very operation of the cause, the effectivity of the production of the effect' (Hume, 1739–40). We have seen it imposing itself as much on the analyst as on the analysand faced with the negative of the trauma. The causation emerges from the negative of the infantile trauma, which is irrepresentable and atemporal, and becomes causality 'his majesty is naked' or 'Christmas tree coffin'. The causal relation itself could only occur in a representational register involving the temporo-spatiality of the preconscious.

In fact, we are trying to approach something paradoxical that seems to be constitutive of the psyche: a processual causality in which cause and effect do not succeed each other, but are simultaneous. This idea is obviously incompatible with the empirical and positivist tradition of thought. Hume said: 'We only see successions, never causations.' It is a processual causality that was handed down to us by Freud who defended, throughout the whole of his work, the need to take into account the simultaneity of psychical processes in the dream-work.

If we are seeking intelligibility with regard to the functioning of two psyches in a retrogressive state due to the analytic situation and if we adopt a standpoint comprising the primordial, hallucinatory, perceptual and representational processes as a whole, at this level, meaning is engendered in simultaneity, in the non-separability between the movement, form and content of the processes.

Our hypothesis, then, is that there exist general precursors of bindings, corresponding to vast instinctual movements of perception bearing the trace of their quest for satisfaction which, in their qualitative identity between that which produces and that which is produced, deploy what may be considered as operations of causation. Confronted with an abrupt rupture in the bindings of representations, it is through the actualisation of the processual simultaneity, in the non-separability between hallucinatory movement, perceptual form and over-determined representational content that meaning emerges, for example, the regressive, sensory form, with anal characteristics, of a hallucinated smell of 'fir'.

The analyst has to gain access, without a code, to this psychic reality. Where the issue is no longer one of a conflict inscribed, repressed, of something 'already there' waiting to be revealed, corresponding to the notion of interpretation as set out in the first topography, we are closer to the conception of the second, as we have developed it earlier; that is to say, of an entanglement between the agencies, having the value of processes, which characterise it. Ego, id and superego are thus conceived both as agencies and processes being constantly reconstituted; and the drive is considered as being able to actualise itself under the configuration of the id itself, but also under that of the superego or the ego. The meaning of 'fir' traversed all the psychical levels.

It seems to us that there is a theoretical field here that opens up considerable explanatory possibilities – a field suited to the study of the drive in its relation to hallucinatory and perceptual activity, to what is representable, and to what is inscribed, following an order that is still difficult for us to grasp.

What we can say for now, and we will end with this, is that, if we distinguish the order of processes from the order of agencies, we will necessarily have to take into consideration two levels of psychic reality whose relations with material reality are quite different. There would be the predominantly representational psychic reality, that of the systems, which Freud described so well. The preconscious plays a cardinal role in it with its networks of connections between representations, with its temporo-spatial causalities. Then there would be the predominantly processual psychic reality, marked by hallucinatory and perceptual activity, deploying itself towards the traces of satisfaction and, to be more exact, those of the quest for the lost object of hallucinatory satisfaction, taking shape in what Freud called the dream-work. Everything here is causational potentiality, power capable of creating meaning, causality is in a state of becoming.

The evolution of the treatment, and more broadly of the psyche, may be said to take place in the interaction between these two psychic realities: on one side, the lifting of repressions involving the revelation of their temporal causalities, their infantile meaning; and, on the other, the 'dream-work' of the operations of causation capable of creating meaning.

It is this confluence between past meaning and future meaning that may be said to qualify the processual nature of analytic treatment.

NOTES

Introduction to the English edition

1 We know that *Die Rücksicht auf Darstellbarkeit (Considerations of Representability)* is one of the four principal factors of the dream, the three others being the work of condensation, the work of displacement and secondary elaboration.
2 *Dictionnaire de la langue française Emile Littré,* vol 3. Edited by Encyclopaedia Britannica France, 2003.
3 In the *Grand Dictionnaire Universel du XIX siècle* edited by P. Larousse in 22 volumes in 1872 one also finds *figurabilité* with a similar definition: 'property essential to matter of having a shape'. The dictionary adds a citation by Virey: 'the essential properties of matter are extension, impenetrability, figurability and inertia'.
4 It is clear that in the limited space of this introduction we cannot take into account the complexity of the relations between *figurabilité,* word-presentations and affects.
5 Translator's note: In the *Ecrits mise en scène* is justifiably translated (p. 161) as 'representation', but for the purposes of this introduction I have preferred 'dramatization'.

Chapter 1

1 Translator's note: This term, in its substantival form, was introduced as a metapsychological notion in 1990 by C. and S. Botella 'in an attempt to broaden an analytic theory overly centred on the notion of representation'. *Dictionnaire International de Psychanalyse,* under the direction of Alain de Mijolla, Paris: Calmann-Lévy, 2002.

Chapter 2

1 Translator's note: throughout this book, I have generally used the term 'investment' rather than the Latinised form 'cathexis'.

2   We do not wish at all to use quantum physics as an argument to validate our hypothesis. Naturally, what counts here is above all the fact that our understanding of the duality corpuscule–wave, whether right or wrong, has enabled us to formulate our analytical hypothesis. It is this that has to be evaluated in itself. Concepts are often approximate and incomplete in relation to what the author has grasped intuitively.

3   Translator's note: *représentation d'objet* (S.E. 'object-presentation'). In this book I reserve the use of presentation for word- and thing-presentations and otherwise use the term 'representation' for the German *Vorstellung*, rather than idea or presentation, except in quotations from the *Standard Edition*.

Chapter 4

1   René Thom's conception of *pregnance* is not far removed: 'The *pregnance*, which is always the memory of an earlier satisfaction (or pain), is also an anticipation of this same satisfaction (or pain). The action triggered by the *pregnance* is aimed at obtaining this satisfaction (or at avoiding the pain)' (Thom, 1988: 29).

2   Translator's note: Thom's term: roughly, a process whereby a single unity is broken down into several unities.

3   Also in the analysand, but since the economic conditions are not identical for the two partners, he often uses other means than the formal regression of thought. See also Chapter 7.

Chapter 6

1   By that, we mean that the 'social' instincts are not really sublimated instincts; they have not abandoned their directly sexual aims, but are 'held back' from attaining them. (See Freud, 1923b: S.E. XVIII, 235.)

2   Concerning this notion of a bisexual sun, we have come across some intermediary phantasies, uncovered in the course of treating young children, between the first drawings of round shapes and drawings of the sun. Initially, there are rounded forms with a few pod-marks depicting for the child 'large devouring beasts'. This is the stage of nightmares, of the fear of being bitten, devoured by large animals: crocodiles, lions, wolves and so on. Next, the drawing becomes smaller and the small circle will be filled with numerous marks all around; it will make us think of the sun but the child will say 'spider' or 'there are hairs'. This is the stage of having phobias of small animals; the child is at the height of the phallic phase. The horror accompanying the drawing of the spider is related to castration, to the horror of the mother's genitals and later on to what remains of a bad mother figure. For us, these drawings evoke the representation of the head of Medusa. Later, the 'spider' will move up to the top of the drawing, above the house; it will become the sun, an idealised paternal image marking a glorious victory over what is terrifying. In this sense, it may be noted that certain representations of Helios, notably towards the end of paganism, bear an astonishing resemblance with those of the head of Medusa. It is as though the myth that, in an attempt at syncretism, progressively established the sun cult,

had followed the same path as that of the children's drawings. The monsters, the heads of Medusa, will be relegated to the back of the memory so that only the sun, the symbol of an ideal father, is represented.

It is worth noting that in this text on Leonardo da Vinci, Freud shows that the representation of Athena, including the head of Medusa, has its origin in an Egyptian divinity, Neith de Saïs, which, like many others, was originally androgynous, hermaphrodite.

3   Muhye al-Din Ibn'Arabi, spiritual master of Muslim mysticism: 'In reality, there is neither union nor separation, just as there is neither distancing nor nearness. There is union without unification, nearness without proximity and distancing without any idea of far and near.' *Le traité d'unité*, Paris: Editions Orientales, 1977.

4   'The double is a creation dating back to a very early mental stage, long since surmounted – a stage, incidentally, at which it wore a more friendly aspect' ('The "uncanny"', *S.E.* XVII, 236).

5   Eric Valentin has told us about the case of a female paranoiac patient whose delusional activity ceased from the moment she heard her mother tell her, while looking at a photo of her daughter, 'What a pretty body you have!'

6   This clinging to the external object, a consequence of an auto-erotic deficiency, is not exclusive to the paranoiac and can be found at work in other structures.

Chapter 7

1   Translator's note: the title in French is *Le travail en double*. This chapter is based on an article of 1984, 'L'homosexualité inconsciente et la dynamique du double en séance', *Revue Française de Psychanalyse*, 1984, 4. It was revised and extended in 1995: 'La dynamique du double en séance' in *Monographies de la Revue Française de Psychanalyse*.

2   Nevertheless, Freud lets it be understood in 1927 (*The Future of an Illusion*) that he has already interpreted the disturbance on the Acropolis.

3   Translator's note: the title in French is 'Les morts-vivants', in English 'The Night of the Living Dead' (1968), directed by George A. Romero.

Chapter 8

1   This chapter originated in an article published in the *Revue Française de Psychanalyse*, 1985, 4: 'Pensée animique, conviction et mémoire'.

2   It is to the honour of Denise Braunschweig, Michel Fain and Michel Neyraut that, for several years now, they have been drawing attention to the importance of animistic thought in the psychical economy. M. Neyraut, 1973, *Le transfert* and, in 1979, *Les logiques de l'inconscient*. M. Fain, 1982, *Le désir de l'interprète*; D. Braunschweig and M. Fain, 'Un aspect de la constitution de la source pulsionnelle', 1981; and 'Symptôme névrotique, symptôme de transfert', 1983.

3   We do not understand 'outside–inside' in the bodily sense, but as signalling the boundaries between 'ego and non-ego', which are not only always hypothetical and constantly in need of being reconstituted, but also constantly menaced by the

possibility of animistic regression. Moreover, defining the sense of reality as a consequence of a magic technique is a considerable problem. This idea becomes more acceptable if we take account of the fact that all evolution in the psyche is based on what the latter is at this very moment, on the use of what prevailed formerly without impediment.

4   No clinical work can claim to demonstrate theoretical hypotheses. It is another way of expressing the author's intuition. In the last analysis, analytic theory, a representation, and so-called objective clinical work, stand in a relation: perception 'confirmation' of the presentation, itself a 'reproduction of perception'. As one recreates the other and vice versa, it is in the mutual elucidation, within the narrow confines of the intricate relations between theory and clinical work that a 'truth' emerges rather than being discovered.

Chapter 9

1   This chapter furthers our ideas expounded in one of the sessions of the seminar that we ran with Claude Smadja at the Paris Institute of Psychosomatics (IPSO) between 1996 and 1998, published in *Actualités psychosomatiques* 1999, 2, AGEPSO, Geneva. Jasmine's case was presented at the Conference of the Institut Claparède in 1999, and was published in a collective work under the direction of S. Decobert and F. Sacco: *Psychothérapie psychanalytique de l'enfant et de la famille*. Paris: Erès, 2000.

Chapter 10

1   A conference organised by André Green at UNESCO, in 1989, entitled *La psychanalyse: questions pour demain*. The development of the paper that we presented there gave rise to an article called 'La problématique de la régression formelle de la pensée et de l'hallucination', published in *Les Monographies de la Revue Française de Psychanalyse* (1990): *La psychanalyse: questions pour demain*. It has been revised, corrected and extended and constitutes the essential content of Chapters 10 and 11 of this volume.

Chapter 11

1   This chapter, like the last, takes up and develops the paper given at the UNESCO conference in 1989.
2   We accord a place of prime importance to the modal of traumatic neurosis; it constitutes the most fundamental psychic solution, perhaps the earliest and most primitive form of thinking (Botella, C. and S., 1988).
3   Translator's note: 'l'odeur du sapin' has the specific connotation in French of the smell of a coffin, i.e. of death.
4   To the two psychic paths described by Freud in *The Interpretation of Dreams*, progressive and retrogressive, it is plausible and heuristic to add a third, a so-called 'short' retrogressive path, the model for which would be the course taken by

traumatic neurosis, that of the direct, immediate transformation of a perception into a dream hallucination.

Chapter 12

1 This text was based on the oral exposition presented by one of us during the day conference devoted to Bion in 1989 on the occasion of the 10th anniversary of his death.

2 In his *Spiritual Exercises*, Ignatius de Loyola had already suggested imagining a scene to the point of achieving a *quasi-perception*. He even went as far as setting himself the challenge of imagining the non-representable.

3 We use the term paradigm in Thomas Kuhn's sense: a set of convictions shared by the scientists of a given discipline.

Chapter 13

1 Perhaps this was also a way of reconsidering a crucial problem in connection with perception and already announced in the Project – namely, the conceptualisation of the transformation of the quantitative into the qualitative. On the side of perception 'the structure of the nervous system consists of contrivances for transforming external quantity into quality'; on the side of consciousness that 'gives us what are called *qualities'*, the same question arises: '*How* and *where* do qualities originate?' This was a question that would never really be answered.

2 It is here that one will be able to measure the importance of André Green's works on the metapsychology of limits and on the work of the negative. To facilitate their comprehension, we recommend reading J. E. Jackson's book, *De l'affect à la pensée. Introduction à l'oeuvre d'André Green*. Mercure de France, 1991.

3 Likewise in *Totem and Taboo* (1912b: S.E. XIII, 95): 'There is an intellectual function in us which demands unity, connection and intelligibility from any material, whether of perception or thought, that comes within its grasp; and if, as a result of special circumstances, it is unable to establish a true connection, it does not hesitate to fabricate a false one.'

Chapter 14

1 As early as *The Interpretation of Dreams* (1900) Freud posed the problem of 'sensory elements' in dreams. Certain arousal dreams, provoked by 'somatic material', by excess excitation (micturation, pollution) impede narcissistic regression from pursuing its course and oblige it to find its resolution through particular modes of immediate hallucinatory discharge without being able to reach the cathexes of unconscious wishes. These dreams, which manifest the conflict between the wish to sleep and physical excitation, coincide with typical dreams, a category of dreams for which interpretation is independent of the dreamer's associations and, concerning which, Freud agreed 'with reluctance' that his analytic technique was not applicable.

Nudity, immobility, stiffness or, on the contrary, drunkenness, flying or falling are these not all 'sensory elements' that traverse typical dreams and although they certainly refer to sexual tendencies, in their sensory form, they remain independent and cannot participate in the formation of the 'fine unity' of the dream-work around infantile wishes. Thus, instead of the dream as a wish-fulfilment, there occurs a hypercathexis of what Freud calls the 'currently active perceptual material' in 'On narcissism: an introduction' (1914). Resisting any form of integration, it bears witness to the flaw in the narcissistic unity of the subject's sexual tendencies and, at the same time, renders the analytic technique of dream interpretation inoperative.

BIBLIOGRAPHY

[* Entries preceded by an asterisk are those that, once revised and expanded, served the authors as a basis for writing this book.]

Abraham, H. and Freud, E. (1965). *A Psycho-Analytic Dialogue: The Letters of Sigmund Freud and Karl Abraham*. Frankfurt am Main: Fischer.

Abraham, K. (1909). *Rêve et mythe*. In *Oeuvres Complètes*, Vol 1. Paris: Payot.

Adde, A. (1998). *Sur la nature du temps*. Paris: Presses Universitaires de France.

Aisenstein, M. (1992). De 'l'art du tir à l'arc' à celui de la psychanalyse. *Revue Française de Psychanalyse*, 56, 2.

Aisenstein, M. (1992). Des régressions impossibles? *Revue Française de Psychanalyse*, 56, 4.

Aisenstein, M. (1993). Limites de l'analyse et idéal psychanalytique. *Bulletin du Groupe Toulousin de la S.P.P.*, 5.

Aisenstein, M. (1994). Du corps souffrant au corps érotique: l'école de la chair. *Revue Française de Psychosomatique*, 5.

Aisenstein, M. (1996). Le corps, limite ou cœur de la cure? In *Psychanalyse, neurosciences, cognitivismes*. Coll. Débats de la psychanalyse de la *Revue Française de Psychoanalyse*. Paris: Presses Universitaires de France.

Aisenstein, M. (1999). Des douleurs dans le rêve. *Revue Française de Psychosomatique*, 15.

Aisenstein, M. (2000). *Michel Fain*. Paris: Presses Universitaires de France.

Ali, S. (1977). *Le rêve et l'affect. Une théorie du somatique*. Paris: Dunod.

Ali, S. (1980). Langue arabe et langue mystique: les mots aux sens opposés et le concept d'inconscient. *La Nouvelle Revue de Psychanalyse*, 22.

Angelergues, R. (1992). *De l'hallucination au langage*. Monograph no. 2 of the Evelyn and Jean Kestemberg Centre for Psychoanalysis.

Anzieu, D. (1985). *Le Moi-peau*. Paris: Dunod.

Anzieu, D. (1987). Les signifiants formels et le Moi-peau. In *Les enveloppes psychiques*. Paris: Dunod.

Anzieu, D. (1988). *L'auto-analyse de Freud et la découverte de la psychanalyse*. Paris: Presses Universitaires de France.

Anzieu, D. (1994). *Le penser. Du Moi-peau au Moi-pensant*. Paris: Dunod.

Anzieu, D. (1996). *Créer, détruire*. Paris: Dunod.

Aristide, A. (1986). *Les discours sacrés*. Paris: Macula.

Atlan, H. (1979). *Entre le cristal et la fumée. Essai sur l'organisation du vivant*. Paris: Seuil.

Aulagnier, P. (1975). *La violence de l'interprétation*. Paris: Presses Universitaires de France. [Trs. A. Sheridan (2001). *The Violence of Interpretation*. London: Brunner- Routledge.]

Aulagnier, P. (1986). *Un interprète enquête de sens*. Paris: Ramsay.

Auroux, S. (1991). *Encyclopédie philosophique universelle*, Vol. 1, *Les notions philosophiques*, under the direction of André Jacob. Paris: Presses Universitaires de France.

Balier, C. (1988). *Psychanalyse des comportements violents*. Coll. Le fil rouge. Paris: Presses Universitaires de France.

Barande, I. (1977). *Le maternel singulier. La psychanalyse prise au mot*. Paris: Aubier-Montaigne.

Barande, R. (1975). *La naissance exorcisée*. Paris: Denoël.

Barande, R. (1989). *Parcours d'un psychanalyste. Son esthétisme et son éthique*. Paris: PromÉdi.

Baranger, W. and M. (1969). *Problemas dei campo psicoanalítico*. Buenos Aires: Kargieman.

Barbaras, R. (1994). *La perception. Essai sur le sensible*. Paris: Hatier.

Barrois, C. (1988). *Les névroses traumatiques*. Paris: Dunod.

Bayle, G. (1996). Ombres adorables. *Revue Française de Psychanalyse*, 1996.

Benveniste, E. (1956). Remarques sur la fonction du langage dans la découverte freudienne. In *Problèmes de linguistique générale*, Vol. 1. Coll. Tel. Paris: Gallimard.

Berger, D. (tr.) (1967). *L'interprétation des rêves*. Paris: Presses Universitaires de France.

Bergeret, J. (1984). *La violence fondamentale. L'inépuisable Œdipe*. Paris: Dunod.

Berman, A. (1984). *L'épreuve de l'étranger*. Paris: Gallimard.

Berman, A. (1985). *La traduction de la lettre ou l'auberge du lointain*. Paris: Seuil.

Bernat, J. (1996). *Le processus psychique et la théorie freudienne*. Paris: L'Harmattan.

Bernat, J., Bessis, M. and de Bru, C. (1990). *Soi et non-soi*. Paris: Seuil.

Billiard, I. (1994). *Somatisation, psychanalyse et sciences cognitives*. Paris: Eshel. [Organised by MIRE (Mission Interministérielle Recherche-Expérimentation) under the direction of Lucien Brams.]

Bion, W. R. (1965). *Transformations: Change from Learning to Growth*. London: Heinemann. [Reprinted (1984). London: Karnac Books.]

Bion, W. R. (1970). *Attention and Interpretation*. London: Tavistock. [Reprinted (1984). London: Karnac Books.]

Bion, W. R. (1975–9). *Une mémoire du futur*. Lyon: Césura.

Bion, W. R. (1983). *Second Thoughts. Selected Papers on Psychoanalysis*. London: Heinemann. [Reprinted (1984). London: Karnac Books.] (*Refléxion faite*. Paris: Presses Universitaires de France.)

Bitbol, M. (1998). *Physique et philosophie de l'esprit*. Paris: NBS Flammarion.

Bleger, J. (1984). *Simbiosis y ambigüiedad*. Buenos Aires: Paidos.

Bokanowski, T. (1998). *De la pratique psychanalytique*. Coll. Épîtres. Paris: Presses Universitaires de France.

Bonnefoy, Y. (1999). *Lieux et destins de l'image. Un cours de poétique au Collège de France (1981–1993)*. Paris: Seuil.

Borges, J. L. (1949). *L'aleph. O.C.*, Vol. I. Coll. La Pléiade. Paris: Presses Universitaires de France. [Trans. (1998). *The Aleph*. London: Penguin Books.]

Botella, C. (1980). Le fil continu. Quelques interrogations au sujet de la notion de conflit infantile dans l'oeuvre de S. Freud. *Revue Française de Psychanalyse*, 44, 5–6.

Botella, C. (1997). La(s) homosexualidad(es), vicisitud del narcismo. Communication à la table ronde sur l'homosexualité au Congrès de l'IPA, 1997. Barcelona. *Revista de Psicoanálisis*, TLV 98, 3. [Reprinted (1999) in *Revue Française de Psychanalyse*, 4.]

Botella, C. and S. (1978). Two cases of anorexia nervosa. *Journal of Child Psychotherapy*, 4, 4.

*Botella, C. and S. (1982). Sur la carence auto-érotique du paranoiaque. *Revue Française de Psychanalyse*, 1.

*Botella, C. and S. (1983a). Notes cliniques sur la figurabilité et l'interprétation. *Revue Française de Psychanalyse*, 3.

Botella, C. and S. (1983b). Notes cliniques sur l'investissement de la représentation de mot. *Les cahiers du centre de Psychanalyse et de Psychothérapie*, 7.

*Botella, C. and S. (1984). L'homosexualité inconsciente et la dynamique du double en séance. *Revue Française de Psychanalyse*, 4.

*Botella, C. and S. (1985). Pensée animique, conviction et mémoire. *Revue Française de Psychanalyse*, 4.

Botella, C. and S. (1988). Trauma and topique: Aspects techniques de l'abord du trauma en séance. *Revue Française de Psychanalyse*, 6.

Botella, C. and S. (1990). L'analyse d'enfant et la métapsychologie. *Journal de la Psychanalyse de L'enfant*, 8.

Botella, C. and S. (1991a). La mémoire sans souvenir. In *Avancés méta-psychologiques*. Paris: Éditions Apsygée.

*Botella, C. and S. (1991b). Mystique, connaissance et trauma. *Hommage à Bion: W. A. Bion, une théorie pour l'avenir*. Paris: Éditions Métallié.

Botella, C. and S. (1992a). Névrose traumatique et cohérence psychique. *Revue Française de Psychosomatique*, 2.

*Botella, C. and S. (1992b). Le statut métapsychologique de la perception et l'irreprésentable. *Revue Française de Psychanalyse*, 1.

Botella, C. and S. (1993). Image mémorielle, trace mnésique et deuil. Publication interne du Séminaire de Perfectionnement.

Botella, C. and S. (1994). Interprétation et hallucinatoire. *Bulletin du Groupe Lyonnais*, 2, 32.

Botella, C. and S. (1995a). A propos du processuel (automate ou sexuel infantile?). *Revue Française de Psychanalyse*, 4.

*Botella, C. and S. (1995b). La dualité négative du psychisme. In *Le négatif, perspectives analytiques*. *Journées Occitanes de Psychanalyse*. Paris: L'Esprit du Temps.

*Botella, C. and S. (1995c). La dynamique du double: animique, auto-érotique, narcissique. Le travail en double. Monographie de la *Revue Française de Psychanalyse*, 'Le double'.

*Botella, C. and S. (1995d). Sur le processus analytique: du perceptif aux causalités psychiques. *Revue Française de Psychanalyse*, 2.

Botella, C. and S. (1996). La tendance convergente de la regression narcissique. *Revue Française de Psychosomatique*, 9.

Botella, C. and S. (1997a). L'inachèvement de toute analyse. *Revue Française de Psychanalyse*, 4.

Botella, C. and S. (1997b). *Mas allà de la representación*. Valencia: Édiciones Promo-Libro.

*Botella, C. and S. (1997c). Le perceptif en tant que concept limite en psychanalyse. In *Concepts limites en psychanalyse*. Coll. Textes de base en psychanalyse. Lonat: Delachaux et Niestlé.

Botella, C. and S. (1997d). Pulsions, représentations, langage et travail du négatif. *Pulsions, représentations, langages*. Conference of the G.E.P.C. Lonat: Delachaux et Niestlé.

Botella, C. and S. (1998a). Le problème du monisme psyché–soma. *Revue Française de Psychanalyse*, 5.

Botella, C. and S. (1998b). *El trauma psiquico. Conceptualization y la formulation del hecho clínico psicoanalítico.* Buenos Aires: Promo Libro.

Botella, C. and S. (1998c). *L'unité fondamentale de l'être humain*: Quatrième Journée de l'AGEPSO. *Actualités psychosomatiques*, 1. Geneva: Georg Éditeur.

*Botella, C. and S. (1999). La thérapie de Jasmine, une communauté dans la régression de la pensée. Mouvements d'organisation et de désorganisation pendant l'enfance. *Actualités psychosomatiques*, 2. Geneva.

Botella, C. and S. (2001). La figurabilité. Report to the 61st Congress of French-speaking Psychoanalysts. *Bulletin de la Société Psychanalytique de Paris.* [Reprinted (2001) in *Revue Française de Psychanalyse*, special congress edition.]

Botella, C. and S. (2002). *Irrepresetável.* Porto Alegre: Editora Criaçao Humana.

Botella, C. and S. (2003). *La figurabilidad psíquica.* Buenos Aires: Amorrortu Éditores.

Botella, C. and S. (2004). *La raffigurabilità psichica.* Rome: Borla.

Botella, C. and S. and Haag, G. (1977). En deçà du suçotement. *Revue française de Psychanalyse*, 5–6.

Botella, S. (1983). Notes cliniques sur l'investissement de la reprépresentation de mot. *Cahiers du Centre de Psychanalyse de de Psychothérapie*, 7.

*Botella, S. (2000). Régression de la pensée dans une cure d'enfant. *Psychothérapie psychanalytique de l'enfant et de sa famille.* Romainville-St. Agne: Erès.

Bourguignon, A. (1994). *L'homme imprévu, l'homme fou (histoire naturelle de l'homme)*, Vols 1 and 2. Paris: Presses Universitaires de France.

Bourguignon, A., Cotet, P., Laplanche, J. and Robert, F. (1989). *Traduire Freud.* Paris: Presses Universitaires de France.

Bouvet, M. (1968). *Œuvres psychanalytiques*, Vol. 1, *La relation d'objet. Avant propos de M. de M'Uzan*; Vol. 2, *Résistances–Transfert.* Paris: Payot.

Brabant, E., Falzeder, E. and Giampieri-Deutsch, P. (eds). (1993–2000). *The Correspondence of Sigmund Freud and Sándor Ferenczi*, Vol. 1, 1908–1914. [Trs. Peter Hoffer. Cambridge, MA: Belknap Press of Harvard University Press.] (Freud: Letter to S. Ferenczi, 6 October 1910, p. 221.)

Braier, E. (1990). *Tabúes en teoría de la técnica. Metapsicología de la cura.* Buenos Aires: Nueva Visión.

Braier, E. (2000). *Gemelos. Narcisismo y dobles.* Buenos Aires: Paidos.

Braunschweig, D. and Fain, M. (1975). *La nuit, le jour.* Paris: Presses Universitaires de France.

Braunschweig, D. and Fain, M. (1981a). Un aspect de la constitution de la source pulsionnelle. *Revue Française de Psychanalyse*, 1.

Braunschweig, D. and Fain, M. (1981b). Bloc et lanterne magique. *Revue Française de Psychanalyse*, 5.

Braunschweig, D. and Fain, M. (1983). Symptôme névrotique, symptôme de transfert. *Revue Française de Psychanalyse*, 2.

Brusset, B. (1988). *Psychanalyse du lien. La relation d'objet.* Paris: Le Centurion.

Brusset, B. (1996). Les sciences de l'esprit et la psyché. In *Psychanalyse, neurosciences, cognitivismes.* Coll. Débats de la psychanalyse de la *Revue Française de Psychanalyse*.

Cahn, R. (1991). Du sujet. Report to the Congress of French-speaking Psychoanalysts. *Revue Française de Psychanalyse*, 6.

Cela, C. J. (1990). Interview in *Le Figaro*, 27 August 1990.

Changeux, J.-P. and Ricoeur, P. (1998). *Ce qui nous fait penser. La nature est la règle*. Paris: Odile Jacob.

Chasseguet-Smirgel, J. (1975). *L'idéal du Moi. Essai psychanalytique sur la 'maladie d'idéalité'*. Paris: Tchou.

Chasseguet-Smirgel, J. (1984). *Ethique et esthétique de la perversion*. Paris: Champ Vallon.

Chauvin, R. (1992). *La biologie de l'esprit*. Paris: du Rocher.

Chemama, R. and Vandermersch, B. (1998). *Dictionnaire de la psychanalyse*. Larousse.

Chevalley, C. (1990). *Dualité (onde-corpuscle)*. *Encyclopédie Universelle. Les Notions Philosophiques*. Dictionnaire 1. Paris: Presses Universitaires de France.

Cournut, J. (1991). *L'ordinaire de la passion. Névrose du trop, névroses du vide*. Coll. Le fil rouge. Paris: Presses Universitaires de France.

Cournut-Janin, M. and Cournut, J. (1993). La castration et le féminin dans les deux sexes. *Revue Française de Psychanalyse*, special edition 53 (Congrès des Psychanalystes de Langues Romanes).

Damasio, A. (1995). *L'erreur de Descartes. La raison des émotions*. Paris: Odile Jacob.

Danon-Boileau, L. (1996). Psychanalyse et cognition: ce que la clinique construit de leurs relations. In *Psychanalyse, neurosciences, cognitivismes*. Coll. Débats de la psychanalyse de la *Revue Française de Psychanalyse*. Paris: Presses Universitaires de France.

David, C. (1971). *L'état amoureux*. Paris: Payot.

David, C. (1992). *La bisexualité psychique*. Paris: Payot.

Debray, R. (1992). *Vie et mort de l'image. Un histoire du regard en Occident*. Paris: Gallimard.

Degoumois, C. (1992). Le vol d'Icare; paradoxe du somnambule. [Reprinted (1998) in Sortie de nuit. *Revue Française de Psychosomatique*, 14.]

Deleuze, G. (1983). *L'image-mouvement*. Paris: Éditions de Minuit.

Deleuze, G., Foucaud, M. and Lyotard, J.-F. (1997). *L'image*. Paris: Vrin.

Delrieu, A. (1997). *Sigmund Freud, Index Thématique*. Paris: Anthropos.

Denis, P. (1997). *Emprise et satisfaction: les deux formants de la pulsion*. Coll. Le fil rouge. Paris: Presses Universitaires de France.

Diatkine, R. (1974). Rêve, illusion et connaissance. Report to the Congress of French-speaking Psychoanalysts. *Revue Française de Psychanalyse*, 5–6.

Diatkine, R. (1979). Le psychanalyste et l'enfant. *La Nouvelle Revue de Psychanalyse*, 19.

Diatkine, R. (1994). *L'enfant dans l'adulte ou l'éternel capacité de rêverie*. Lonat: Delachaux et Niestlé.

Diatkine, R. (2000). Le surmoi culturel. Report to the Congress of French-speaking Psychoanalysts. *Revue Française de Psychanlyse*, special edition.

Dods, E. R. (1959). *Les Grecs et l'irrationnel*. Paris: Champs Flammarion.

Donnet, J.-L. (1995). *Le divan bien tempéré*. Coll. Le fil rouge. Paris: Presses Universitaires de France.

Donnet, J.-L. (1999). Patients limites, situations limites. In *Les états limites*. Paris: Presses Universitaires de France.

Donnet, J.-L. and Green, A. (1973). *L'Enfant de ça*. Paris: Éditions de Minuit.

Dorey, R. (1995). La problématique homosexuelle masculine: une approche structurale. *Bulletin de la Psychanlyse en Europe*, 44.

Dufour, D.R. (1990). *Les mystères de la Trinité*. Bibliothèque des Sciences Humaines. Paris: Gallimard.

Duparc, F. (1995). *L'image sur le divan. Comment l'image vient au psychanalyste*. Paris: L'Harmattan.

Dupuy, J. P. (1994). *Aux origines des sciences cognitives*. Paris: La Découverte.

Enriquez, M. (2000). L'enveloppe de mémoire et ses trous. In *Les enveloppes psychiques*. Paris: Dunod.

Erdelyi, M. H. (1985). *Psychoanalysis: Freud's Cognitive Psychology*. New York: W. H. Freeman.

d'Espagnat, B. (1985). *Une incertaine réalité*. Paris: Gauthiers-Villars.

d'Espagnat, B. (1990). *Penser la science ou les enjeux du savoir*. Paris: Dunod.

d'Espagnat, B. (1994). *Le réel voilé*. Coll. Le temps des sciences. Paris: Fayard.

Faimberg, H. (1989). Pour une théorie (non narcissique) de l'écoute du narcissisme: comment l'indicible devient-il dicible? In *Monographies: la psychanalyse, questions pour demain*. Paris: Presses Universitaires de France.

Faimberg, H. (1996). Listening to listening. *International Journal of Psychoanalysis*, 4.

Fain, M. (1982). *Le désir de l'interprète*. Paris: Aubier-Montaigne.

Fedida, P. (2000). *Par où commence le corps humain. Retour sur la régression*. Paris: Presses Universitaires de France.

Ferenczi, S. (1914). L'homoérotisme: nosologie de l'homosexualité masculine. In *Œuvres Complètes*, Vol. II. Paris: Payot.

Ferenczi, S. (1932). *Journal clinique*. Paris: Payot.

Ferenczi, S. (1955). *Final Contributions to the Methods and Problems of Psycho-Analysis*. New York: Basic Books.

Ferro, A. (2000). *La psychanalyse comme œuvre ouverte*. Romainville-Saint-Agne: Erès.

Flaubert, G. (1880). *Bouvard et Pécuchét*. Paris: Gallimard. [Trs. (1905). *Bouvard and Pecuchet*. In *Flaubert's Works*, Vol. IX. Cleveland, OH: St Dunstan Society.]

Fliess, R. (ed.) (1948). *Psychoanalytic Reader*. New York: International Universities Press.

Frazer, J. G. (1911). *The Golden Bough*. London: Macmillan.

Freud, E. L. (ed.) (1960). *Letters of Sigmund Freud, 1873–1939* (trs. T. and J. Stern). London: Hogarth Press.

Freud, E. L. (ed.) (1970). *The Letters of Sigmund Freud and Arnold Zweig* (trs. E. W. Robson-Scott). New York: Harcourt, Brace and World Inc.

Freud, S. (1895). Project for a scientific psychology. *S.E.* I.

Freud, S. (1900). *The Interpretation of Dreams*. *S.E.* IV–V. [Trs. D. Berger (1967). *L'interprétation des rêves*. Paris: Presses Universitaires de France; trs. I. Meyerson (1926). *La science des rêves*. Paris: Alcan.]

Freud, S. (1905a [1901]). Bruchstück einer Hysteria-Analyse. *G.W.* V.

Freud, S. (1905b [1901]). Fragment of an analysis of a case of hysteria. *S.E.* VII.

Freud, S. (1905c). *Three Essays on Theory of Sexuality*. *S.E.* VIII.

Freud. S. (1905d). *Der Witz und seine Beziehung zum Unbewussten*. *G.W.* VI. [*Jokes and their Relation to the Unconscious*. *S.E.* VIII.]

Freud, S. (1908). The sexual theories of children. *S.E.* IX.

Freud, S. (1910a). The antithetical meaning of primal words. *S.E.* XI.

Freud, S. (1910b). Leonardo da Vinci and a memory of his childhood. *S.E.* XI.

Freud, S. (1911a). Formulations on the two principles of mental functioning. *S.E.* XII.

Freud, S. (1911b). Psycho-analytic notes on an autobiographical account of a case of paranoia (dementia paranoides). *S.E.* XII.

Freud, S. (1912a). The dynamics of the transference. *S.E.* XII.

Freud, S. (1912b). *Totem and Taboo. S.E.* XIII.

Freud, S. (1914). On narcissism: an introduction. *S.E.* XIV.

Freud, S. (1914–18). Wolf Man. From the history of an infantile neurosis. *S.E.* XVII.

Freud, S. (1915a). A case of paranoia running counter to the psycho-analytic theory of the disease. *S.E.* XIV.

Freud, S. (1915b). *Instincts and their Vicissitudes. S.E.* XIV.

Freud, S. (1915c). The unconscious. *S.E.* XIV.

Freud, S. (1916–17). *Introductory Lectures on Psycho-Analysis. S.E.* XV.

Freud, S. (1917a [1915]). Metapsychological supplement to the theory of dreams. *S.E.* XIV.

Freud, S. (1917b). *Mourning and Melancholia. S.E.* XIV.

Freud, S. (1919). The 'uncanny'. *S.E.* XVII.

Freud, S. (1920). *Beyond the Pleasure Principle. S.E.* XVIII.

Freud, S. (1921a). Group psychology and the analysis of the ego. *S.E.* XVIII.

Freud, S. (1921b). Psychoanalysis and telepathy. *S.E.* XVIII.

Freud, S. (1922a). Dreams and telepathy. *S.E.* XVIII.

Freud, S. (1922b). Some neurotic mechanisms in jealousy, paranoia and homosexuality. *S.E.* XVIII.

Freud, S. (1923a). *The Ego and the Id. S.E.* XIX.

Freud, S. (1923b). Two encyclopaedia articles. *S.E.* XVIII.

Freud, S. (1924a). The economic problem of masochism. *S.E.* XIX.

Freud, S. (1924b). The loss of reality in neurosis and psychosis. *S.E.* XIX.

Freud, S. (1924c). Neurosis and psychosis. *S.E.* XIX.

Freud, S. (1925a). *Inhibitions, Symptoms and Anxiety. S.E.* XX.

Freud, S. (1925b). Negation. *S.E.* XIX.

Freud, S. (1927a). Fetishism. *S.E.* XXI.

Freud, S. (1927b). *The Future of an Illusion. S.E.* XXI.

Freud, S. (1929). *Civilization and its Discontents. S.E.* XXI.

Freud, S. (1932a). Dissection of the personality. In *New Introductory Lectures. S.E.* XXII.

Freud, S. (1932b [1933]). *New Introductory Lectures on Psychoanalysis. S.E.* XXII.

Freud, S. (1936). A disturbance of memory on the Acropolis. *S.E.* XXII.

Freud, S. (1937a). Constructions in analysis. *S.E.* XXIII.

Freud, S. (1937b). *Moses and Monotheism. S.E.* XXIII.

Freud, S. (1938a). *Findings, Ideas, Problems. S.E.* XXIII.

Freud, S. (1938b). *An Outline of Psychoanalysis. S.E.* XXIII.

Freud, S. (1940 [1938]). Splitting of the ego in the process of defence. *S.E.* XXIII.

Freud, S. (1950–74). *Standard Edition (S.E.)* (of the *Complete Psychological Works of Sigmund Freud*). London: Hogarth Press.

Freud, S. (1999). *Gesammelte Werke (G.E.).* Frankfurt am Main: Fischer.

Freud, S. and Breuer, J. (1895). *Studies on Hysteria. S.E.* II.

Gadamer, H. G. (1996a). *La philosophie herméneutique.* Paris: Presses Universitaires de France.

Gadamer, H. G. (1996b). *Vérité et méthode.* Paris: Seuil.

Gagnebin, M. (1999). *Du divan à l'écran. Montages cinématographiques, montages interprétatifs.* Paris: Presses Universitaires de France.

Gammil, J. (1998). *A partir de Melanie Klein* (Introduction de Geneviève Haag). Lyon: Césura.

Garma, A. (1970). *Le rêve, traumatisme et hallucination.* Bibliothèque de Psychanalyse. Paris: Presses Universitaires de France.

Gervereau, L. (2000). *Les images qui mentent (Histoire du visuel au XXe siècle).* Paris: Seuil.

Gibeault, A. (1989). Destins de la symbolisation. Report to the 47th Congress of French-speaking Psychoanalysts, Paris. *Revue Française de Psychanalyse*, special congress edition.

Gimenez, G. (2000). *Clinique de l'hallucination psychotique.* Paris: Dunod.

Godfrind, J. (1993). *Les deux courants du transfert. Le fait psychanalytique.* Paris: Presses Universitaires de France.

Green, A. (1973). *Le discours vivant. La conception psychanalytique de l'affect.* Coll. Le fil rouge. Paris: Presses Universitaires de France. [Trs. Alan Sheridan (1999). *The Fabric of Affect in the Psychoanalytic Discourse.* London: Routledge.]

Green, A. (1974). L'analyste, la symbolisation et l'absence dans le cadre analytique: à propos des changements dans la pratique et l'expérience analytiques. *Nouvelle Revue de Psychanalyse*, 10. [Trs. A. Sheridan (1986). *On Private Madness.* London: Hogarth Press.]

Green, A. (1975). The analyst, symbolization and absence in the analytical setting (trs. K. Lewison and D. Pines). *International Journal of Psychoanalysis*, 56.

Green, A. (1976). Un, autre, neutre: valeurs narcissiques du même. *Nouvelle Revue de Psychanalyse*, 13. [Trs. in Weller (2001).]

Green, A. (1983). *Narcissisme de vie, narcissisme de mort.* Paris: Éditions de Minuit. [Trs. in Weller (2001).]

Green, A. (1986a). *On Private Madness.* London: Hogarth Press.

Green, A. (1986b). Pulsion de mort, narcissisme négatif, fonction désobjectalisante. In *La pulsion de mort.* Paris: Presses Universitaires de France.

Green, A. (1990). *La folie privée.* Paris: Gallimard. [Trs. A. Sheridan (1986). *On Private Madness.* London: Hogarth Press.]

Green, A. (1993). *Le travail du négatif.* Paris: Éditions de Minuit. [Trs. A. Weller (2002). *The Work of the Negative.* London: Free Association Books.]

Green, A. (1995a). *La causalité psychique. Entre nature et culture.* Paris: Odile Jacob.

Green, A. (1995b). *ProPédeutique. La métapsychologie revisitée.* Paris: Champ Vallon.

Green, A. (1996a). Cognitivisme, neurosciences et psychanalyse: Un dialogue difficile. In *Psychanalyse, neurosciences, cognitivismes.* Coll. Débats de la psychanalyse de la *Revue Française de Psychanalyse.* Paris: Presses Universitaires de France.

Green, A. (1996b). Philosophie de l'esprit et psychanalyse. In *Psychanalyse, neurosciences, cognitivismes.* Coll. Débats de la Psychanalyse de la *Revue Française de Psychanalyse.* Paris: Presses Universitaires de France.

Green, A. (1998). *L'intrapsychique et l'intersubjectif en psychanalyse.* Québec: Éditions Lanctôt. [Trs. A. Weller (1998). The intrapsychic and the intersubjective in psycho-analysis. *Psychoanalytic Quarterly*, 69.]

Green, A. (1999a). *The Fabric of Affect in the Psychoanalytic Discourse.* London: Routledge.

Green, A. (1999b). Genèse et situation des états limites. In *Les états limites.* Paris: Presses Universitaires de France.

Green, A. (1999c). *The Work of the Negative*. London: Free Association Books.

Green, A. (2000a). Le cadre psychanalytique: son intériorisation chez l'analyste et son application à la pratique. In *L'avenir d'une désillusion*. Coll. Petite bibliothèque de psychanalyse. Paris: Presses Universitaires de France.

Green, A. (2000b). *La diachronie en psychanalyse*. Paris: Éditions de Minuit. [Trs. A. Weller (2003). *Diachrony in Psychoanalysis*. London: Free Association Books.]

Green, A. (2000c). *Le temps éclaté*. Paris: Éditions de Minuit. [Trs. A. Weller (2002). *Time in Psychoanalysis: Some Contradictory Aspects*. London: Free Association Books.]

Green, A. (2002). *Life Narcissism. Death Narcissism* (trs. A. Weller). London: Free Association Books.

Greenacre, P. (1953). *Traumatisme, croissance et personnalité*. Paris: Presses Universitaires de France.

Greenson, R. R. (1967). *The Technique and Practice of Psychoanalysis*. London: Hogarth Press.

Grondin, J. (1999). *Introduction à H. G. Gadamer*. Paris: Éditions du Cerf.

Grunberger, B. (1971). Le narcissisme. Essai de psychanalyse. Paris: Payot. [Trs. (1979). *Narcissism: Psychoanalytic Studies*. New York: International Universities Press.]

Guignard, F. (1996). *Au vif de l'infantile*. Lonat: Delachaux et Niestlé.

Guignard, F. (1997). *Épître à l'objet*. Coll. Épîtres. Paris: Presses Universitaires de France.

Guillaumin, J. (1979). *Le rêve et moi*. Coll. Le fil rouge. Paris: Presses Universitaires de France.

Guillaumin, J. (1983). *Psyché. Études psychanalytiques sur la réalité*. Coll. Le Fil Rouge. Paris: Presses Universitaires de France.

Guillaumin, J. (1987). *Entre blessure et cicatrice. Le destin du négatif dans la psychanalyse*. Coll. L'or d'Atalante. Paris: Champ Vallon.

Guillaumin, J. (1996). *L'objet (l'objet, l'absence et l'ombre)*. Coll. Perspectives psychanalytiques. Paris: L'Esprit du Temps.

Guillaumin, J. (1998). *Transfert, Contretransfert*. Coll. Perspectives psychanalytiques. Paris: L'Esprit du Temps.

Guttman, S. A., Parrish, S. M., Ruffing, J. and Smith, P. H. Jr. (1995). *Konkordanz zu den Gesammelten Werken von Sigmund Freud*. Ontario: North Waterloo Academic Press.

Haag, G. (1990). Le dessin préfiguratif de l'enfant: quel niveau de représentation? VIIIe Journées Occitanes de Toulouse. *Journal de la Psychanalyse de l'Enfant*, 8.

Haag, G. (1995). Moi corporel et formation de l'écran des rêves. In *Le rêve, l'enfant et le psychanalyste* (under the direction of S. Decobert and F. Sacco). Colloque de l'Institut Édouard Claparède, Janvier: La vie onirique chez l'enfant. Paris: Erès.

Haag, G. (2000). La pratique psychanalytique avec les enfants autistes: aménagements techniques, processus possibles, développements métapsychologiques. *Pratiques de la psychanalyse* (under the direction of J. Cournut and J. Schaeffer). Paris: Presses Universitaires de France.

Haag, G. and Botella, C. and S. (1977). En deçà du suçotement. *Revue Française de Psychanalyse*, 5–6.

Hadamard, J. (1993). *Essais sur la psychologie de l'invention dans le domaine mathématique*. Paris: Éditions Jacques Gabay.

Hegel, G. W. (1804–1805). *Logique et Metaphysique (Jena 1804–1805)*. Paris: Gallimard.

Hegel, G. W. (1807). *Phänomenologie des Geistes*. [Trs. J. P. Lefebre (1991). *Phénoménologie de l'esprit*. Paris: Aubier; trs. A. V. Miller (1910). *The Phenomenology of Spirit*. Oxford: Blackwell.]

Hegel, G. W. (1812–16). *Wissenschaft der Logik*. [Trs. B. Bourgeois (ed.). *Logique d'iena – la science de la logique*. Paris: Vrin; English edn 1874, *The Logic of Hegel*.] *The Encyclopaedia of Philosophical Sciences* (1830). Oxford: Clarendon.

Hinshelwood, R. D. (1989). *A Dictionary of Kleinian Thought*. London: Free Association Books.

Hobson, J. A. (1988). *Le cerveau rêvant*. Bibliothèque des sciences humaines. Paris: Gallimard.

Hochmann, J. and D. M. (1996). *Esprit, où es-tu? Psychanalyse et neurosciences*. Paris: Odile Jacob.

Hulin, M. (1993). *La mystique sauvage. Perspectives critiques*. Paris: Presses Universitaires de France.

Hume, D. (1739–40). *A Treatise of Human Understanding*. London: Penguin Classics. [Trs. (1995). *L'entendement. Traité de la nature humaine*. Paris: Flammarion.]

Ibn'Arabi, Muhye al-Din (1977). *Le traité d'unité*. Paris: Editions Orientales.

Jackson, J. E. (1991). *De l'affect à la pensée. Introduction à l'œuvre d'André Green*. Paris: Mercure de France.

Jacob, A. (1990). *Encyclopédie Philosophique Universelle*, Vol. I, *Les notions philosophiques* (under the direction of Sylvain Auroux). Paris: Presses Universitaires de France.

Jacob, F. (1970). *La logique du vivant. Une histoire de l'hérédité*. Bibliothèque des Sciences Humaines. Paris: Gallimard.

James, T. (1995). *Vies secondes*. Coll. Connaissance de l'inconscient. Paris: Gallimard.

Janin, C. (1996). *Figures et destins du traumatisme*. Coll. Le fait psychanalytique. Paris: Presses Universitaires de France.

Jarczyk, G. (1999). *Le négatif ou l'écriture de l'autre dans la logique de Hegel*. Paris: Ellipses.

Jeammet, P. (1996). Sciences cognitives, thérapies cognitives et psychanalyse. In *Psychanalyse, neurosciences, cognitivismes*. Coll. Débats de la psychanalyse de la *Revue Française de Psychanalyse*. Paris: Presses Universitaires de France.

Jeanneau, A. (1985). L'hystérie. Unité et diversité. Report to Congress of French-speaking Psychoanalysts. *Revue Française de Psychanalyse*, 1.

Jeanneau, A. (1990). *Us dilires non psychotiques*. Coll. Le fait psychanalytique. Paris: Presses Universitaires de France.

Jeannerod, M. (1993). *Le cerveau machine*. Paris: Fayard.

Jeannerod, M. (1996a). *De la physiologie mentale. Histoire des relations entre biologie et pychologie*. Paris: Odile Jacob.

Jeannerod, M. (1996b). Un tremplin pour les sciences cognitives. *La Recherche, Actualité des Sciences*, 289.

Jones, E. (1955). *The Life and Work of Sigmund Freud*, Vol. 2. London: Hogarth Press.

Juignet, P. (1999). *La psychanalyse, une science de l'homme*. Coll. Champs psychanalytiques. Lonat: Delachaux et Niestlé.

Kerstemberg, E. and J. (1965). Report to the Congress of French-speaking Psychoanalysts. *Revue Française de Psychanalyse*, special congress edition.

Klein, M. (1921–45). *Essais de psychanalyse*. Paris: Payot.

Klein, M. (1957). *Envy and Gratitude*. London: Tavistock.

Koestler, A. (1947–93). *Oeuvres autobiographiques*. Paris: Laffont.

Koestler, A. (1954). *The Invisible Writing: Autobiography 1931–53.* Worcester and London: Trinity Press.

Kohut, H. (1971). *The Analysis of the Self.* New York: International Universities Press.

Kohut, H. (1979). *Les deux analyses de M.Z.* Paris: Navarin.

Kohut, H. (1984). *How does Analysis Cure?* Chicago: University of Chicago Press.

Korff-Sausse, S. (2000). La mémoire en partage. *Revue Française de Psychanalyse*, 1.

Koyré, A. (1968). *Études Newtoniennes.* Paris: Gallimard.

Kristeva, J. (1974). *La révolution du langage poétique.* Paris: Seuil.

Kuhn, T. S. (1977). *La tension essentielle. Tradition et changement dans les sciences.* Bibliothèque des Sciences Humaines. Paris: Gallimard.

Lacan, J. (1957). *L'instance de la lettre dans l'inconscient ou la raison depuis Freud.* In *Ecrits.* Paris: Seuil. [Trs. A. Sheridan (1977). The agency of the letter in the unconscious or reason since Freud. In *Ecrits: A Selection.* London: Routledge.]

Lacan, J. (1966). *Écrits.* Paris: Seuil.

Lacan, J. (1973). *Le séminaire.* Paris: Seuil.

Laplanche, J. (1970). *Vie et mort en psychanalyse.* Coll. Nouvelle bibliothèque scientifique. Paris: Flammarion.

Laplanche, J. (1987). *Nouveaux fondements pour la psychanalyse.* Paris: Presses Universitaires de France.

Laplanche, J. (1992). *La révolution copernicienne inachevée. Travaux 1967–1992.* Paris: Aubier.

Laplanche, J. (1993). *Le fourvoiement biologisant de la sexualité chez Freud.* Coll. Les empêcheurs de penser en rond. Paris: Institut Synchélabo.

Laplanche, J. (1999). *La sexualité humaine. Biologisme et biologie.* Coll. Les empêcheurs de penser en rond. Paris: Institut Synchélabo.

Laplanche, J. and Pontalis, J.-B. (1967). *Vocabulaire de la psychanalyse.* Paris: Presses Universitaires de France. [Trs. (1973). *The Language of Psychoanalysis.* London: Hogarth Press.]

Lavallee, G. (1999). *L'enveloppe visuelle du moi, perception et hallucinatoire.* Paris: Dunod.

Lebovici, S. (1979). *Un expérience du psychanalyste chez l'enfant et chez l'adulte devant le modèle de la névrose infantile et de la névrose de transfert.* Report to the 3rd Congress of French-speaking Psychoanalysts, Paris. Paris: Presses Universitaires de France.

Lechevalier, B. and Lechevalier, B. (1998). *Le corps et le sens. Dialogue entre une psychanalyste et un neurologue.* Lonat: Delachaux et Niestlé.

Le Guen, C. (1982). *La dialectique freudienne. 1 Pratique de la méthode psychanalytique.* Coll. Le fil rouge. Paris: Presses Universitaires de France.

Le Guen, C. (1989). *La dialectique freudienne. 2 Théorie de la méthode psychanalytique.* Coll. Le fil rouge. Paris: Presses Universitaires de France.

Levy, P. (1998). *Qu'est-ce que le virtuel?* Paris: La Découverte.

Lewin, B. D. (1946). Le sommeil, la bouche et l'écran du rêve. *Nouvelle Revue de Psychanalyse*, 1972, 5.

Lewin, B. D. (1968). Le passé en images. *Revue Française de Psychanalyse*, 1990, 4.

Lewin, B. D. (1968). La vie dure de l'image. *Revue Française de Psychanalyse*, 1991, 44.

Little, M. (1986). *Des états limites. L'alliance thérapeutique.* Paris: Éditions des Femmes/Antoinette Fouques.

Luquet, P. (1961). Les identifications précoces. *Revue Française de Psychanalyse*, 1962.

Report to the 20th Congress of French-speaking Psychoanalysts. *Revue française de Psychanalyse*, special congress edition.

Lussier, M. (2001). Court plaidoyer pour 'figurabilité'. *Revue Française de Psychanalyse*, 4, special congress edition.

Lutenberg, J.-M. (1993). *La ilusion vaciada. Reflexiones cerca de la experiencias reales y virtuales*. Buenos Aires: Infinto Lassùs.

Lutenberg, J.-M. (1998). *El psicoanalista y la verdad*. Buenos Aires: Publikar.

Lyotard, J.-F. (1985). *Discours, Figure*. Paris: Klincksieck.

McCulloch, W. (1948–53). Tenth Macy Conference on Cybernetics (ed. Heinz von Foerster).

McDougall, J. (1978). *Plaidoyer pour une certaine anormalité*. Paris: Gallimard. [Trs. (1980). *Plea for a Measure of Normality*. London: Free Association Books.]

McDougall, J. (1982). *Théâtres du je*. Paris: Gallimard. [Trs. (1986). *Theatres of the Mind: Illusion and Truth on the Psychoanalytic Stage*. London: Free Association Books.]

McDougall, J. (1989). *Théâtres du corps*. Paris: Gallimard. [Trs. (1990). *Theatres of the Body: A Psychoanalytic Approach to Psychosomatic Illness*. London: Free Association Books.]

McDougall, J. (1996). *Eros aux mille visages*. Paris: Gallimard.

Mahler, M. S. (1994). *Infantile Psychosis and Early Contributions: The Selected Papers of Margaret Mahler*, Vol. 1, *Psychose infantile*. Paris: Payot.

Maldavsky, D. (2000). *Lenguaje, pulsiones, defensas*. Buenos Aires: Nueva Vision.

Mallet, J. (1964). De l'homosexualité psychotique. *Revue Française de Psychanalyse*, 5–6.

Mallet, J. (1966). Une théorie de la paranoïa. *Revue Française de Psychanalyse*, 1.

Marett, R. R. (1909). *The Threshold of Religion*. London: Longman.

Marty, P. (1976). *Les mouvements individuels de vie et de mort. Essai d'économie psychanalytique*. Paris: Payot.

Marty, P. (1980). *L'ordre psychosomatique*. Paris: Payot.

Marty, P., de M'Uzan, M. and David, C. (1963). *L'investigation psychosomatique*. Paris: Presses Universitaires de France.

Marucco, N. (1999). *Cura analítica y tranferencia. De la represion à la desmentida*. Buenos Aires: Amorrortu.

Masson, J. M. (ed.) (1985). *The Complete Letters of Sigmund Freud to Wilhelm Fliess, 1887–1904*. London: Belknap Press.

Mayr, E. (1997). *Qu'est-ce que la biologie?* Paris: Fayard.

Meltzer, D. (1967). *The Psychanalytic Process*. London: Heinemann. [Trs. (1971). *Le processus psychanalytique*. Paris: Payot.]

Meltzer, D. (1972). *Les structures sexuelles de la vie psychique*. Paris: Payot.

Meltzer, D. (1983). *Dream Life. A Reexamination of the Psychoanalytic Theory and Technique*. Perthshire: Clunie Press. [Trs. (1993). *Le monde vivant du rêve*. Paris: Césura.]

Meltzer, D., Bremner, J., Hoxter, S., Weddel, D. and Wittenberg, I. (1975). *Explorations dans le monde de l'autisme*. Paris: Payot.

Menahem, R. (1986). *Langage et folie. Essai de psycho-réthorique*. Paris: Les Belles Lettres.

Merleau Ponty, M. (1964a). *L'Œil et l'Esprit*. Paris: Essais Folio.

Merleau-Ponty, M. (1964b). *Le visible et l'invisible*. Paris: Gallimard.

Meyerson, I. (tr.) (1926). *La science des rêves*. Paris: Alcan.

de Mijolla, A (1981). *Les visiteurs du Moi*. Paris: Les Belles Lettres.

de Mijolla, A. (ed.) (2000). *International Dictionary of Psychoanalysis*. Paris: Calmann-Levy.

Miller, J. (1997). *Une mémoire pour deux. Le virtuel des transferts.* Coll. Le fait psychanalytique. Paris: Presses Universitaires de France.

Minazzoli, A. (1996). *L'homme sans visage. Une anthropologie négative.* Coll. perspectives critiques. Paris: Presses Universitaires de France.

Music, Z. (1995). *Rétrospective.* Catalogue de l'exposition du Grand Palais en 1995.

de M'Uzan, M. (1976). *De l'art à la mort.* Paris: Gallimard.

de M'Uzan, M. (1994). *La bouche de l'inconscient.* Paris: Gallimard.

Neyraut, M. (1973). *Le transfert.* Coll. Le fil rouge. Paris: Presses Universitaires de France.

Neyraut, M. (1979). *Les logiques de l'inconscient.* Paris: L'Harmattan.

Neyraut, M. (1996). La mémoire inconsciente comme limite épistémologique. In *Psychanalyse, neurosciences, cognitivismes.* Coll. Débats de la psychanalyse de la *Revue Française de Psychanalyse.* Paris: Presses Universitaires de France.

Neyraut, M. (1997). *Les raisons de l'irrationnel.* Coll. Le fil rouge. Paris: Presses Universitaires de France.

Nicolaïdis, N. (1984). *La représentation. Essai psychanalytique.* Paris: Dunod.

Nicolaïdis, N. (1993). *La force perceptive de la représentation de la pulsion.* Paris: Presses Universitaires de France.

Ody, M. (1989). Œdipe comme attracteur. *Monographie de la Revue Française de Psychanalyse,* 1990, Psychanalyse: questions pour demain. Paris: Presses Universitaires de France.

Papaionnou, K. (1962). *Hegel.* Paris: Éditions Seghers.

Parat, C. (1988). *Dynamique du sacré.* Lyon: Césura.

Parat, C. (1995). *L'affect partagé.* Coll. Le fait psychanalytique. Paris: Presses Universitaires de France.

Pascal, B. (1658). *De l'esprit géométrique* et *Pensées.* Coll. La Pléiade. Paris: Presses Universitaires de France. [Trs. (1904–14). Of the geometrical spirit. In *Blaise Pascal: Minor Works.* Harvard Classics.]

Pascal, B. (1966). *Pensées* (trs. A. J. Krailsheimer). Harmondsworth: Penguin Classics.

Pasche, F. (1962). L'ascèse psychanalytique. In *A partir de Freud.* Paris: Payot.

Pasche, F. (1969). *A partir de Freud.* Paris: Payot.

Pasche, F. (1981). Métaphysique et inconscient. *Revue Française de Psychanalyse,* 1. [Reprinted in Pasche, 1988.]

Pasche, F. (1983). L'imago zéro. Une relation de non-dialogue. *Revue Française de Psychanalyse,* 4. [Reprinted in Pasche, 1988.]

Pasche, F. (1988). *Le sens de la psychanalyse.* Coll. Le fil rouge. Paris: Presses Universitaires de France.

Pasche, F. (1999). *Le passé recomposé. Pensées, mythes, procès.* Coll. Le fil rouge. Paris: Presses Universitaires de France.

Penot, B. (1982). Interprétation et déni. Colloque de Deauville 1982: L'interprétation. *Revue Française de Psychanalyse,* 3.

Penot, B. (1989). *Figures du déni. En deçà du négatif.* Paris: Dunod.

Perron, R. (2000). *Épître aux enfants qui se cachent dans les grandes personnes.* Coll. Épîtres. Paris: Presses Universitaires de France.

Perron-Borelli, M. (1997). *Dynamique du fantasme.* Coll. Le fil rouge. Paris: Presses Universitaires de France.

Piaget, J. (1945). *La formation du symbole chez l'enfant. Imitation, jeu et rêve, image et représentation.* Lonat: Delachaux et Niestlé.

Piaget, J. (1947). *La représentation du monde chez l'enfant*. Paris: Presses Universitaires de France.

Poincare, H. (1908). *L'invention mathématique*. Paris: Éditions Jacques Gabay.

Pommier, G. (2000). Pour l'amour du père et du phallus. L'homosexualité en première ligne. *Revue Internationale: La clinique lacanienne. Les homosexualités 2000*, 4. Paris: Erès.

Pontalis, J.-B. (1977). *Entre le rêve et la douleur*. Paris: Gallimard.

Pontalis, J.-B. (1986). *L'amour des commencements*. Paris: Folio.

Pontalis, J.-B. (1988). *Perdre de vue*. Paris: Gallimard.

Pontalis, J.-B. (1990). *La force d'attraction*. Paris: Seuil.

Pontalis, J.-B. (1997). *Ce temps qui ne passe pas*. Paris: Gallimard.

Pontalis, J.-B. (2000). *Fenêtres*. Paris: Gallimard.

Porret, J.-M. (1997). *L'arrière-scène du rêve*. Paris: L'Harmattan.

Porte, M. (1994). *La dynamique qualitative en psychanalyse*. Coll. Psychopathologie. Paris: Presses Universitaires de France.

Potamianou, A. (1995). *Processus de répétition et offrandes du Moi*. Coll. Champs psychanalytiques. Lonat: Delachaux et Niestlé.

Pragier, G. and Faure-Pragier, S. (1990). Un siècle après l'Esquisse: nouvelles métaphores? Métaphores du nouveau. Report to the 50th Congress of French-speaking Psychoanalysts, Madrid. *Revue Française de Psychanalyse*, special congress edition.

Press, J. (1999). *La perle et le grain de sable. Traumatisme et fonctionnement mental*. Lonat: Delachaux et Niestlé.

Prochiantz, A. (1997). *Les anatomies de la pensée: A quoi pensent les calamars?* Paris: Odile Jacob.

Racamier, P. C. (1966). Esquisse d'une clinique psychanalytique de la paranoïa. *Revue Française de Psychanalyse*, 1.

Racamier, P. C. (1980). De l'objet–non objet. *Nouvelle Revue Française de Psychanalyse*, 20.

Rallo Romero, J., Ruiz de Bascones, M. T. and Zamora de Pellicer, C. (1974). Les rêves comme unité et continuité de la vie psychique. Report to the Congress of French-speaking Psychoanalysts. *Revue Française de Psychanalyse*, special congress edition.

Rank, O. (1914). *Le double*. Paris: Payot. [Trs. (1989). *The Double: A Psychoanalytic Study*. London: Karnac Books.]

Rascovsky, I. (1976). Un sueño de dos y dos sue nos de uno. *Revista de Psicoanalisis*, 1.

Ricoeur, P. (2003). *Sur la traduction*. Paris: Bayard.

Rolland, J.-C. (1998). *Guérir du mal d'aimer*. Paris: Gallimard.

Rorty, R. (1979). *L'homme spéculaire*. Coll. L'ordre philosophique. Paris: Seuil.

Rose, D. (1996). *L'endurance primaire*. Coll. Le fil rouge. Paris: Presses Universitaires de France.

Rosenberg, B. (1991). Masochisme mortifere et masochisme gardien de la vie. *Monographies de la Revue Française de Psychanalyse*.

Rosenberg, B. (1997). Le moi et son angoisse. Entre pulsion de vie et pulsion de mort. *Monographies de la Revue Française de Psychanalyse*.

Rosolato, G. (1978). *La relation d'inconnu*. Paris: Gallimard.

Rosolato, G. (1985). *Éléments de l'interprétation*. Paris: Gallimard.

Rosolato, G. (1996). *La portée du désir ou la psychanalyse même*. Paris: Presses Universitaires de France.

Rosolato, G. (1999). *Les cinq axes de la psychanalyse*. Paris: Presses Universitaires de France.

Roudinesco, E. and Plon, M. (1997). *Dictionnaire de la psychanalyse*. Paris: Fayard.

Roussillon, R. (1991). *Paradoxes et situations limites de la psychanalyse*. Coll. Le fait psychanalytique. Paris: Presses Universitaires de France.

Roussillon, R. (1995). La métapsychologie des processus et la transitionnalité. *Revue Française de Psychanalyse*, special congress edition.

Roussillon, R. (1995). Perception, hallucination et solution 'biologique' du traumatisme. *Revue Française de Psychosomatique*, 8.

Roussillon, R. (1999). *Agonie, clivage et symbolisation*. Coll. Le fait psychanalytique. Paris: Presses Universitaires de France.

Rousso, H. (1998). *La hantise du passé*. Coll. Conversations pour demain. Paris: Texture.

Sami, A. (1970). *De la projection*. Paris: Payot.

Sami, A. (1974). *L'espace imaginaire*. Paris: Gallimard.

Sami, A. (1977). *Corps réel, corps imaginaire*. Paris: Dunod.

Sami, A. (1997). *Le rêve et l'affect. Une théorie du somatique*. Paris: Dunod.

Sazzo, R. (1993). *Reflets de miroir et autres doubles*. Paris: Presses Universitaires de France.

Schaeffer, J. (1997). *Le refus du féminin (La Sphinge et son âme en peine)*. Paris: Presses Universitaires de France.

Schapiro, M. (2000). *Les mots et les images*. Préface d'Ho Damisch, La peinture prise au mot. Paris: Macula.

Schmid-Kitsikis, E. (1999). *W. R. Bion*. Coll. Psychanalystes d'aujourd'hui. Paris: Presses Universitaires de France.

Schmid-Kitsikis, E. (2000). La mémoire du traumatisme ou comment nier l'oubli pour ne pas se souvenir. *Revue Française de Psychanalyse*, 1.

Schreber, D. P. (1955). *Memoirs of My Nervous Illness*. London: Dawson & Sons Ltd.

Searles, H. (1986). *Mon expérience des états-limites*. Paris: Gallimard..

Segal, H. (1981). *Délire et créativité*. Paris: Éditions des Femmes.

Silberer, H. (1909). Rapport sur une méthode permettant de provoquer et observer certains phénomènes hallucinatoires symboliques. *Ornicar*, 31.

Smadja, C. (1993). À propos des procédés auto-calmants du moi. *Revue Française de Psychosomatique*, 4.

Smadja, C. (1998). Le fonctionnement opératoire dans la pratique psychosomatique. Report to the ELE Congress, Lausanne. *Revue Française de Psychanalyse*, 5.

Starobinski, J. (1999). *Action et réaction*. Paris: Seuil.

Steiner, G. (1976). *After Babel*. Oxford: Oxford University Press.

Steward, J. (1994). *Somatization: Psychanalyse et sciences du vivant*. Paris: Eshel.

Szwec, G. (1998). *Les galériens volontaires. Essais sur les procédés auto-calmants*. Coll. Épîtres. Paris: Presses Universitaires de France.

Tadie, J.-V. and Tadie, M. (1999). *Le sens de la mémoire*. Paris: Gallimard.

Tausk, V. (1919a). *Oeuvres Psychanalytiques*. Paris: Payot.

Tausk, V. (1919b). On the origin of the 'influencing machine' in schizophrenia. *Psychoanalytical Quarterly*, 1933, 2. [Also in Fliess (ed.), 1948.]

Thom, R. (1988). *Esquisse d'une sémiophysique*. Paris: InterÉditions. [Trs. (1990). *Semio-Physics*. New York: Addison Wesley.]

Thom, R. (1993). *Prédire n'est pas expliquer*. Paris: Champs Flammarion.

Tisseron, S. (1997). *Psychanalyse de l'image. Des premiers traits au virtuel*. Paris: Dunod.

Tustin, F. (1972). *Autisme et psychose de l'enfant*. Paris: Seuil.

Tustin, F. (1986). *Le trou noir de la psyché*. Paris: Seuil.

Valabrega, J.-P. (1994). *La formation du psychanalyste* (1979 edition). Coll. Bibliothèque scientifique. Paris: Payot.

Varela, F. (1988). *Connaître les sciences cognitives*. Paris: Seuil.

Varela, F. (1994). Sciences cognitives et psychanalyse: questions ouvertes. In *Somatisation, psychanalyse et sciences du vivant*. Paris: Eshel.

Varela, F., Thompson, E. and Rosch, E. (1993). *L'inscription corporelle de l'esprit*. Coll. Sciences cognitives et expérience humaine. Paris: Seuil.

Vernant, J.-P. (1985). *Mythes et pensées chez les Grecs*. Paris: La Découverte.

Viderman, S. (1970). *La construction de l'espace analytique*. Paris: Denoël.

Viderman, S. (1977). *Le céleste et le sublunaire*. Coll. Le fil rouge. Paris: Presses Universitaires de France.

Vincent, J.-D. (1986). *Biologie des passions*. Paris: Odile Jacob.

Vincent, J.-D. (1996). *La chair et le diable*. Paris: Odile Jacob.

Voltaire, F. (1734). *Lettres philosophiques, 14e lettre*. Paris: Flammarion. [Trs. L. Tancock (1964). *Letters on England, letter 14* ('On Descartes and Newton') and *letter 15* ('On the system of gravitation'). Harmondsworth: Penguin Classics.]

Weller, A. (tr.) (2001). *Life Narcissism. Death Narcissism*. London: Free Association Books.

Widlocher, D. (1986). *Métapsychologie du sens*. Coll. Psychiatrie ouverte. Paris: Presses Universitaires de France.

Widlocher, D. (1996). *Les nouvelles cartes de psychanalyse*. Paris: Odile Jacob.

Wilgowicz, P. (1991). *Le vampirisme: de la Dame Blanche au Golem: essai sur la pulsion de mort et sur l'irreprésentable*. Lyon: Césura.

Winnicott, D. (1940–70). *Conversations ordinaires*. Paris: Gallimard.

Winnicott, D. (1969). *Through Paediatrics to Psychoanalysis*. London: Hogarth Press and The Institute of Psychoanalysis. [*De la pédiatrie à la psychanalyse*. Paris: Payot.] [Reprinted (1992). London: Karnac Books.]

Winnicott, D. (1971). *Playing and Reality*. London: Tavistock. [*Jeu et réalité. L'espace potentiel*. Paris: Gallimard.]

Winnicott, D. (1974). Fear of breakdown. *International Review of Psychoanalysis*, 1. [Reprinted (1989). *Psychoanalytic Explorations*. London: Karnac Books.]

Woscodoinik, J. (1996). *El alma de 'El Aleph'*. Buenos Aires: Nuevo Hacer.

Zaltzman, N. (1998). *De la guérison psychanalytique*. Coll. Épîtres. Paris: Presses Universitaires de France.

INDEX

negatisation of 137–8; and object representation 27; and reality testing 136, 137; self-perception 105, 146, 170–1, 172, 173; traumatic 22; unknowableness of 142; *see also* non-perception; representation–perception; sensory experience
perception–consciousness 160–4; initial 170–1
perceptual causality 175–80
perceptual identity 71, 83, 101, 106, 124
perceptual process 164–6
perceptual traces 116
persecutor 66
perversion 157, 162
phantasies 60, 71, 102, 164–5; primal 132, 175, 176; *see also* fantasies
pictograms 47
pictorial language 47
Pitts 159
pleasure ego 29–30, 173
pleasure principle 102, 127, 142
point O 139–40, 147, 153
polar oppositions 24
Pontalis, J.-B. 3, 7, 46, 164
Porret, J.-M. 47
Porte, Michèle 39
positivism 18, 25, 140, 154
'possibility of action' 7
pre-animistic states 79, 102–4, 105–6, 137
preconscious 11, 12, 21, 23, 26, 33, 83, 92, 94, 95, 127, 141, 146, 160, 164, 178, 180; auto-erotic 95, 96, 98; ego 98; reason for the existence of 135; temporo-spatiality of 110–12, 136, 179; and the unconscious 95, 110, 136
présentabilité 4–5, 7
presentation 46
primal matrices 175
primal phantasies 132
primal scene 175
primal trace 171–2
primitive man 78, 86, 88, 93, 96, 98, 103

primitive psyche 137
primitive scene 76
primitive states 135
primordial abstraction 43, 44
prisoners 142–4
projection: neurotic 133; paranoic 65, 66; psychotic 133
projective identification 85
projective repudiation 103
Proust, M. 134
psyche 11–12, 18–19, 27, 30, 84, 85, 174, 175, 180; first task of (work of figurability) 42; general functioning 177–8; primitive 137; and the real world 155, 157; role of negativity in 39–44
psychic causality 175–80
psychic quality 10–12, 13
psychoanalysis 157–8, 159
psychoanalytic asceticism 141
psychoneurosis 81, 84, 115, 124, 140–1, 142
psychosis 48, 54, 88, 145, 157; hallucinations of 116–17, 127, 132–4

quality, psychic 10–12, 13
quantum physics 22–4, 119–20, 154
quasi-hallucinatory 102, 119, 122, 126, 127

Racamier, P. C. 64, 65
racial difference 101, 102
Rank, O. 77
Rascovsky, I. 105
reaction formation 94
reality: creation of the sensation of 9, 10; denial 137; disavowal 90, 91; events of 39; knowledge of 153; material 180; psychic 179–80; quantum 22–4; ultimate 139; unknowableness 22–3, 139, 152, 155
reality ego 29–30, 137, 162, 173
reality principle 91, 127, 142
reality testing 30, 41, 68, 79, 86, 90–1, 92, 97, 98, 117, 133, 134, 136–8, 142, 163, 172